EMERGING CENTRAL ASIA

MANAGING GREAT POWER

RELATIONS

Edited by

Kashif Hasan Khan and Halil Koch

CENTRAL ASIA

MANAGING GREAT POWER

RELATIONS

Edited by

Kashif Hasan Khan and Halil Koch

Published by Blue Dome Press
335 Clifton Ave,
Clifton, NJ 07011
www.bluedomepress.com

Library of Congress Cataloging-in-Publication Data available

ISBN: 978-1-68206-030-8

Contents

LIST OF TABLES, FIGURES AND MAPS

LIST OF ABBREVIATIONS

AIIB	Asian Infrastructure Investment Bank
ASEAN	Association for South East Asian Nations
BRI	Belt and Road Initiative
CADGAT	Central Asia Data-Gathering and Analysis Team
CAR	Central Asia Region
CCP	Chinese Communist Party
CGD	Center for Global Development
CIS	Commonwealth of Independent States
CKU	China-Kyrgyzstan-Uzbekistan
CPEC	China–Pakistan Economic Corridor
EAEU	Eurasian Economic Union
EU	European Union
FDI	Foreign Direct Investment
FTA	Free Trade Agreement
GEP	Greater Eurasian Partnership
IOM	International Organization for Migration
IOR	Indian Ocean Region
ITEC	Indian Technical and Economic Cooperation
ODA	Official Development Assistance
PRC	People's Republic of China
QUAD	Quadrilateral Security Dialogue
RCSC	Russian Centers of Science and Culture
SCO	Shanghai Cooperation Organization
SREB	Silk Road Economic Belt
TAR	Trans-Asian Railway
TICA	Turkish International Cooperation Agency
TRACECA	Transport Corridor Europe-Caucasus-Asia
TÜBİTAK	Scientific and Technological Research Council of Turkey
USSR	Union of Socialist Soviet Republics
XUAR	Xinjiang Uyghur Autonomous Region

FOREWORD

A central question for the study of Central Asia's international environment since 1991 has been whether the local states have real agency in developing independent, sovereign foreign policies or whether they just have to adapt to the push and pull of large regional or global powers and powerful transnational forces. In the 1990s the challenge for the five new states of this region was to try to substantiate their sovereignty, for local leaders to bolster their political legitimacy, to manage the damaging fallout of the dissolution of integrated Soviet systems, to contain local cross-border tensions and to renegotiate relations with Moscow on respectable terms.

These preoccupations were affected by the sudden and irresistible, increase in American influence from the early 1990s after the 9/11 attacks and the onset of military action in Afghanistan, which also offered Central Asian leaders some opportunities to balance Russia's continued assertion of special rights over Central Asian foreign affairs. However, in this period China was still very much a secondary, lower profile presence in the region, Turkish relative economic weakness limited its potential as a partner for the new Turkic states, while India was hardly visible.

This contrasts to Central Asia's contemporary international environment, revealed in the chapters of this fascinating volume. To be sure prominent features of the Central Asian states' foreign policy strategies have not been transformed: for example, Kazakhstan's multi-vector policy; Uzbekistan's bilateralism; Turkmenistan's isolation in the guise of neutrality. The region has also remained impressively stable overall, despite fears over transnational Islamist influences, over possible leadership succession crises and failures in governance. However, a profound process of reconnection of landlocked and seemingly remote interior Central Asian territories to the wider world has gathered pace. It is precipitated by a scale of investment and infrastructure development which could not be imagined twenty years earlier. This new opening of Central Asia, especially to the east and west, has happily coincided with the local states resolving many border frictions among themselves, a new interest in intergovernmental consultations and a proactive approach by Uzbekistan, arguably the key state for region-wide developments.

The authors in this book highlight major features of what are tectonic shifts in the geo-economics and international ties of Central Asian states thirty years on from the Soviet collapse. The development of Central Asia's new ties of course reflects the wider priorities and resources available to major powers with interests in the region. The United States under the Biden administration continues to seek disengagement from Afghanistan and the American security policy imprint in Central Asia, a secondary concern, diminishes with that. The European Union in turn remains preoccupied by threats to its cohesion among member states and is better aware of the limited prospects it has to advance any transformational normative agenda in Central Asia.

In contrast, China is fast becoming the dominant investor in the region, the largest trade partner, a rival to Russia in access to Central Asian energy reserves and the primary enabler of far-reaching new transport and communications links, under the aegis of the Belt and Road Initiative (BRI). For China, as a chapter in this book confirms, domestic security is now increasingly bound up with this international outreach. Yet the very scale of this Chinese presence in Central Asia creates worries among Central Asian elites about a new form of dependency. On the other hand, this reinforces Russia's image as a known and familiar neighbour. However, Russia continues to unsettle its Central Asian partners by empowering separatism in Ukraine and Georgia and even hinting at doubts over Kazakhstan's statehood, while the Russian economy does not offer a shining prospect of modernisation. Moscow and Beijing have been speaking a win-win language of cooperation between the Eurasian Economic Union and the BRI, and of common commitment to Eurasianism, elevated in the Russian lexicon to the notion of 'Greater Eurasia'. But common projects between these rather different macro-regional frameworks seem hard to identify. A crucial if publicly unvoiced question for local officials and elites, is how far over time China will supplant Russia regionally, and whether Chinese dominance in trade may spill over eventually into attempts to shape Central Asian foreign policy preferences. This uncertainty is only likely to be reinforced by the global pandemic, which has further boosted China's economic growth relative to Russia's, while Russia and China have both emerged as major players in the new field of vaccine diplomacy.

At the same time geo-economic and geostrategic flux in Central Asia may offer opportunities for other second order powers. So the chapter in this book reviewing Turkish-Central Asian relations is timely. With Turkey's successful support of Azerbaijan in the 2020 war over Nagorno-Karabakh it is not fanciful to conceive of a higher Turkish profile in Central Asia in the 2020s. Equally, a chapter devoted to India's efforts at greater economic access to Central Asia, in some competition with the BRI, speaks to the new geo-economics of the 2020s, and foreshadows the growing Chinese-Indian rivalry in wider Asian diplomacy.

However, for a book entitled *Emerging Central Asia: Managing Great Power Relations*, the scholarly question of how much agency Central Asian states can exert in the force field of major powers remains important. Given the centrality of Uzbekistan, bordering all the other Central Asian states, yet insulated from the direct border influence of Russia or China and the more activist recent diplomacy of Tashkent, it is not surprising that two chapters are devoted to the position of this state: to the effects of nationalism in Uzbekistan and to the implications if Uzbekistan were to join the Eurasian Economic Union. A larger book might extend the coverage of Central Asian states' efforts to manage the changing matrix of great power relations. However, the editors perform a valuable service in helping open out a wide agenda for future research and study in the 2020s, as the Central Asian region deepens its connectivity in an increasingly inter-connected world.

Prof. Roy Allison
Director, Russian and Eurasian Studies Centre,
St. Antony's College, Oxford University

ACKNOWLEDGEMENTS

One fine morning in our weekly meetings on Monday, over coffee at 8am in Koch's office, -15 temperature outside, we were discussing the CAR (Central Asian Republics) - its people, culture and history. That discussion led us to think further on coming up something more concrete. Several sessions of discussions over one and half year period have ended up bringing out the volume you have in your hand now.

Both editors have gained immensely from experiences of living in the region for many years. Our regular interactions with many young and senior scholars - who are studying the region for many years and many of them have lived in the region, studying regional languages, and collaborating closely with locals – give us in depth understanding not from the local but also International perspectives.

In working on this book project, we have enjoyed the intellectual engagement and support of many people. We have benefited from many people in finishing this book. Many people have read chapters of the book and provided helpful comments. Murray Eldred read all the chapters and gave us very useful advice, both content-wise and editorially.

The assistance of our capable GLODEP Erasmus Mundus Joint Master student and intern, Laila Jiwani from Dallas, USA, at Silk Road Research Center was integral to the development of our Introduction and Conclusion as well as for language editing throughout the book.

We extend our gratitude to our esteemed colleagues at Ala-Too International Unversity, Dr. Rustam Umarov, Dr. Kiyalbek Akmoldoev, and Mr. Firdavs Amakov for providing valuable information about the region. Many thanks to Prof. K Atyshov for sharing his insightful understanding of the region.

We are also very thankful to all learned contributors from different parts of the world. Their scholarly chapters address significant questions often posted to the region and raise several points which pave way for further explorations.

Both editors are very thankful to the Team of Blue Dome Press for helpfulness during editorial process.

Last but not least, we thank our families, without whose support and love this book project would not have been finished. We dedicate this book to our sons Yaqub Hasan and Asym Hasan. Their smiles give us immense strength to continue doing ethical academic work.

Regardless the great number of contributions and influences of all those who have served and aided this process, we stay answerable for the likely lapse of numerous elements containing those beyond the scope of our study. Obligation for whatever problems remain is ours. We hope that this book contributes to the ongoing literature on Central Asia.

Kashif Hasan Khan
Halil Koch

Contributors

Dr. Kashif Hasan Khan is the Director of Silk Road Research Center at Ala-Too International University in Bishkek, Kyrgyzstan. He has previously worked in the corporate sector as an international business consultant. He has worked in Turkey, Philippines, England, and India. His research and teaching interests include international business, international trade theories, and the political economy of Central Asia and history of economic thoughts. Dr. Kashif has written a number of articles and participates in and hosts a number of national and international conferences in India and elsewhere. His latest publications include 'India and Central Asia: The Strategy of Re (connectivity)' (KW Publishers, New Delhi, 2020), and 'India and Central Asia: Emerging Extended Neighbourhood (New Century Press, New Delhi, India. 2020).

Dr. Halil Koch serves as Vice Rector of Ala-Too International University in Bishkek, Kyrgyzstan and is one of the leading educators of Kyrgyzstan. He earned his PhD in Economics from the National Academy of Science of the Kyrgyz Republic. Dr. Koch has dedicated over 25 years to the development of education in the Kyrgyz Republic. He was awarded a "Certificate of Honor" by the Kyrgyz Ministry of Education in 2004. He has also held several significant positions at Turkish-Kyrgyz educational institutions. Dr. Koch also has several articles to his credit.

Dr. Alexey Fominykh studied History at Mari State University in Yoshkar-Ola, Russian Federation and received a Candidate of Sciences (Кандидат наук) degree in Political Science from the University of Nizhny Novgorod in 2003. He lectures on International Relations at the Department of Intercultural Communications of Mari State University, and heads the International Project Office at Volga State University of Technology in the same city. He has been working in international education since 1999. In 2007, he was among the first Russian international academic administrators to travel to the Teachers College, Columbia University and the University of Minnesota on a specialized Fulbright Program. His research interests center on international education and public and cultural diplomacy, with special focus on the post-Soviet area. One of his recent publications includes "Russian Public Diplomacy Through Higher Education" published in "Russia's Public Diplomacy: Evolution and Practice" (Palgrave Macmillan, 2020).

Prof. Lere Amusan is Head of the Department of Political Studies and International Relations at North West University in South Africa. As of July 2020, Lere has published eighty-two articles in reputable and globally recognised journals spanning six continents. He has also published two monographs titled *Mercy Killing and Thanksgiving: Food Security with Tears in Africa* (2019) and *Africa and Climate Change in the Era of Complex Interdependent Globalised International System* (2009). He co-edited two books, *Political Instability in Africa* (2020) and *Contemporary Security Issues in Africa* (2020). Professor Lere Amusan has alsocontributed twenty-one chapters in edited books. His area of research focus is food politics and food policy. He has been a member of various professional associations such as the South African Association of Political Science, the Midwest Political Science Association in the U.S., and the International Political Science Association. He has received many awards as an outstanding researcher in his university, and has attended forty-four conferences locally and internationally. Amusan was one of the eighteen scholars selected globally for the 2019 Study of the U.S. Institute (SUSI). Lere is a reviewer and editorial board member of twenty-one journals, including Space Policy, Regional and Federal Studies, Africa Today, Indian Quarterly, and the Journal of Asian and African Studies, among others. He has graduated eleven masters and four PhD candidates. Amusan serves as an external examiner for various universities in South Africa and beyond.

Mr. Ryan Schweitzer received his bachelor's degree in Political Science from Columbia University in New York City. His focus on nationalism and identity led him to carry out extensive studies on Central Asia. He has a deep understanding of the region, with multiple in-country work experiences in Uzbekistan, including his most recent Fulbright research grant. His Fulbright research on Uzbekistan's alphabet and language policies were published at GW University's Central Asia Program.

Ryan has also received the Melikian Scholarship, Harriman Institute Summer Language Fellowship, and a U.S. Department of State Foreign Language Area Studies Fellowship for the Uzbek language. His interests in Central Asia include regional security, migrant issues, and human rights.

Dr. Aizada Nuriddenova is currently a Senior Lecturer in the Department of Social Sciences at Suleyman Demirel University in Almaty. She obtained her master and PhD degrees in International Relations with a focus on China's foreign policy from the School of International and Public Affairs at Jilin University in People's Republic of China. Aizada has taught at the Gumilyov Eurasian National University in Nur-Sultan at the Department of Oriental Studies and served as a Visiting Lecturer at Allameh Tabataba'i University in Iran for one semester, where she delivered two graduate courses on international organizations in Central Asia and the cultural features of the Central Asian region. She has authored and co-authored over a dozen articles and book chapters. Her current research combines Chinese foreign policy and regionalism in Central Asia by focusing on normative aspects of Chinese foreign policy such as 'Community of Common Destiny', recent consultative meetings in the Central Asian region, and the impact of the Chinese Belt and Road Initiative in Central Asia.

Assoc. Prof. Halim Nezihoglu is head of the Department of International Relations at Ala-Too International University in Bishkek, Kyrgyzstan. He earned his PhD at the Diplomatic Academy under Ministry of Foreign Affairs in Kyrgyzstan. His research interests include national identity, ethnic relations and great power politics in Central Asia. His latest publications include "The Importance of India for Multi-vector Foreign Policy of Kyrgyzstan," In Khan, K H (ed) 'India and Central Asia: The Strategy of Re (connectivity)' (KW Publishers, New Delhi, 2020). He also coordinated national and international conferences on Central Asia.

Dr. Anirban Chatterjee is an Assistant Professor at the Department of Political Science, Plassey College, University of Kalyani, West Bengal, India. He earned his PhD entitled "Russian Response towards

Western Democracy Promotion in the Post-Soviet Space, 2003-2015" from the Centre for Russian and Central Asian Studies at the School of International Studies at Jawaharlal Nehru University (JNU) in New Delhi. He also received his MPhil from the same Centre. The title of his MPhil dissertation was "State Capacity and Governance in Tajikistan, 1991-2013". He has worked as a Research Intern at the Indian Council of World Affairs (ICWA) in New Delhi, India's leading foreign policy based think tank. He also received a Gold Medal for securing the first position in his MA examination from Babasaheb Bhimrao Ambedkar Central University in Lucknow, Uttar Pradesh. He has published book reviews and articles in peer-reviewed journals and recently contributed a chapter in an edited volume by Dr. Kashif Hasan Khan titled 'Central Asia and India: Emerging Extended Neighbourhood'.

Dr. Fabrizio Vielmini is a Senior Research Fellow on Silk Road Connectivity at the Center for Policy Research and Outreach (CPRO) of Westminster International University in Tashkent. He has specialized in the affairs of the Caucasus and Central Asia since 1995, and from 2002 onwards lived in the two regions, where he worked for the OSCE, the EU Special Representative (EUSR) for Central Asia, the EU Monitoring Mission in Georgia (EUMM), as well as a number of other commercial and analytical projects.

Mr. Tola Amusan is a PhD candidate in the Politics department at the University of Otago in Dunedin, New Zealand. His research interest centers around China's foreign policy and geoeconomics. He was awarded a doctoral scholarship by the University of Otago and is a member of the Golden Key Society. He has thus far published one article titled "China and Saharan Africa Economic Relations: A Neo-Mercantilist Perspective" in African Renaissance (2019).

MANAGING GREAT POWER RELATIONS:

AN INTRODUCTION

Kashif Hasan Khan and Halil Koch

Academics, historians and political scientists often refer to the Great Game." This term is the subject of much debate in the literature on Central Asia. In this context, the word "game" refers to seeking to promote stability while reaping the maximum benefits in the region by stopping other powers from gaining influence. The term was first popularized by the writer Rudyard Kipling in his novel, *Kim*, published in 1901[1]. Many have argued, however, that it is not only a "Great Game", but a "Great Gain" for the countries of the Central Asian Region (CAR), as they stand to benefit greatly from the competition of major powers in the region.

Throughout history, people from many nations have journeyed through the region, attracted by its silk and spices as well as its people's knowledge of irrigation, animal husbandry, music, religion, science, mathematics and philosophy. During the Soviet period, however, the influence of the USSR prevented the rest of the world from forming ties with Central Asia. Since their independence in the 1990s, the CARs have required capital investment assistance and international support, but there was very little knowledge about the region within the international community. Many efforts have since been made to increase international recognition and build goodwill by reconnecting with the rest of the world and implementing a range of economic reforms. Despite these measures, lasting peace and prosperity has proved elusive. There is still a need for strengthened governance and increased transparency, accountability, and inclusion in the region, as well as environmentally sustainable growth policies.

---

[1] Although Kipling popularized it, the term "Great Game" was first seen even before Kipling's work. An officer from the British East India Company, Arthur Connolly, used the term long before Kipling.

The end of the Cold War era has led to drastic changes in Eurasian geopolitics, particularly regarding energy politics in Central Asia and the Caspian Sea Region. The emergence of the newly independent Republics - including Kazakhstan, Kyrgyzstan, Tajikistan, Turkmenistan and Uzbekistan - shifted control from the Soviet Union and led to increased competition and cooperation between the regional and extra-regional powers for the rich energy and mineral resources of these states.

The population of all the CAR states combined is about 60 million people composed of various ethnic and religious groups. The majority of Central Asians are made up of Turkic-speaking (Kyrgyz, Kazakh, Karakalpak, Tatar, Uighur) and Farsi-speaking (Tajik) linguistic groups. The CAR states also have some variety in religious identities. 90% of Central Asians identify as Sunni Muslims with secular and communist mindsets, while the remainder mostly identifies as Orthodox Christian. The CAR states generally maintain peaceful relations with one another as they have a common Islamic heritage, secular states, some degree of authoritarian governance, and all face similar challenges with corruption and drug trafficking. (Papkova and Dimitry, 2011).

In this volume, the authors argue that in the twenty-five years since independence, several major events have had long term consequences for the region. Xi Jinping announced the One Belt One Road (OBOR) project in 2013; the Eurasian Economic Union was created in 2015; Russia established military bases in Kyrgyzstan, Tajikistan, and Kazakhstan; and Russian-CAR cooperation in Afghanistan grew. Currently, today's superpowers - the US, Russia, and China - have much at stake in Central Asia. China has a strong interest in the region's vast national gas reserves. Russia is increasing trade with many countries in Central Asia for military and geostrategic purposes. The U.S. seeks to bring democracy and stability to Central Asia to prevent the region from becoming a cradle for terrorism (Soliev, 2019). This volume focuses on how Central Asia has once again become a focal point for the entire world. For example, since the U.S.'s declaration of a so-called "War on Terrorism" following the attacks of September 11, 2001, many

U.S. delegations in the region have established relations with Central Asian secret services and military forces.

In response to these developments, Russia began attempts to regain influence in the region in order to prevent Western interests from gaining clout. The growth of the Chinese presence in the region also accelerated through increased access to various commodities and funding infrastructure projects. At the same time, other countries such as Japan, Turkey, India, Iran, and the EU also wanted to engage with the CAR. Western powers like the EU and USA seek to advance their agendas with regard to democratic governance and civil structures like freedom of speech and human rights policies. India, whose foreign policy is characterized by a resurgence of the principle of non-violence – the same approach promoted by Mahatma Gandhi to balance national and international relations - has begun to view the region as its extended neighbor (Khan & Kuszewska, 2020). Turkey has also tried reviving its historic cultural and linguistic ties, while Iran and Japan are most interested in expanding business relations. Central Asia's resources and strategic importance are attracting growing interest from a diverse range of actors, each with unique interests in the region. All these developments are described in post-Soviet literature as the emergence of a new "Great Game" between the great powers, which the editors of this book argue that these developments stand to benefit CARs. To support the argument, this volume discusses a number of infrastructure projects and trends.

Today, U.S. strategists seem to be resigned to a modest and pragmatic role in Central Asia. The Trump administration has given some indications about the future contours of U.S policy in Central Asia. In May 2017, U.S. Secretary of State Rex Tillerson announced that democratic values would not impede the advancement of U.S. national security and economic interests. The U.S. global retreat on human rights would favor a more pragmatic approach to the militarization of the region and even less focus on civil liberties. Furthermore, foreign assistance to Central Asian countries, with the exception of Uzbekistan, has been significantly reduced. If this trend continues, Central Asia will be increasingly dependent on Russia and China, whose political agendas do not prioritize democratic principles or promote open civil societies (Romanowski, 2017). The Trump Administration's stance towards Central Asia has led to concern that interest in the region may again decline. European interest in Central Asia has also decreased from high levels 20 years ago in the immediate aftermath of 9/11. The European Union's involvement in the region has diminished to a small number of value-based projects. Moreover, Iran and Turkey, although they continue their policies in the region, are also not delivering as much to the region as expected.

Chinese interest in Central Asia is also not focused on the region, Rather, it centers on establishing global routes to connect China to the Middle East and Europe as well as the Xinjiang region, whose population is ethnically Central Asian. In order to curb the so-called terrorist activities by Uighurs and ensure the cooperation of CAR border security, China continues to invest in the CA region to keep the region under their influence (Khan H.K., 2020a).

As China's focus on its security agenda in the region increases, reports of a growing presence of Chinese private security firms are emerging. There are also more overt displays of strength occuring, like the construction of new military bases, joint training exercises with Tajik, Kyrgyz, and Uzbek forces, and the provision of equipment for Tajik forces along the Chinese border with Afghanistan. This begs the question: is Russian supremacy in the region intact? Willa common language and increasing cross-border labor mobility help Russia to maintain its hegemony and monopolize military sales?

On the other hand, there are many reservations about China's presence in Central Asia. In Kyrgyzstan, for example, there are high levels of public disdain toward the Chinese resulting from China's acquisition of Tajik land in the aftermath of Tajikistan's default on Chinese debt. China's considerable role in the region is rapidly expanding. Beijing holds 41 percent and 53 percent of Kyrgyzstan's and Tajikistan's external government debt, respectively. Over half of China's debt to Tajikistan was disbursed between 2007 and 2010. Roman Kozhevnikov, a Tajik journalist, wrote in an article for Reuters that a Chinese company has purchased a majority share in Tajikistan's largest gold mine. "This process is capable of stirring up tension within the local population, who perhaps cannot accept such a mass influx of Chinese," said Tajik political analyst Zafar Abdullayev (Khan, K.H, 2020).

The rise of nationalism as a political force in Central Asia concerns China in a number of ways. At the most basic level, China wishes to avoid instability on its border that would inevitably accompany nationalists challenging or replacing existing governments. Chinese leaders are also concerned that nationalist governments in Central Asia could serve as examples for Uighur separatists and be less cooperative with China in suppressing the activities of separatists on the border (Burles, 1999).

Beijing and Moscow act as individual and distinct actors, each pursuing their own agendas in the region. Both share some perspectives on Central Asia, which is visible in multilateral organizations and, more broadly, in relation to a "declining West" (see Conclusion). In 2001, Russia and China signed the Treaty of Good Neighborliness and Friendly Cooperation which set forth a bilateral relationship based on "mutual respect of sovereignty and territorial integrity," non-interference in internal affairs, equality and mutual benefit. Years of negotiations on their borders culminated in China receiving almost 340 square kilometers of disputed territory from Russia in return for Beijing dropping all other land claims against Moscow. Today, neither sees major threats emanating from across their common border. Rather, Moscow is much more concerned about NATO activities on its Western flank, or about threats coming to Russia from the Middle East or Afghanistan coming through the Caucasus or Central Asia. Beijing also appears worried about instability coming across the border from Afghanistan and Central Asia and is intensely focused on shoring up its geopolitical position amid territorial disputes in the South China Sea and East China Sea (Stronski, Ng et. al., 2018).

In light of these considerations, this book aims to explore how the Central Asian Republics have managed their relations with small and major powers during the 25 years following the collapse of the USSR. The authors identify and discuss the questions like: what are the Central Asian states' interests and how they are pursuing them? What are the CAR states' relationships with these powers, and what is changing? Are the great powers outsourcing policing or security responsibilities to the CAR?

By exploring the above-mentioned points, the book looks at the role of the major players in Central Asia and the region's response to the "New Great Game." This volume is especially focused on the current challenges and opportunities the region faces. The contributors also touch upon other crucial topics like security challenges, historical relations with other major powers, the immigration of labor and students, the rise of nationalism, the energy sector and the BRI.

Overall, this book aims to provide a better understanding of Central Asia's multi-faceted relations in the face of rapidly evolving geostrategic dynamics. It serves as a timely insight into the contours of Central Asian states' policies, emerging trends and the significant features of these interactions. The chapters are authored by academics and researchers from Central Asia and other parts of the globe to provide a wide spectrum of opinion and analysis on the subject.

In the opening chapter, **Aizada Nuriddenova,** in her article "Russian and Chinese versions of 'Eurasianism': A Response from Kazakhstan," points out that the idea of connecting Eurasia is by no means new. It was actively advocated by the former President of Kazakhstan Nursultan Nazarbayev in the early 1990s as the concept of "Eurasianism" and has become one of the major components of Kazakhstan's foreign policy today. This idea started to come to fruition in early 2010s after the Global Financial Crisis gave rise to a Russian concept of Eurasianism along with its new regional framework – the Eurasian Economic Union (EAEU). In 2013, Chinese President Xi Jinping proposed to "join hands in building a Silk Road Economic Belt (SREB) with innovative cooperation," thus offering a Chinese view of Eurasianism. These three conceptions of Eurasian integration, discussed in detail in the chapter, merged, and the notion of connecting Eurasia became larger in scope and more ambitious in its objectives.

In his chapter, "The Importance of Central Asia in China's Domestic Security", **Lere Amusan** emphasizes that terrorism has gone global. It is a phenomenon that has haunted the international system for some time due to what Samuel P. Huntington describes as "the Clash of Civilizations" and aptly conceived by Dominique Moisi as "the geo-politics of emotion" shaped by cultures of fear, humiliation, and hope in contemporary global politics. Great, emerging and weak powers in international relations are all affected by it to differing degrees. As a state, China is seen by some as a great power, while others see it as an emerging nation, and others perceive it as a pivotal state in the context of geopolitics. The issue of domestic terrorism in China, centered around the Turkic Uighur ethnic group in the Xinjiang Autonomous Region, has captured global media and diplomatic attention. With borders close to several Central Asian states like Kazakhstan, Kyrgyzstan and Tajikistan, China, through the Shanghai Cooperation Organization (SCO), strives to cooperate with Central Asian members to have cordial relations. This paper examines the importance of Central Asian states in China's domestic political stability.

Tola Amusan's paper "China's Geo-Economic Inroads into Central Asia: An Asymmetric Interdependence Vulnerability Approach" discusses the fact that China's rise to what might arguably be termed superpower status is so prominent that talking about international relations without mentioning the phrase "the rise of China" could almost be considered taboo. China's rise resonates more on the level of economy, which has extended to strategic, military, political, diplomatic and cultural dimensions. China has expanded its footprint across all corners of the global system since it shifted to a more outward-looking stance at the beginning of the 21st century. This economic strength has given Beijing an increased level of strategic, political and diplomatic leverage which enhances China's ability to directly compete for influence in Central Asia with Russia. China's encroachment in the region is based solely on its national interest which revolves predominantly around energy resources. The Belt and Road Initiative (BRI) is the key to understanding China's geo-economic intent in the Central Asian subregion as it directly connects Central Asia to China. Utilizing the concept of asymmetric interdependence vulnerability, this piece examines the role that geo-economics plays in China's international relations in Central Asia as well as how it impacts Russian interests in the context of the initiation of a "New Great Game".

In "Nationalism through Fear: Uzbekistan" **Ryan Michael Schweitzer** argues that since independence, the population of Uzbekistan has seen a growing shift towards nationalistic tendencies through new policies in religion, economy, government and language. Through this process of self-determination and self-realization, Uzbekistan is moving away from its Soviet history, and is instead embracing the resurgence (and reinvention) of its cultural identity. This chapter asks where this movement is heading, and what made this phenomenon occur? Is it a response to the perceived threat of Russia or simply an expression of Uzbek identity? It is unclear whether this new approach towards nationalistic tendencies comes from the will of the people of Uzbekistan, or if the government and elite are creating nationalistic narratives in response to security concerns. This paper examines these important questions, and attempts to explain the rise of nationalism in Uzbekistan as an expression of de-Russification.

Halim Nezihoglu argues in his paper, "Turkey and Central Asia: A Historical-Geopolitical Context of the Relations "that Central Asia has come to the fore in the agenda of world politics after the dissolution of the Soviet Union. Central Asian states, situated in a great power-driven regional system have adopted multi-vector foreign policies as their overall foreign policy strategy. The republics have sought to develop good relations and cooperation with different global/regional powers and other states and to balance the diverse interests of various players. One of the important actors in the region has been Turkey, which has historical, cultural, and linguistic ties with the region. High expectations about the progress of relations between these historically connected countries have not been realized, however, and remain limited. Although governments and leaders have changed from time to time in Turkey and the Central Asian republics since the collapse of the Soviet Union, the general framework and direction of the relations between them have remained largely unchanged. This article analyzes Turkish foreign policy towards Central Asia and the general direction of the foreign policies of Central Asian republics toward Turkey in framing their relations in a historical-geopolitical context.

In his paper "Uzbekistan Joining the Eurasian Economic Union: Implications for Central Asia's Regional Balance", **Fabrizio Vielmini** looks at the accession of Uzbekistan to the Eurasian Economic Union (EAEU), which may have the potential to be a game-changer for international relations in Central Asia. Apart from expected material benefits, Tashkent's interest in the Union coincides with the desire of Russia and other Central Asian countries to balance both the excesses of neo-liberal globalization and Chinese inroads into regional affairs. Moreover, the entrance of a relevant demographic and economic player such as Uzbekistan will reinforce the Central Asian dimension of the EAEU, thus moderating the organization's internal imbalance. This is especially true if Uzbekistan finds a mechanism to act in tandem with Kazakhstan. At the same time, full membership in the EAEU represents a difficult choice for Uzbekistan. The consolidated national doctrine of self-reliance could be put under question and problems may arise in Uzbekistan's relations with its Western partners.

Alexey Fominykh's paper "Cross-border Student Migration From, To and Within Central Asia: Pull and Push Factors" refers to the consistently high birth rates in the CAR and, consequently, their having the most mobile student population in the post-Soviet space. In the first decade of the 21st century, the number of Central Asian youth studying abroad almost doubled and continues to grow. This chapter examines the recent and current developments and factors influencing cross-border academic migration from, to and within the five post-Soviet republics of Central Asia. After analyzing the data on cross-border academic migration flows, the author argues that the bulk of Central Asian academic migrants go to Russia, where they currently make up about 40% of the total international student population. The Russian government continues to encourage this development and sponsor academic mobility from the post-Soviet states via scholarships and tuition waivers.

In the last chapter, "Connectivity for Economic Sustainability: India's March towards Eurasia" **Anirban Chatterjee** argues that the importance of "connectivity" in an era of economic interdependence has never been felt as acutely as in recent times. It is even more pertinent for India, one of the world's fastest growing but energy deficient economies, to tap the potential of connectivity to meet its domestic requirements. As a result, the country is increasing engagement with the neighboring regions, and Eurasia in particular. In order to expedite its market diversification strategy and reduce its dependence on traditional sources in the West, together with Russia and Iran, India has launched the International North-South Transport Corridor (INSTC) to increase access and substantially reduce the cost and travel time to the markets of Eurasian countries, and eventually reach up to European markets as well. India's strategic interest in the Eurasian region and the increasing need for economic and energy cooperation with the region requires it to enhance efforts to augment connectivity with the region. India's growing presence in the region is also buttressed by the fact that India has become a full member in the Shanghai Cooperation Organization (SCO) and is also negotiating Free Trade Agreement (FTA) with the Eurasian Economic Union (EAEU). India regards China's Belt and Road Initiative (BRI) with skepticism and advocates the speedy operationalization of INSTC and other connectivity initiatives. Against this backdrop, the proposed paper will be dealing with the following research questions: How does the INSTC serve India's economic interests? Can the INSTC become an alternative to the BRI? How does India perceive the BRI? In what ways can India compete with the BRI? How does India plan to respond to the BRI? How does Eurasia as a region present an opportunity for India to fulfil its geo-strategic interests? How would India's membership in the SCO and cooperation with the EAEU give it a stronger foothold in Central Asia to further bolster the prospects of connectivity with the region?

Overall, the book highlights the current discourse of the major powers towards Central Asia from different perspectives. The work of all the authors points to the conclusion that Central Asia is not only a region that may lead to conflict between the major powers, but that it may also play a pivotal role in de-escalating tensions through negotiations. At the same time, the region seems to be making noticeable progress towards more democratic and open societies based on free markets, the rule of law and respect for human rights. There are four interconnected aspects that comprise the core development of the five countries of Central Asia: good governance, economic challenges, corruption and poor governance in the form of political cruelty. The following works explore these aspects in further detail.

CHAPTER ONE

RUSSIAN AND CHINESE VERSIONS OF "EUR-ASIANISM": A RESPONSE FROM KAZAKHSTAN
Aizada Nuriddenova

Introduction

The term "Eurasianism" remains vague and outdated. In the past, it carried cultural, ethnic, and nationalist connotations, and while this is still the case to some extent, the term is not well defined. In her comprehensive study on Eurasianism, Laruelle (2009) notes that there are several versions of the term in works on Central Asia by the "Eurasianists" of the 1920s and 1930s. This includes but is not limited to the theories of ethnogenesis developed by Lev Gumilyov, writings on Eurasian geopolitics by Aleksandr Dugin, "Eurasianism: An Ideology for the Multipolar World" by Aleksandr Panarin and the national motives expressed by Kazakh poet Olzhas Suleimenov (Laruelle, 2009). Contemporary Eurasianism can be distinguished from its previous forms by its emphasis on economic integration, regionalism and its attempts to physically connect the Eurasian countries. The following study focuses on contemporary forms of Eurasianism with a focus on regional economic integration and regional infrastructure projects that aim to connect Eurasian countries as a whole.

The idea of connecting Eurasia is by no means new. The former President of Kazakhstan, Nursultan Nazarbayev, actively advocated for integration in the early 1990s. Nazarbayev supported this agenda within the former Soviet Republics as a means of ameliorating the negative consequences of the dissolution of the Soviet Union. Common borders, opening vital supply routes and increased demand for one another's exports were seen as clear advantages of such a union. This concept gained further popularity in the early 2010s as a result of the global financial crisis, giving rise to a Russian concept of Eurasianism and a new regional framework – the Eurasian Economic Union (EAEU). A Chinese view of Eurasianism appeared as well, with Chinese President Xi Jinping proposing to "join hands in building a Silk Road Economic Belt (SREB) with innovative cooperation mode" in 2013 (Ministry of Foreign Affairs of the PRC, 2013). Central Asian, Russian and Chinese perspectives of Eurasian concepts are now coinciding with one another as the notion of connecting and integrating Eurasia becomes larger in scope and more ambitious in its objectives.

Kazakhstan, due to its geostrategic location and size, presents itself as a major bridge in connecting the countries of Eurasia via economic corridors. Due to its geography, Kazakhstan has to balance relations with the two regional powers – Russia and China. This raises the question: how is Kazakhstan responding to the Belt and Road Initiative (BRI), given its commitment to the Russia-led EAEU? The purpose of this study is to explore Kazakhstan's response to the Russian and, more recently, Chinese visions of Eurasianism. This paper applies a hedging strategy framework to understand the decision making processes of Kazakhstan's governing bodies and analyze ways in which they might affect the initiatives of its northern and eastern neighbors.

This paper argues that Kazakhstan aims to take advantage of Russian and Chinese concepts of Eurasianism for their own economic benefit. Given the uncertain economic situation of the former Soviet republics caused by the drastic fall of oil prices and western sanctions towards Russia, Kazakhstan needs strong external mechanisms for boosting and strengthening its economy. As a less influential nation acting within the framework of two larger powers, Kazakhstan seeks to avoid taking sides and demonstrate strong commitment to a multi-vectored foreign policy. The Kazakh view thus reflects the vision that these two understandings of Eurasianism can be complementary in organizing the new economic and infrastructural landscape of Eurasia.

The relationship between these two concepts of Eurasianism can be understood in terms of "hardware" and "software". The hardware element includes tangible support for infrastructure and economic stimulus projects. The software side includes "soft power" dimensions of influence like policy influence or conditional funding for projects. In the case of Kazakhstan, Russia and China project spheres of influence comprised of the software of the EAEU's rules and regulations and the hardware of the SREB's highways, railways and bridges.

In order to fulfill its purpose and objective, this paper uses the principle of a hedging strategy to explore Kazakhstan's response to the Russian and Chinese Eurasian integration projects. The hedging strategy framework is often applied in the context of foreign policy behavior of small states with powerful neighbors. For instance, many scholars tend to use this framework to describe Japan's strategy vis-a-vis the US and China (Kang, 2007) as well as the relationship between ASEAN countries and China. (Chung, 2004). This paper employs the hedging strategy framework to the post-Soviet space to explore its applicability in this context.

Hedging Strategy: A Conceptual Discussion

The concept of hedging remains one of the undertheorized aspects of International Relations (IR) Theory. This fact is widely recognized by IR scholars who continue to have difficulty elaborating the exact conditions under which states are prone to hedge and the concrete methods of conducting this strategy. IR scholars are divided into two camps in terms of defining a hedging strategy. One group emphasizes a hedging country's middle position between balancing and bandwagoning whereas another group stresses that hedging includes both engagement and containment elements and can thus be understood as a hybrid strategy. Koga and Kang are described as belonging to the former group while Korolev, Wohlforth, and Hemmings lean towards the latter.

According to Kei Koga, the concept of hedging should be understood within Balance of Power Theory, in which a hedging strategy lies in the middle of the continuum between balancing and bandwagoning as a third option for hedging states (Koga, 2018). This strategy is common in the foreign policy of states that seek to maintain strategic ambiguity in order to reduce risks, uncertainties and negative consequences caused by balancing or bandwagoning (Koga, 2018). According to Kang, hedging is one of several strategies in a wide spectrum between balancing and bandwagoning. He views hedging as distinct from these other strategies in that it is more likely to be used when there is fear of a rising adversary. Countries may prefer hedging when they do not see a need to balance power, but are still skeptical of another country (Kang, 2007).

Chung hypothesizes that hedging can be "motivated by the need to optimize economic benefits and minimize security risks in response to an environment of uncertainty" (Chung, 2004, p. 35). In light of an analysis that finds China-Russia relations characterized by cooperation on global issues and disagreements on regional approaches, Korolev sees hedging as a strategy of simultaneous engagement and containment (Korolev, 2016).

Wohlforth in particular notes the ambiguous nature of the hedging strategy and views it as a coping mechanism deployed by middle countries. In this sense, a hedging strategy would "allow them to cooperate with the potential hegemon even as they encourage other states to pay the costs of balancing it" (Wohlforth, 2004, p. 227).

This illustrates the contradictory nature of hedging, in which states may simultaneously carry out two contradictory policies such as balancing and engagement to prepare for a variety of possible future scenarios. The worst case scenario will be met with balancing, while the best case will be handled by engaging (Hemmings, 2013).

This paper adopts the first version of hedging, which emphasizes the middle ground between balancing and bandwagoning. This view is well suited to this context, because it takes into account the fact that states may try to avoid the strategic ambiguity of the second view in order to avoid being hurt or exploited.

Russian and Chinese Versions of "Eurasianism"

Although the idea of Eurasianism in Russia has been on the rise since the beginning of the 2000s (Laruelle, 2009), it came into fruition in the 2010s in the form of a Customs Union. Since early 2009, three former Soviet countries – Russia, Belarus, and Kazakhstan – met to discuss the launch of the Customs Union in order to establish unified customs tariffs. On the 1st of January of 2010, the participating countries announced the establishment of the Customs Union. In July of 2011, they removed all the customs controls between them and enacted a common customs code, and in January of 2012, introduced a common economic space.

It is estimated that the Customs Union established a common market with a population of 170 million and aggregate industrial potential of $600 billion, as well as 90 billion barrels of oil reserves and agricultural production valued at $112 billion. The agreement would enable the three countries to achieve 15% GDP growth by 2015, and eventually reach an economic union based on the EU model (European Bank for Reconstruction and Development, 2012). Such an economic union eventually emerged in 2015, grouping together Russia, Belarus, Kazakhstan, Armenia, and Kyrgyzstan into a regional trade bloc.

According to Arbatova, this model of Russian Eurasianism with its focus on regional economic integration stems from a period of uncertainty about Russia's prospects for modernization. She postulates that the Global Financial Crisis led Vladimir Putin to conclude that Russia should not emulate the West as a path to prosperity. Instead, there was a shift towards the view that Russia should revive its economy and establish a unified political, economic, military and cultural space with its partners in the post-Soviet space (Arbatova, 2019). Laruelle notes that this "neo-Eurasianism" takes a pragmatic turn, as the form of the EAEU can represent several dimensions. One of them is the inevitability of the Russia-led regional integration process, articulated by Putin when he stated that: "reintegrating the post-Soviet space under its leadership is Russia's 'natural' geopolitical destiny and that the country cannot be denied this vocation" (Bassin, Glebov & Laruelle, 2015).

The Russian Eurasian vision was extended further in June 2016 when President Putin proposed a "Greater Eurasian Partnership" (GEP) encompassing the EAEU, the states of the Commonwealth of Independent States (CIS), China, India, Pakistan, and Iran. Rolland argues that this move was a result of the Russian leadership's intention to show that Russia is still the key player in Eurasia's integration projects, since it faces a challenge in the form of China's Belt and Road Initiative (Rolland, 2019).

It can thus be seen that the previous versions of Russian Eurasianism have been transformed to suit the contemporary needs of Russian foreign policy and its regional stance. While one cannot disregard the previous Eurasianism models, one can be certain that its latest version - with its emphasis on regional economic integration and competition to secure Russian influence in Eurasia - is becoming more prevalent.

How does the Chinese version of Eurasianism in the form of the BRI differ from the Russian one? Although there is no official conceptual Chinese Eurasian doctrine that elaborates China's vision for the continent, we can note one thing that differentiates Chinese Eurasianism from Russian namely, the scope of what China offers under the banner of Eurasianism. Whereas the Russian Eurasianism (i.e. Customs Union and later the EAEU) initially focused on the economic integration of selected post-Soviet countries, the Chinese version aims to physically connect Europe to Asia. Building on the glorious history of the Silk Road during the Han Dynasty, regional expansion during the Tang Dynasty and the naval expeditions of the Ming Dynasties, China emphasizes its contribution to the advancement of all humankind within the framework of Eurasianism. One can thus conclude that China envisions a grander role for itself that links it to the realm of global governance.

Harper argues that the BRI means China's return to Eurasia takes into consideration the long-term involvement of various Chinese dynasties in Eurasia through the Silk Road, as well as defense measures against nomadic tribes from the Northern and Western Chinese frontiers. He also notes the importance of the post-Cold War period, since it allowed China to reshape a region that was previously dominated by Russia (Harper, 2019).

During his state visit to Kazakhstan in 2013, Chinese President Xi Jinping proposed to 'join hands building a Silk Road Economic Belt with innovative cooperation mode and to make it a grand cause benefiting people in regional countries along the route' (Ministry of Foreign Affairs, 2013). In his speech titled "Promote People-to-People Friendship and Create a Better Future" at Kazakhstan's Nazarbayev University, he further outlined the five main steps that need to be taken to implement this project. They include: 1) strengthening communication among partners, i.e. countries along the road should communicate with each other and consult on plans for future economic development; 2) improving road connectivity to allow participating countries to form a transportation network which connects Asian and European countries from the Pacific to the Baltic sea; 3) facilitating trade among the partner-countries; 4) enhancing monetary circulation in order to avoid financial risks and economic competitiveness; 5) strengthening people-to-people exchanges (Ministry of Foreign Affairs, 2013). The BRI has thus undoubtedly become an ambitious and comprehensive framework aimed at building connectivity and cooperation among the Eurasian countries, as well as facilitating the movement of goods, services, and people across borders.

One interesting aspect of these two visions of Eurasianism is that they have not led to a regional Sino-Russian rivalry. Conversely, as noted by Harper, the "image of Eurasia has shifted from being a largely Russian entity to a Sino-Russian partnership" (Harper, 2019, p.117). The two countries expressed their willingness to work together in May of 2015 during the Putin-Xi Summit in the Russian capital. The two heads of state signed a Joint Russian-Chinese declaration on linking the EAEU and SREB initiatives, while committing to promote regional economic integration and maintain peace and stability (Rolland, 2019).

Despite their distinct origins, these two versions of Eurasianism highlight the importance of the Eurasian landmass to Russia and China's respective regional and global aspirations. Even though the scope of both the GEP and BRI is grand, the Central Asian region is pivotal to their success. Exploring the response of Kazakhstan, the largest Central Asian country involved in these models of Eurasianism, thus carries tremendous importance.

Kazakhstan's Response

President Xi's announcement of the BRI initiative in the Kazakhstani capital during his Central Asian tour clearly illustrates the importance of Kazakhstan in promoting the land-based "Silk Road Economic Belt" project in Eurasia as one of the main components of its successful implementation. Kazakhstan, due to its unique geographic location, size and logistics has the potential to become a major bridge in connecting the countries along this economic belt. Indeed, some observers of Kazakhstan have already noted that it is 'the buckle of One Belt, One Road' initiative given that Kazakhstan's future economic growth depends on the development of transport infrastructure and regional trade (Runde, 2015). Moreover, Kazakhstan was one of the 21 founding members of the Asian Infrastructure Investment Bank (AIIB), a development bank aimed at funding the infrastructure projects, in October 2014. This demonstrates Kazakhstan's embrace of the new Chinese initiative from the initial stages of the project despite its commitments to the Russia-led EAEU.

The idea of connecting Eurasia is by no means alien to Kazakhstan. In March 1994, the then Kazakhstani President proposed the idea of creating a Eurasian Union among former Soviet republics. Common borders, vital supply routes and greater demand for one another's exports were seen as major potential advantages to such a union.

The reasons behind this proposal were hidden in Kazakhstan's domestic economic policy, where the Eurasian idea was extremely popular in the 1990s. After the Soviet collapse and the associated wide-spread economic crisis, the only solution to Kazakhstan's economic predicament was seen to be cooperation with Russia and the former Soviet republics in the form of new confederation or some other form of regional institution.

Although President Nazarbayev's proposal was not met with enthusiasm by other post-Soviet countries, he continued to emphasize Kazakhstan's willingness to work with Russia and the CIS countries. As President Nazarbayev pointed out in 1997: "I have formulated and will continue to promote the idea of Eurasian unity which, I believe, has a strategic future. Kazakhstan alone cannot realize its great transit potential, nor can any other neighboring country do so. This should be done jointly, in close and mutually beneficial cooperation", thus Kazakhstan was deeply committed to the idea of connecting Eurasia (Nazarbayev,

1997). Fast forward to 2009 and 2013, and the Russian proposal of creating a customs union and the Chinese idea of implementing BRI both represented means of realizing this proposal, albeit in partnership with regional powers.

As Kazakhstani officials have repeated on several occasions, Kazakhstan seeks to complement both the Russian EAEU and China's BRI – in order to capitalize on the possible economic benefits. This paper argues that Kazakhstan is trying to hedge between the two projects by being a stable contributing partner to China's BRI while maintaining its commitments to the Russia-led EAEU.

Kazakhstan represents itself as an enthusiastic supporter of the Chinese grand vision in Eurasia, and Kazakhstani officials continue to express their support towards the project. Furthermore, they highlight its commonality with Kazakhstan's 'Nurly Zhol' ('Bright road') program, which in turn aims at developing domestic infrastructure. The Nurly Zhol program seeks to connect the capital to the main economic regions by building highways toward the South, East and West. By the same token, it is intended to create jobs in light of the past economic crisis caused by the sharp falls in oil prices and the western economic sanctions against Russia, which have had a very negative impact on Kazakhstan's economy

The complementary nature of these two programs was officially stated during President Nazarbayev's state visit to the People's Republic of China (PRC) in September of 2015, when he announced that "the synergy of the two programs – 'Bright Road' and the 'New Silk Road' – are to open new opportunities for strengthening the strategic partnership between the two countries" (Kapital, 2015). Since then, the 'Bright Road' project has at times been described by Kazakhstan as part of the 'Silk Road Economic Belt' project. The rationale behind such bold statements is the fact that Kazakhstan has already become a major conduit of the transcontinental logistics project. Currently, 250,000 containers travel from the Chinese port of Lianyungang to Europe through the territory of Kazakhstan with this volume expected to double in 2020 (Kazinform, 2015).

One reason why Kazakhstan welcomes Chinese projects is that they enhance connectivity and the diversification of economic activities and trade routes, a strategic priority in light of its landlocked location. However, the longevity of Kazakhstan's geostrategic advantage in trade is concerning to some observers who stress the high costs associated with being a trade hub. Currently, the transportation of Chinese products by land is sponsored by the Chinese government and it is unclear how long the Chinese government will be willing and able to continue this support (Kassenova, 2017).

Another indication of the hedging strategy applied by Kazakhstan can be observed in Baitabarova's study, which argues that Nur-Sultan went beyond a passive response to the Chinese initiative and "exercised active agency to fill it with a concrete plan" (Baitabarova, 2018, p. 161). The decision to link the Kazakhstani project of Nurly Zhol and the SREB is the most appropriate example of this. Baitabarova also mentions that Kazakhstan views the SREB as an opportunity to gain new access to capital and technology that can be utilized to advance domestic economic and developmental agendas (Baitabarova, 2018).

It can be concluded that Kazakhstan's behavior is likely to be motivated by the possibility of capitalizing on the Chinese economic presence in Central Asia and the associated capital inflows and infrastructure projects in order to avoid the negative consequences of being excluded from the ambitious Chinese initiative. At the same time, Kazakhstan attempts to maintain its special relationship with Moscow with the aim of avoiding definitively taking sides and any strategic uncertainty it might entail.

The Two Eurasianisms and Regional Powers

There have been differing responses from the European Union countries, Turkey and India to the Russian and Chinese initiatives in Central Asia and Eurasia in general. China's BRI has produced stronger feedback compared to the EAEU due to its larger scope, ambitious agenda and its effects on the aforementioned regional powers. These major regional powers have taken neutral stances regarding the establishment and further development of the EAEU by acknowledging that Russia is defending its interests in its "near abroad" and will continue to do so in the future. Moreover, the EAEU has narrow and clearly defined economic goals such as trade creation, free movement of people, goods and capital and, hence, does not seem to project large structural changes in the region. Therefore, the resurgence of Russian Eurasianism in the post-Soviet region has not significantly changed Russia's relations with other major regional powers.

In the meantime, China's Eurasian project has produced a range of supporters and opponents among the major regional powers. For example, Turkey showed strong support for the BRI with its announcement of a "Middle Corridor Initiative" that aims to build a transport route from Turkey to China through Central Asia. Consequently, in November of 2016, Turkey and China signed a memorandum of understanding on aligning BRI and the Middle Corridor Initiative (Guo, 2018).

Some argue that the EU's initial enthusiasm towards the BRI is gradually fading as the project could undermine European unity. The Belt and Road Initiative is more appealing towards the Central and Eastern European countries that are greatly in need of investment. Such disunity is seen within the framework of 16+1 which brings together Central and Eastern European countries and China together outside of the EU (Mohan, 2018). The 16+1 format that initially included Albania, Bosnia and Herzegovina, Bulgaria, Croatia, the Czech Republic, Hungary, Latvia, Lithuania, Macedonia, Montenegro, Poland, Romania, Serbia, Slovakia, and Slovenia plus China was joined by Greece in 2019, turning it into the 17+1 framework. This development is linked to the significance of Greek ports in implementing the BRI in Europe (Kavalski, 2019). Countries like France and Germany have thus grown more skeptical of the initiative and are voicing their concerns regarding the BRI and its adherence to the rules of free trade (Brattberg & Soula, 2018). Nevertheless, the EU and China seek to find common ground in their approaches towards BRI, as indicated by a memorandum of understanding on the EU-China Connectivity Platform signed in 2015, which is intended to promote synergy between the BRI and EU initiatives such as the Trans-European Transport Network Policy (European Commission, 2015).

By contrast, India displays clear opposition to the Chinese initiative. India's major concerns with the BRI are related to its existing territorial disputes with China as well as the potential geopolitical advantages that China would gain through access to South Asia and the Indian Ocean. Moreover, India argues that the BRI is not based on the principles of good governance, rule of law, and transparency, while emphasizing that this project will create debt burdens in recipient countries (Baruah, 2018). India's disapproval of the BRI was made clear by its absence from the First and the Second Belt and Road Forums that took place in 2017 and 2019. However, the Chinese emphasize that this will not affect Sino-Indian bilateral relations (Kamdar, 2019).

Although the Chinese Eurasianism project, in the form of the BRI with its various corridors, has strained Beijing's relations with the EU and India, other major regional powers are demonstrating their willingness to work with China in order to attain constructive solutions.

Regarding the potential benefits that can be gained from the two Eurasianism projects by Russia and China, it is pertinent to point out that both projects were launched in order to revive their respective pasts as they relate to the countries' respective goals and ambitions. For Russia, it is a way of reasserting its past influence and reestablishing its economic dominance in as many former Soviet republics as possible. For China, the BRI presents a framework through which it will be able to play the role of a regional hegemon. Both initiatives are clearly defined in scope, and the potential for Russia and China to respectively benefit from them is likely to be determined by that scope.

Conclusion

This paper argues that the hedging strategy can best explain Kazakhstan's response to the Russian and Chinese grand projects in Eurasia, since clear external balancing and bandwagoning do not match the fundamental approach of Kazakhstan's foreign policy, which is based on a multi-vector orientation. This way, Kazakhstan can avoid the risk of falling out with both regional powers in the face of uncertainty.

This study highlights that the Chinese infrastructure initiative is without doubt unprecedented in its scope and goals. Some states have received the proposal guardedly, while many of the countries that lie at the heart of the project have welcomed it by viewing it as the start of the new creative era of connectivity and inter-state interaction. Kazakhstan is not an exception in this respect, since it has expressed self-conscious support for the initiative by recognizing its own role as a major transit country.

However, some observers doubt Kazakhstan's enthusiasm, arguing that Nur-Sultan's commitment towards the EAEU would not allow Kazakhstan to approve of the BRI, let alone participate in its realization. This paper argues, rather, that Kazakhstan has become China's main contributing partner in its BRI project, in particular its continental component – the "Silk Road Economic Belt." In doing so, the two regional projects - the EAEU and the BRI – can be complementary in organizing the new economic and infrastructural landscape of Eurasia. As many have noted, the coexistence of the Trans-Pacific Partnership (TPP) and the 21st century Maritime Silk Road in the Asia-Pacific Region, and the coexistence of EAEU and "Silk Road Economic Belt" is quite possible. This seems plausible, since both the EAEU and SREB share the common goals of enhancing the free movement of goods, services, people and capital. If these two overlapping regional projects can work in harmony, they may comprise the software (the EAEU with its rules and regulations) and hardware ("Silk Road Economic Belt" with its highways, railways and bridges) of the structure of economic activities in the Eurasian continent.

CHAPTER TWO

THE IMPORTANCE OF CENTRAL ASIA IN CHINA'S DOMESTIC SECURITY

Lere Amusan

Introduction

Global terrorism gained prominence after the 9/11 attacks weakened the preeminent global power, the United States of America (USA). Before the 9/11 attacks, terrorism occurred but was considered a second-tier national security threat, and non-state actors were, for the most part, not taken seriously. The 9/11 events increased awareness amongst nations about the salience of the threat of terrorism to the sovereignty and territorial integrity of nation-states. With the acceleration of globalization and the rise of non-state actors', it can be argued e that states have been weakened, as their borders are more porous and governments are less able to control the movements of goods and persons across borders. The volume of academic discourse on terrorism has increased and governments have developed comprehensive counter-terrorism policies with varying degrees of success. The nature and impact of terrorism brings about competing interpretations, which is common in the field of social sciences.

When researching terrorism in China, it is very likely that an academic will look into the situation in the Xinjiang Uighur Autonomous Region (XUAR), where Muslim ethnic Uighur groups comprise 45 percent of the population (BBC, 2018; Liu & Peters, 2017). This area receives the most attention from the Chinese Communist Party (CCP) in its counter-terrorism efforts. Like the majority of the countries in the international system, China's attitude towards terrorism was altered by the events of 9/11, after which the central government initiated its war on terror (Chung, 2002, p. 8; Sutter, 2016). Such efforts have been successful, but have also harmed China's image due to various human rights issues (Tuttle, 2015). China's 2002 National Defense White Paper labeled terrorism in the post-9/11 era as the preeminent threat to global and regional stability. The document further stated that China will 'unremittingly' combat terrorism in whatever form it appears (Information Office of the State Council, 2002).

The main crux of this paper can be summarized by the following thesis: to protect one's household, one needs to create a stable outer environment. In this analogy, nations recognize the importance of conditions in neighboring countries. China has stressed the importance of cooperation/multilateralism when it comes to tackling global threats such as terrorism. To tackle terrorism within its claimed territory, Beijing must cooperate with the international system and its regional neighbors in particular. Regional cooperation in tackling terrorism has so far focused on coordinatingpolicies between China, Kazakhstan, Kyrgyzstan, Tajikistan, Uzbekistan, and Russia (Omelicheva, 2007), via international or regional institutions. Since this is a more liberal stance of international relations (Jackson & Sorensen, 2013, p. 110), so this paper will look into Central Asian-Sino terrorism cooperation through the Shanghai Cooperation Organisation (SCO).

Terrorism in a Nutshell

Terrorism is defined by Amusan and Adeyeye as using violence to achieve political ends through the creation of fear, uncertainty, and apprehension (Amusan & Adeyeye, 2014; Amusan, Adeyeye & Oyewole, 2019; Heywood, 2011). Another way of seeing terrorism is as an irregular form of warfare that uses hard force to air out grievances and discontent through targeting non-combatants (Mansbach & Rafferty, 2008). While acknowledging the fact that terror has no internationally accepted definition, the Global Terrorism Index (GTI) defines terrorism as 'the threatened or actual use of illegal force and violence by a non-state actor to attain a political, economic, religious, or social goal through fear, coercion, or intimidation' (Institute for Economics and Peace, 2019, p. 6). However, these definitions ignore the important concept of ideology. Another way of seeing terrorism is as the phenomenon of using violence against civilians to achieve political or ideological objectives (Office of the United Nations High Commissioner for Human Rights, 2008, p. 5). However, this paper will employ an academic consensus definition of terrorism as developed by (Schmid & Jongman, 1988, p. 28):

Terrorism is a method of using repeated violent action to inspire fear, employed by (semi-) clandestine individual, group or state actors, for idiosyncratic, criminal or political reasons, whereby - in contrast to assassination - the direct targets of violence are not the main targets. The immediate human victims of violence are generally chosen randomly (targets of opportunity) or selectively (representative or symbolic targets) from a target population, and serve as message generators. Threat- and violence-based communication processes between terrorists or terrorist organizations, victims, and main targets are used to manipulate the main target audience(s), turning it into a target of terror, a target of demands, or a target of attention, depending on whether intimidation, coercion, or propaganda is the primary goal.

Theoretical framework

This study will employ a strand of liberalism known as institutional liberalism. An example of this thinking is Woodrow Wilson's approach to international relations. Wilson described his vision for the international system as creating a zoo instead of a jungle, i.e. where the states (animals) are regulated and cooperative. This led to the creation of the League of Nations (LON) after the First World War. Institutional liberals contend that international institutions facilitate cooperation between states (Jackson & Sorensen, 2013). In other words, institutions and the rules that arise from them help to facilitate mutually beneficial state-to-state interactions in various important issues that affect all of humanity. This, in turn, can ensure beneficial effects for security, welfare and liberty (Keohane, 2012). The ultimate goal is the creation of a peaceful, free, and prosperous world for all those who reside in it. To achieve this, institutional liberalism depends on the role of common goals and interests to create international institutions and foster cooperation, leading to a more regulated, peaceful, and prosperous world. In the context of this paper, an institution is defined as a formal international multilateral organization that sets constitutive, regulative, and procedural rules and norms that govern the actions of states and thus state-to-state relations in particular areas of international relations (Duffield, 2007).

A Brief Overview of the China and Uyghur Xinjiang Story

Most of China's terrorism problems are asymmetrically located in the XUAR (Clarke, 2018; Sutter, 2016). This warrants a summary of who the Uyghur people are and how they came to be under China's control.

The Uyghur ethnic minority group is predominantly located in the province of Xinjiang, found in the Northwest part of China, where they make up roughly half of Xinjiang's 23 million inhabitants (Feng, 2018). The Uyghur people are identified as a Turkish Muslim minority group that originates from and is culturally aligned with Central Asia (CA) (Castets, 2003, p. 1). The Uyghur are ethnically Turkic and practice a moderate form of Sunni Islam with a collective Muslim identity (Mahmut, 2019, p. 24). Uyghurs are considered to be indigenous people of Central Asia. Xinjiang has been under Chinese control and influence since the Qing Dynasty annexed Xinjiang in 1759 after the Dzungar–Qing Wars between 1687–1757 (Castets, 2003). However, the collapse of the Qing Dynasty in the early twentieth century saw a rise in the Uyghur community's will for self-determination. This led to the creation of an independent East Turkestan Republic in the 1930s and 1940s as the central government was unable to effectively control the region. The creation of the People's Republic of China (PRC) resulted in a strong centralized government that then re-gained control of Xinjiang (Castets, 2003). This tumultuous history has led both sides to make contradicting claims as to who has sovereign rights over Xinjiang. The CCP claims that Xinjiang has been an inalienable part of China since ancient times, while the Uyghurs claim that they have inhibited Xinjiang for six thousand years (Tschantret, 2018).

The Uyghur discontent towards the Chinese state started in the early 1760s when its annexation began a period of ethnic, religious, social, economic and political tension between the local indigenous people and the state (Frankel, 2017).

Terrorism in China

China, like many states in the international system, has a history of terrorism. Terrorism in China is mostly related to the issues of ethnicity and self-determination which have been sources of intra- and interstate conflict throughout history. This is the case when it comes to studying terrorism in China, a topic often linked to ethnic minority groups like the Uighurs, Kazakhs, Koreans, Mongols, Tibetans and other groups who constitute of 8 percent of the total population, or about 120 million Chinese citizens (Potter, 2013; Tuttle, 2013). The majority of terrorist activities in China can be characterized as low-level violence by Islamic groups like the East Turkestan Islamic Movement (ETIM), which fights for an independent Xinjiang state or, as they see it, an independent East Turkestan. For Beijing, the issue of territorial integrity is of utmost importance. Thus, Beijing labels those fighting for an independent East Turkestan as terrorists and part of an international Islamic terrorist network (Chung, 2002). Based on the 2017 GTI reports, China, along with other countries such as Saudi Arabia, Germany, and the United Kingdom, are described as low conflict states with high levels of terrorism (Institute for Economics and Peace, 2017). The low-level violence generally included knife attacks, vehicle rampages, and bombings. Below, Figure 1 shows the number of terrorism-related deaths in China from 2003-2017.

Figure 1: Terrorism Fatalities in China (2003-2017)

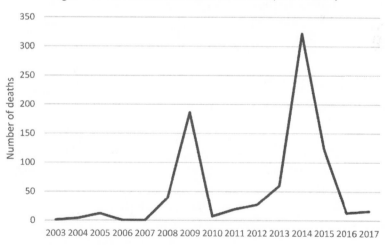

Source: (Ritchie, Hasell, Appel, & Roser, 2020)
*Data was collected from Global Terrorism Database (GTD); RAND Database of Worldwide Terrorism Incidents; Integrated Network for Societal Conflict Research (INSCR) and International Terrorism: Attributes of Terrorist Events (ITERATE). Data for 2006 and 2007 was not found.

From the above diagram, 2009 and 2014 show the highest numbers of terrorism related deaths. The 2009 death rates resulted from the riots in Urumqi while the 2014 death rates resulted from various attacks from bombings and knife attacks (Byman & Saber, 2019). Prior to 2003, the collapse of the Soviet Union played a role in the rise of Uyghur nationalism in Xinjiang. This is due to the fact that the collapse of the Soviet Union led to the creation of various Muslim states[2] neighboring Xinjiang along the western part of the Chinese border, . These newly independent states "...contain titular populations with ethnic and religious characteristics more closely resembling those of western China's long-restive non-Han populations, and this has contributed to an upsurge in Uyghur nationalism" (Potter, 2013, p. 72). The longing to also experience independence like their neighboring Muslim brothers and sisters in former Soviet Central Asia, and Beijing's refusal to award such independence, led to increasing tensions between separatists and government forces. These tensions erupted in the 1990s, particularly in 1995 and 1997 (Dillon, 2014), culminating in the creation of the Turkestan Islamic Party (TIP) and ETIM in 1997. These events were decisive in shaping the development of China's counterterrorism policy.

Counter-terrorism in China

Different states have different strategies for countering terrorism, with varying degrees of success. Counterterrorism (CT) can be seen as the complex set of strategies, policies, and programs that are proposed to counter terrorists, their supporters, and their sponsors (Bellasio, et al., 2018). These measures span a variety of fields, the most important of which include politics, law, finance, communication, defense and intelligence. In the case of China, counterterrorism consists of both domestic and international components. On the domestic front, it includes passing and implementing national security and counterterrorism laws, repression through societal controls and

---

[2]   These states are what form the bulk of Central Asia: Kazakhstan, Kyrgyzstan, Uzbekistan, and Tajikistan.

heavy policing in Xinjiang. This heavy policing has led to Xinjiang being labeled as a police or security state in where technological control (i.e. Integrated Joint Operations Platform (IJOP)) is exerted over the Uyghur population (Human Rights Watch, 2019; Dirks & Cook, 2019). This has created an intrusive social system that monitors nearly every aspect of an individual's life. There exists a "surveillance state" where "facial-recognition software and iris scanners at checkpoints, train stations and petrol stations; biometric data-collection for passports; mandatory apps to cleanse smartphones of potentially subversive material; surveillance drones" are used (Clarke, 2019). CT centers around China's armed forces, particularly the People's Armed Police (PAP), which has a mandate to combat violence and terrorism (Information Office of the State Council, 2019). Over the years, the number of security personnel has increased as the number of police force recruitments rise. This has increased exponentially under the leadership of Chen Quanguo, the Regional Party Secretary as of August 2016. Within the first year of Quanguo's leadership, 100,680 police recruits were sent out, higher than at any time between 2009-2015 (Zenz & Leibold, 2019). This trend became especially apparent after the 2009 Urumqi riots where it was said that the "Chinese authorities have ratcheted up control through a massive expansion of its security apparatuses" (Leibold & Zenz, 2016).

Most of China's counterterrorism activities are directed towards "identified" terrorist groups like the Eastern Turkistan Islamic Movement (ETIM), East Turkistan Liberation Organization (ETLO), World Uighur Youth Congress (WUYC) and East Turkistan Information Center (ETIC) that are perceived to be active in Xinjiang (Permanent Mission of the People's Republic of China to the United Nations, 2003). A significant indicator of the CCP's emphasis on the XUAR in terms of public security is the amount of resources put into domestic security spending. Security spending in Xinjiang is increasing at a higher rate than national spending (Greitens, Lee, & Yazici, 2019). According to the Jamestown Foundation, a U.S.-based think tank, Xinjiang's domestic security spending per capita (measured in Renminbi) ranks second out of all China's regions, behind the Tibet Autonomous Region (TAR). However, between 2006-2017, domestic security spending in Xinjiang increased faster than other regions, growing by 411% compared to 404% in Tibet (Zenz, 2018; Feng, 2018).

Though China's anti-terrorism activities had started before 9/11, after 9/11,China started to engage in international anti-terror cooperation (Guang, 2004). Before 9/11, the need for counterterrorism measures reached its peak during the East Turkestan movement of the 1990s. After 9/11, various anti-terror institutions were formed as part of policies and strategies designed to help reduce China's vulnerability to terrorism. Beijing's counterterrorism plan includes the following:

- ► strengthening counterterrorism legislation;
- ► expanding the counterterrorism bureaucracy;
- ► increasing law enforcement operations in Xinjiang;
- ► promoting economic growth and other development initiatives in Xinjiang; and
- ► promoting ethnic unity and combating religious extremism (Tanner & Bellacqua, 2016).

In December 2001, the Standing Committee of the National People's Congress (NPC) amended China's criminal law to cover terrorist activities (Article 120). This amendment includes founders, leaders, and participants of terrorist groups and activities. Another legislative landmark came in August 2015 when the ninth amendment of the criminal law was passed, and then in December 2015 when the Counterterrorism law was also passed. The Counterterrorism law defined terrorism through the eyes of the CCP. The CCP defines terrorism as the following:

The term 'terrorism,' as it is used in this law, refers to advocacy or behavior (zhuzhang he xingwei which is aimed at realizing political or ideological objectives through means of violence, destruction, intimidation, or other methods or creating social panic, endangering public safety, violating persons or infringing property, or coercing state organs or international organizations (Article 3).

The 9th amendment of the PRC Criminal Law [Article 120(3) to 120(6)] describes terrorist or extremist actions and their punishments (Tanner & Bellacqua, 2016, p. 39).

With regards to bureaucracy, there are two national-level organizations: the National Counterterrorism Leading Small Group and Ministry of Public Security's (MPS) Counterterrorism Bureau. These organizations create a platform for institutional coordination and ensuring all elements of the bureaucracy work together to combat terrorism. The former ensures the coordination of counterterrorism policy while the latter strives to improve the terrorism intelligence collection (Tanner & Bellacqua, 2016).

Law enforcement is a critical component of any state's counterterrorism arsenal. In China, the PAP and the People's Liberation Army (PLA) are responsible for this area. The CCP has increased its security presence in Xinjiang, as well as deploying an extensive security artificial surveillance system. Xinjiang has experienced a disproportionately heavy presence of security forces, surveillance, checkpoints and security cameras (Chin & Burge, 2017). China's "Strike Hard" security campaign, which started in 1996, and wastermed in 2014 as the "Strike Hard Campaign Against Violent Terrorism," were designed to target terrorism, extremism, separation, and religious activities that incite the former three (Human Rights Watch, 2018). These programs increased the presence of security personnel, establishing a permanent heavy security presence in XUAR. This has led to various claims that Xinjiang has become a 'Police State' (Human Rights Watch, 2019).

Another section of China's counterterrorism policy is the creation of ethnic unity, which the CCP views as integral to limiting ethnic separatism and religious extremism (Tanner & Bellacqua, 2016). Such attempts have drawn numerous criticisms, however, one being that the central government has repressed the Uyghur national identity and Islamic religion/practice (Meyer, 2016). In line with relevant international law, minoritie sare qualified to be addressed as indigenous peoples with certain rights (Amusan, 2017; Lennox & Short, 2016). Article 36(1) - (4) of the PRC constitution ensures religious freedom and forbids religious discrimination. Section 36(3) states that religion must not be used to incite protest or violence, however, which has been used as the basis for the religious crackdown on the Uyghur ethnic minority. Moreover, religious groups in China are constrained under the iron fists of the communist party, and religion cannot be used as the basis to oppose the central government in any way, shape or form, and religious groups must be 'registered'. In the case of the Uyghurs, Islam is normally singled out and discriminated against as a religion that incites extremism. This brings into light the 'vocational training' or re-education centers which the government portrays as re-educating the Muslim minority. Estimates suggest that such camps have roughly 1 million Uyghur residents. (Amnesty International 2018; Human Rights Watch, 2018; Zenz, 2018). Based on the accounts of Uyghur people who fled China and gave a rough account of the conditions in these camps, "Detainees are forced to pledge loyalty to the CCP and renounce Islam, they say, as well as sing praises for communism and learn Mandarin" (Maizland, 2019).

In the course of China's counterterrorism efforts, Beijing realized that the "war-on-terror" cannot be fought in isolation when coterminous states of CA are involved. This led to the inevitable move toward regional cooperation to address terrorism activities in Xinjiang.

Terrorism in Central Asia

Terrorism is a transnational issue in many geographical areas. Central Asia is no exception, and terrorism is considered to be a top national security issue for all five Central Asian states (Lain, 2016). Throughout the fall of the Soviet Union and subsequent attempts at nation-building, terrorist activities have become a staple in the region's security discourse (Jin & Dehang, 2019, p. 67). In particular, the nation-building explanation for terrorism has resulted in a heightened threat of terrorism in Central Asia, as there are various groups (political, economic, and religious) that seek to challenge what they consider an illegitimate *status quo* (Borkoev, 2013). Central to this challenge to the status quo is the religious aspect, with groups such as *Hizb ut-Tahrir* and Islamic Movement of Uzbekistan (IMU) being proponents of the creation of a Caliphate (Amanbayeva, 2009). However, terrorist attacks in Central Asia have been categorized as low-scale, rare, ineffective and sometimes exaggerated (Lewis, 2014). However, these unconventional security threats are still central to the security discourse of these states due to the perception of underground networks and the penetration of terrorists from neighboring terrorist hubs such as Afghanistan and Pakistan (Institute for Economics & Peace, 2016; Cheng, 2010). The region has elements of various groups designated as international terrorist organizations like the Islamic Jihad Union (IJU), IMU, and Jund Al-Khilafah which have links with major terrorist groups like the Taliban and Al-Qaeda (Lewis, 2014). However, there is a lack of concrete empirical data about the nature and extent of terrorist activities in Central Asia (Lewis, 2014). Figure 2 below, shows the terrorist impact ranking of CA states from 2012-2019.

Figure 2: Terrorist Impact Ranking of CA States from 2012-2019

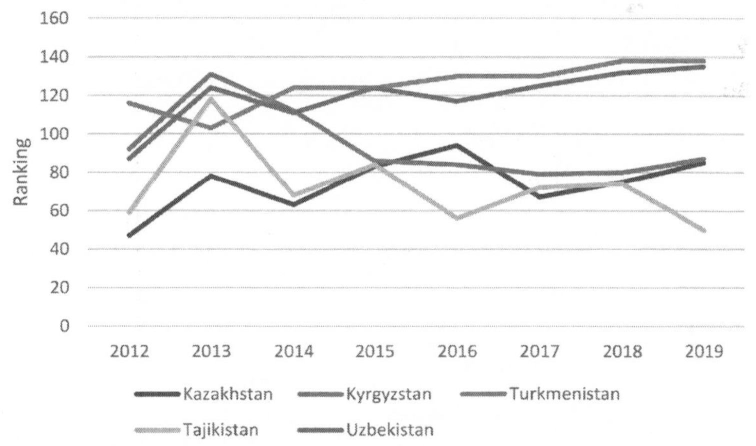

Source: Global Terrorist Index (2012, 2013, 2014, 2015, 2016, 2017, 2018, 2019)

For China, this is a problem as the Uyghur ethnicity "has extensive diaspora links throughout Central Asia, particularly in Kazakhstan, Kyrgyzstan, Uzbekistan, and Turkey" (Tanner & Bellacqua, 2016). Thought the states of Central Asia and China have a number of common security interests, terrorism is certainly one of the foremost issues of shared concern. Since 9/11, Beijing has shifted from viewing terrorism as a domestic issue to a more transnational outlook where it is understood as a threat at the global level (Reeves, 2016). The Xinjiang issue places extra pressure on Beijing to take a more cooperative route on tackling terrorism, as the presence of religious sectarianism, terrorism, separatism, and ethno nationalism in Central Asian states has the potential to 'inspire' the Uyghur people (Panda, 2006, p. 36). Thus, to China, the threat comes not only from Uyghur militants, but also from external terrorist groups and the ethnic, cultural, and historical connections the Uyghurs have with these groups (Clarke, 2018). This concern is intensified by the initiation of the Belt and Road Initiative (BRI) which has been received with enthusiasm, but has also elicited security concerns, as Central Asia is an important component of the project (Reccia, 2018).

Regional Cooperation: Regional Anti-Terrorism Structure (RATS) and counterterrorism in Central Asia

Domestic counterterrorism measures are important, but these measures are incomplete without complimentary efforts on the international level due to the transnational nature of terrorist networks. Terrorists can function in different states due to the porous nature of state borders resulting from globalization and technological advancements. Transnational terrorism has implications for more than two states, unlike domestic terrorism which is strictly confined to the border of the specific state (Rosendorff & Sandler, 2005). Terrorism requires a concerted international and regional effort from all states affected by it. For this reason, counterterrorism cooperation among states is crucial, as states cannot tackle this issue unilaterally, as shown by the USA's "war on terror". The facilitation of such cooperation is normally found in institutions that are vital to the global fight against terrorism. States have used international institutions to suppress and prevent terrorism, and these effots have generally been effective, especially if they are backed by global powers, which has realist connotations (Amusan

& Oyewole, 2016; Romaniuk, 2010). Regional cooperation is normally done through regional organizations, which are organizations that "only allow states to join that fulfil criteria related to their geographical location" (Panke, 2019). The main hypothesis is that China, to an extent, relies on the stability of neighboring Central Asian states to create stability in Xinjiang through the gradual eradication of domestic terrorism which could spill over into China. According to the Global Times, former RATS director Zhang Xinfeng noted, "It is a fact that violent attacks seen in Northwest China's Xinjiang Uyghur Autonomous Region were also influenced by terrorist groups hiding in Central Asia, due to their close ties in history, ethnicity and religion" (Xiang, 2013). This ultimately shows the importance of the Central Asian states in China's quest to promote domestic stability by limiting terrorism in Xinjiang via the SCO. China is heavily invested in these efforts and plays a leading role in counterterrorism through the SCO and RATS, because it cannot face transnational terrorism alone (Jin & Dehang, 2019).

The SCO is an intergovernmental international organization whose main priority is found in the realm of interstate relations. Its creation was announced on June 15, 2001 and its charter signed in June, 2002. The organization entered into force on September 19, 2003 (Shanghai Cooperation Organization, 2020). Its membership is concentrated mainly in Asia, and Central Asia in particular, as 4 (Kazakhstan, Kyrgyzstan, Tajikistan, and Uzbekistan) out of 6 of the founding member states (excepting Russia and China) of the SCO are geographically located in CA.[3] Other permanent members include India and Pakistan. The SCO is concentrated on issues related to non-conventional security, i.e. terrorism, separatism, and regional extremism (European Parliament, 2015, p. 2). SCO counterterrorism

---

[3] There are other states that are involved with the SCO. There are four observer states, namely the Islamic Republic of Afghanistan, the Republic of Belarus, the Islamic Republic of Iran and the Republic of Mongolia. There are also six dialogue partners, namely the Republic of Azerbaijan, the Republic of Armenia, the Kingdom of Cambodia, the Federal Democratic Republic of Nepal, the Republic of Turkey, and the Democratic Socialist Republic of Sri Lanka.

efforts were formalized by the *Shanghai Convention on Combating Terrorism, Separatism and Extremism*. Its crucial first step was the formulation of an agreed-upon definition of terrorism, separatism, and extremism in Article 1. While Article 2 states that the states "shall cooperate in the area of prevention, identification, and suppression of acts referred to in Article 1," Article 8 additionally posits that "Co-operation among central competent authorities of the Parties within the framework of this Convention shall be carried out in a bilateral or multilateral format on the basis of a request for assistance as well as by way of providing information upon the initiative of the central competent authority of a Party" (Shanghai Cooperation Organisation, 2001). Cooperation ranges across a range of areas, including "trade, the economy, research, technology, and culture, as well as in education, energy, transport, tourism, environmental protection" (Shanghai Cooperation Organisation, 2020).

Central to the SCO's counterterrorism efforts is the RATS, a permanent body of the SCO which was legally created in 2001 in accordance with the *Agreement on Regional Anti-Terrorist Structure between the Member States of the Shanghai Cooperation Organisation* of June, 2002. The function of this permanent body is found in Article 3, which states: "RATS shall be the permanent body of the SCO intended to assist in the coordination and collaboration of the Parties' competent agencies in combating terrorism, separatism, and extremism as defined in the Convention" (Shanghai Cooperation Organisation, 2002). States that are part of the convention are required to assist each other in combating terrorism, mainly at the request of one of the parties (Article 6 (2) of the RATS agreement). According to (Wallace, 2014) RATS's functions can be divided into five thematic functions, based on Article 6 of the RATS agreement: Information exchange, information integration and production (Article 6 (3), (4), and (5)), external relations (Article 6 (12)), training and exercise coordination (Article 6 (6), (7), and (8)), and legal and jurisdictional (Article 6 (9)). This is shown by the various important anti-terrorism measures in areas of financing, cybersecurity/information sharing, and combat exercises that are covered by various RATS conventions as summarized in table 1. These measures have enhanced counterterrorism cooperation between SCO member states (Jin & Dehang, 2019).

Table 1: Anti-Terrorism Measures

Anti-Terrorism measures	Conventions
Financing	Agreement on Cooperation in Combating Illicit Traffic of Narcotic Drugs, Psychotropic Substances, and Precursors
Weaponry movement	Agreement over Cracking Down Smuggling Weapons, Explosives and Ammunition
Information sharing/cybersecurity	Agreement on the Database of the Regional Anti-Terrorist Structure of the Shanghai Cooperation Organization
Combat exercises	Agreement on the Procedure for Organizing and Conducting Joint Anti-Terrorist Exercises by Member States of the Shanghai Cooperation Organization

Source: (Shanghai Cooperation Organisation, 2020)

This has contributed significantly to counterterror activities in the Central Asian states, as such cooperation means member states are required to support each other to combat terrorism (Omelicheva, 2009). This provides a win-win opportunity for all sides as they are better able to pool together the necessary military, financial, and intelligence resources to combat terrorism. This is clearly shown by the various multilateral anti-terror military drills which have taken place, in which China has been the most active participant (Jin & Dehang, 2019). Table 2 illustrates some of the multilateral military anti-terror drills between 2003-2018.

Table 2: Multilateral Military Anti-Terror Drills Between 2003-2018

Year	Code	Participants	Host(s)
August 6-12, 2003	Coalition-2003	China, Kazakhstan, Kyrgyzstan, Russia, and Tajikistan	Kazakhstan and China
March 5-6, 2006	East-Antiterror-2006	Kyrgyzstan, Uzbekistan, Kazakhstan, China, Tajikistan, Turkmenistan, and Russia	Uzbekistan
May 29-31, 2007	Issyk Kul Anti-Terror-2007	Kyrgyzstan, Kazakhstan, China, Russia, Tajikistan, and Uzbekistan	Kyrgyzstan
August 16–26, 2010	Saratov-Antiterror-2010	Russia, Kazakhstan, and Kyrgyzstan	Russia
September 9–25, 2010	'Peace Mission-2010'	Russia, China, Kyrgyzstan, Tajikistan, Kazakhstan	Kazakhstan
June 8-14, 2012		Kazakhstan, China, Kyrgyzstan, Russia, and Tajikistan.	Tajikistan
August 24–29, 2014	Peace Mission-2014	China, Russia, Kazakhstan, Kyrgyzstan, Tajikistan	China
September 15–17, 2015	CentrAsia-Antiterror-2015	Russia, China, Kyrgyzstan, Kazakhstan, Tajikistan, and Uzbekistan	Kyrgyzstan
August 29, 2018	Peace Mission 2018	China, Russia, Kyrgyzstan, Tajikistan, Kazakhstan	Russia

Source: (de Haas , 2016, pp. 382-386; Jin & Dehang, 2019, p. 73)

China's growing influence and power meant that it played a leading role in the counterterrorism efforts of the SCO. With the functions of the RATS as detailed in Article 6, we find that China has established an avenue to legally help the Central Asian states combat terrorism, something that China appears to be enthusiastic about. This is due to the belief that helping Central Asian states handle their 'terrorist threat' will reduce the ability of Uyghur extremist groups to use Central Asia for aid, refuge, and inspiration (Scobell, Ratner, & Beckley, 2014).

Conclusion

China's involvement in CA is not motivated by altruism, but by the state's interest in economic and political stability in the region. Without the support of Central Asian states, Beijing's domestic terrorism policies could be rendered ineffective in the long term. This is a result of the cultural irredentism that is the hallmark of the state system in developing areas. The need for energy, oil and gas, and political stability despite the repression of minorities in Xinjiang and Xizang (Tibet), as well as the realization of the Silk Road Economic Belt, Maritime Silk Road, and China-Pakistan Economic Corridor necessitate an international security regime, and the SCO is intended to fulfill this role. Transforming this organization into a supra-national institution will go a long way toward helping Beijing achieve domestic political stability.

For meaningful improvement in the two neglected provinces of Xinjiang and Xizang, there is a need to promote human rights, such as rights relating to religion and culture. One expression of these rights may take the form of an educational system that will eventually promote minorities' access to gainful employment on a level similar to that enjoyed by the Han ethnic group, which dominates the political and economic affairs of the state. In achieving this, relevant public laws that guide indigenous rights and responsibilities should be promoted. This will facilitate the socio-economic development of these regions, as well as improving mutual trust between Beijing and the Central Asian states.

CHAPTER THREE

HINA'S GEO-ECONOMIC INROADS INTO CENTRAL ASIA: AN ASYMMETRIC INTERDEPENDENCE VULNERABILITY APPROACH

Tola Amusan

Introduction

The Central Asia Region (CAR) is an essential component in China's foreign relations due to the Chinese central government's various interests in the region. China's relations with the CAR has deep historical roots, extending to the period where China was considered the 'Middle Kingdom'. This relationship has gone through phases of varying degrees of peace and animosity, particularly during the Cold War period. The collapse of the Soviet Union (USSR) resulted in the establishment of five independent states - Kazakhstan, Kyrgyzstan, Tajikistan, Turkmenistan, and Uzbekistan - which collectively form the CAR. Such a separation provided Beijing new avenues to secure its interests, but at the same time augmented the security threat posed by the region: a blessing and a curse. For this reason, since the 1990s China has increased its engagement with the region for two overriding interests; security and economic pursuits. Both domestic and international factors play a role in China's increased attention towards the region. China is not alone when it comes to emphasizing improved relations with the CAR. Other major powers like Russia and the European Union (EU), influential powers like India and Iran, and minor powers like Afghanistan and Pakistan are all vying for a stake in this region.

The relationship between China and the CAR, post-Cold War, has centered around security issues such as border disputes - a cause of friction between the USSR and PRC during the Cold War - as well as promoting economic ties. In shaping its relations with the CAR, China is playing to its strengths and leveraging the economic component of power and influence. Beijing, by many accounts, is considered an economic superpower which allows China to exert considerable political and diplomatic power. When applying this to the case of the CAR, this leverage has allowed China to develop friendly relations and directly challenge other major powers, a situation often attributed to Beijing's geographic proximity and economic affluence. Thus, China has mostly used economic instruments to promote its interests in the region in a form of "geo-economics".

Globalization and interdependency are common characteristics of the modern international system. They promote prosperity and peace, but they can also be used by states as a form of leverage and influence, particularly in situations of asymmetric interdependence vulnerability. For China, there is a consensus on what its interests in the CAR are. This paper investigates the means used in pursuit of those interests. China's strategy in the CAR is centered around the BRI, which advances various objectives for Beijing. One of these objectives is the creation of asymmetric interdependence vulnerability that increases China's geo-economic influence and power. This, in turn, leads to China having greater bargaining power and increases its ability to consolidate and defend its interests in the region.

Conceptual Framework

Geo-economics as a concept has gaps in its conceptual contributions that require further investigation (Scholvin & Wigell, 2018). The term was first coined by Edward Luttwak (1990) who argued that states would pursue their conflicting interests using economic means rather than military power after the collapse of the Soviet Union. In his own words, Luttwak argued that state power is found in "disposable capital in lieu of firepower, civilian innovation in lieu of military-technical advancement, and market penetration in lieu of garrisons and bases" (Luttwak, 1990, p. 17). Geo-economics is the use of economic instruments to promote and defend a state's national interests and achieve desired geopolitical results (Blackwill & Harris, 2016). There is a relationship between economic growth, development, and changes in the geopolitical character of the international system. Another way of seeing geo-economics is as a foreign policy strategy whereby states use economic means of power to achieve strategic objectives (Scholvin & Wigell, 2018). The 'geo' in geo-economics refers to the need to recognize the importance of the geographic dimension. As such, the study and practice of geo-economics is about the use of economic power to achieve strategic objectives within a geographical dimension (Wigell et al., 2019b). Geo-economic power has been described as a new form of power that involves both states and non-state actors such as corporations who use capital to influence state bureaucrats toward making policies that favor corporate interests (Kundnani, 2011).

Geo-economics can be seen from both macro and micro levels. "Macro-level economic power management and the new era's micro-level implications for the system's actors in the shifting global power game, captures the essence of the age of geoeconomics" (Hsiung, 2009). Hsiung defines geo-economics as the acquisition of economic power to diversify the availability of economic instruments that actors can use as a power base. Actors can also use geo-economic strategy as leverage in bargaining positions, as well as to advance and define their national interests within a geographical context.

Economic interdependence is an essential component of International Relations as it covers various aspects of the field. Interdependence can be a source of peace and prosperity, (Jackson & Sørensen, 2013) but it can also be a source of tension and belligerence (Copeland, 2015). Asymmetric interdependence vulnerability posits that when interdependence is unequal, some parties are more dependent on others instead of the utopian ideal of 'mutual dependence'. In this context, vulnerability pertains to the opportunity cost incurred by a state when a relationship is disrupted, even when taking into consideration the availability of an alternative policy and the cost of such policy (Keohane & Nye, 2012). In an asymmetrically interdependent relationship, the degree of vulnerability for one party is higher than the other. Hence, one party stands to bear more of the costs than the other (Esakova, 2012). Coupled with the effects of globalization, interdependence can be used as a potent source of power, and this dynamic is the defining characteristic of asymmetric vulnerability interdependence. In this way, states pursue their interests through the manipulation of the economic ties that bind them together in a globalized world (Keohane & Nye, 2012; Lee, 2014).

China's Interests in Central Asia

China identifies itself as a developing country, and the developing world is becoming more important to China (Scobell et al., 2018). For this reason, China has prioritized other developing countries in its overall foreign policy in the 21st century, particularly within the multilateral framework (Scobell et al., 2018). Developing countries, such as those of Latin America, Asia, Oceania and Africa are more likely to fall into China's orbit of influence than the more developed states.[4] China's presence in the developing world in modern history became a topic of discussion during the Cold War, when Beijing focused on expanding its influence, both ideological and political, to challenge American and Soviet imperialism. Since the end of the Cold War and with the advent of the 21st century, Beijing has made significant strides in the developing world, leading to a more complicated interconnection between its various interests in these regions.

The CAR is an important cog in China's worldwide activities, and China has a wide array of interests in the region. One can argue that the CAR is not only vital to domestic stability and the growth of the Chinese state- it also plays a role in the preservation of the central government (Mitchell, 2014). China's interests in the CAR can be grouped into 2 categories: security and economic interests. This is based on the comments of several scholars, i.e. Mitchell (2014), Peyrouse (2016), Scobell et al. (2018) and Sutter (2012).

---

[4] Developed and developing countries tend to be classified according to their levels of industrialisation, income per capita, and human development. Developed countries tend to rank high in these three areas, while developing countries have lower rankings. In this paper, the United Nation's method of classifying countries as either low and medium human development (developing) or high and very high human development (developed) will be used. The United Nations uses the Human Development Index (HDI) to rank countries on a scale of 0-1 using life expectancy (health quality), education (mean and expected years of schooling for adults and children), and standard of living (Gross National Income per capita). Countries with scores lower than 0.550 are low development countries, between 0.550 – 0.699 are medium human development, between 0.700-0.799 are high human development and more than 0.800 are considered to be very high human development countries (Todaro & Smith, 2015; United Nations Development Programme, 2019)

In the security realm, the most important issues after the formation of the new CAR states, were delimitation and de-militarization of
borders. These issues were one of the main catalysts for Sino-Soviet tensions and conflict during the Cold War, and a priority immediately after
the Cold War (Brown, 2000). For this reason, Beijing wasted no time in
trying to resolve these issues with the creation of the "Shanghai Five,"
a treaty organization that initially included China, Russia, Kazakhstan,
Tajikistan, and Kyrgyzstan (Chung, 2004).

Another issue is the presence of extremists, terrorists and separatist
groups. China worried that the newly formed independent states in the
CAR would become a breeding ground for such groups. Such groups
could infiltrate China, particularly the autonomous Xinjiang region
(Guangcheng, 2015). Hence, peace in the CAR is of vital importance to
China.

Economically, Beijing has various vested interests in the region in
the realms of trade, investment, energy, and natural resources. These
form the crux of Chinese economic engagement with the CAR states.
Not only does this relationship benefit China economically by securing
access to alternative sources of energy and natural resources, additional
markets for Chinese products, and more business for companies, it also
helps China with its Xinjiang issue. The central government has emphasized the rapid development of Xinjiang, which would require opening
up the province's Western border with the CAR states. Thus, economic
cooperation with the CAR is also important for the stability of Xinjiang
(Guangcheng, 2015). On the other hand, the CAR has a role in China's
economic security which is visible in the 'Malacca Dilemma'.[5] Chinese
economic engagement with the CAR states is thus aimed at implementing Beijing's strategic security interests (Jarosiewicz et al., 2013).

---

[5] The Malacca Dilemma is term coined by Hu Jintao that refers to the situation whereby
China's heavy dependence on the Strait of Malacca to receive its energy imports forms
one of its greatest weaknesses as any form of blockade in the Strait can cripple the
Chinese economy and negatively impact the legitimacy of the CCP (Lanteigne, 2008).

China-Central Asia Economic Relations

The following section investigates China's economic engagement with the CAR from 2000, as this period saw an increased emphasis on economic engagement. During the 1990s, China's main interaction with the CAR states was focused on security (border disputes, extremism, separatism and terrorism). This is not to say that economic relations were not important; China and the CAR states had budding economic relations during this period. It was not until the early 2000s, however, with China's 'going out' initiative, that economic relations began to make significant strides. By many accounts, China is the single most important state actor in the region (Mariani, 2013). Beijing has a distinct advantage over other economic competitors, it is geographically close to the region and has the economic strength to forge deep economic relations. This has resulted in China's economic footprint in the region growing significantly in the 21st century, particularly in trade, investment, and finance (Scobell et al., 2018). Since 2013, the BRI has been the crux of China's economic relations with the CAR states. The following subsections detail each aspect of China's economic relations with the CAR, namely trade, foreign direct investments, and financing and aid.

Sino-Central Asia Trade

China's total trade with the states in the CAR has grown from 2000 to 2018, displayed in Figure 3 below.

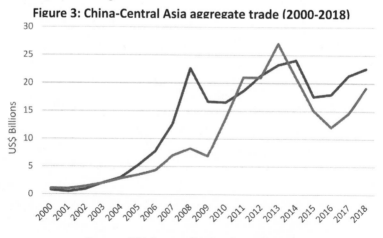

Figure 3: China-Central Asia aggregate trade (2000-2018)

Source: UN Comtrade database (2020)

Figure 4: China's disaggregated trade with Central Asian states

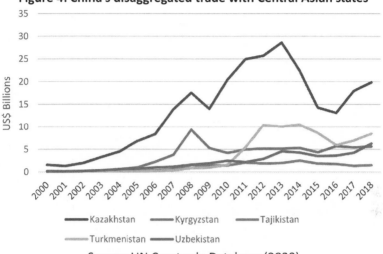

Source: UN Comtrade Database (2020)

	Total inflow (US$ Billions)	China FDI (US$ Billions)	China Share of total FDI (%)
Kazakhstan	24.3	1.5	6.1%
Tajikistan (2017)	0.270	0.095	35%
Kyrgyzstan	0.851	0.338	40%
Uzbekistan	2.4	0.5	20.8

Sources: (National Bank of Kazakhstan, 2020; National Statistical Committee of the Kyrgyz Republic, 2020; News Central Asia, 2019; Saidov, 2019; UNCTAD STAT, 2020; Xinhua, 2020b)

These events are mainly driven by China's quest for a nearby source for natural and energy resources (Scobell et al., 2018). This brings the issue of the 'Malacca Dilemma' and China's economic security into the foreground. China's investments in the CAR are primarily found in energy and natural resources , as well as in infrastructure. The infrastructural investments are largely spurred by the BRI, facilitating the smooth transportation of energy and natural resources between the CAR and mainland China (Scissors, 2018, p. 6). China has been the main driver for the infrastructural development of the CAR states, linking China's western frontier through the development of roads and railways, much like the ancient Silk Road. The Central Asia Data-Gathering and Analysis Team (CADGAT) has examined 261 investment projects under the BRI and gathered empirical data on China's investments in the region. The data is summarized in the table below according to the amount recipient countries received and the total monetary value of the projects per sector.

Table 4: China BRI projects in Central Asia as of 2019

	Total value (US$ billion)	Rail and road connectivity (US$ billion)	Energy connectivity (US$ billion)	Resource exploration and processing (US$ billion)	Other (US$ billion)
Kazakhstan	90.9	14.54	18.5	37.8	20.06
Kyrgyzstan	5.4	1.8	2.7	0.68	0.22
Turkmenistan	24.8	1.4	9.4	14	NA
Uzbekistan	4.6	1.3	0.21	2.23	0.86
Tajikistan	10.5	4.52	4.5	0.465	1
Total (billion) and (% share)	**136.2**	**23.6 (17.3%)**	**35.31 (26%)**	**55.18 (40.51%)**	

Source: (CADGAT, 2019)

According to these data, the majority of China's BRI investment projects are found in the resource exploration and processing sector, accounting for 40.51% of China's investment in the region. Kazakhstan is the highest recipient of these investments, receiving 66.7% of the total value. The importance of natural resource extraction is also evident in the American Enterprise Institute (AEI) data. AEI data, compared to CADGAT data, show different figures but reach the same conclusion, as shown in Table 5.

Table 5: China's FDI and Construction in the Central Asia Energy Sector (2005-2018)

	The total value of FDI and construction contracts (US$ billion)	The total value of Chinese FDI and construction in the energy sector (US$ billions)	% of energy in total FDI and construction contracts
Kazakhstan	33.99	24.28	71.4
Kyrgyzstan	4.73	2.89	61
Uzbekistan	5.44	3.49	64
Turkmenistan	6.8	6.8	100
Tajikistan	1.61	0.75	47

Source: (American Enterprise Institute, 2020)

Most of China's investments and construction activities are in the natural resource sector. Tables 4 and 5, the data displays that Kazakhstan is the main beneficiary of Chinese outward FDI in the CAR and that the energy sector dominates this FDI. China's investment approach focuses on oil and uranium mines in Kazakhstan, gas in Turkmenistan, Uzbekistan, and Kazakhstan and electricity in Kyrgyzstan, Tajikistan, and Kazakhstan. With the CAR as the backbone of China's overland Silk Road, it is predicted that Beijing's bilateral investment engagement with the region will increase considerably (Grant, 2019). China has bought up critical assets in most of the Central Asian states. For instance, in Kazakhstan, China has shares in Petro Kazakhstan, JSC KazMunaiGas E&P, and Kazakhmys. China also acquired Kyrgyzaltyn in Kyrgyzstan, Tajik Aluminum in Tajikistan and Uzbek neftegaz in Uzbekistan (American Enterprise Institute, 2020).

Financing and Aid

In examining Chinese financing, we consider both Official Development Assistance (ODA) and Other Official Flows (OOF). The former abides by a strict OECD definition of aid in which aid is "designed to promote the economic development and welfare of developing countries" (OECD, 2018). The latter constitutes "official sector transactions that do not meet official development assistance (ODA) criteria" (OEDC 2020). Both of these generally take the form of loans. It is important to note, however, that ODA and OOF data from China is very elusive, as such activities are considered secret (Horn et al., 2019). Table 6 presents China's share of the CAR states' external debt in 2018.

Table 6: China's Share of Central Asian External Debt (2018)

	Total external debt (US$ billion)	China's loans (US$ billion)	China's share of external debt (%)
Kazakhstan	158.8	11.6	7.3
Kyrgyzstan	3.82	1.72	44.9
Uzbekistan	17.3	2	11.5
Turkmenistan	0.91	-	-
Tajikistan	2.9	1.2	41

Source: (Kyrgyz Bank, 2020; Levina, 2019; Ministry of Finance of the Republic of Tajikistan, 2019; National Bank of Kazakhstan, 2020; World Bank, 2020a)

Table 6 suggests that in the majority of the CAR states[6] China contributed more than 10% of each state's external debts. When looking at the external debt to China (debt stock as a share of GDP), the top 50 most indebted recipients of Chinese loans included 4 from states in the CAR (Turkmenistan, Uzbekistan, Kyrgyzstan, and Tajikistan). As of 2017, their debt to China made up at least 10% of their GDP, with Kyrgyzstan having the highest debt-GDP ratio and Uzbekistan having the lowest (Horn et al., 2019, p. 15). The majority of these loans are provided by State-Owned Enterprises and Banks and geared towards natural resources, energy resources, and infrastructure (Aid Data, 2020). For the CAR states, a herculean effort may be necessary to repay these loans. According to Jaborov (2018, p. 34), these states will continue to depend primarily on China due to the US backtrack and Russia's lack of financial

---

[6] Data on China's share of Turkmenistan's external debt could not be found.

strength. Additionally, China's loans tend to be cheaper than the other parties, with interest loans as low as 2 percent and repayment periods as long as 20 years.

China's Economic Clout in Central Asia

Having analyzed China's economic involvement in the CAR, the next step is to discuss China's geo-economic influence in the region. To do this, it is important to first examine China's degree of economic importance in the region and the ways in which it leads to asymmetric vulnerability interdependence. Beijing is rising to be the most important economic player in the sub-region in various aspects of international economic relations (Scobell et al., 2018). In terms of total trade, China accounts for a substantial share of each state's trade as of 2018, as shown in Table 7.

Table 7: China's Share of Total Trade in Central Asian States (2018)

	China's share of total trade	Russia's share of total trade
Kazakhstan	12.34	19.54
Kyrgyzstan	28.11	26.1
Uzbekistan	20.05	17
Tajikistan	41.32	25

Source: UN Comtrade database (2020); World Bank (2020)

In 2017, China accounted for 83% and 11% of Turkmenistan export and import respectively (OEC, 2018). Compared to Russia, China accounts for more trade with Kyrgyzstan, Turkmenistan, Uzbekistan, and Tajikistan. Meanwhile, in Kazakhstan, Russia accounts for a marginally larger share of total trade (OEC, 2018; UN Comtrade, 2020). To have an influence over these states by means of trade, trade must play a large role in that state's economy. The states in the

CAR are highly dependent on the external financial flows that come with international trade. In Kazakhstan, trade accounts for 63% of its GDP, Kyrgyzstan, 70%, Turkmenistan, 35%, Tajikistan, 57%, and Uzbekistan, 68%.[7]

China has been a rising force in terms of investment and construction projects, as seen in Tables 3, 4, and 5. There is a consensus that China has become an important source of funding and investment in all the CAR states (Konstantinas, 2013; Peyrouse, 2007; Scobell et al., 2018). Though most of these investments go to the natural resource sector and transportation connectivity, the provision of funds, technological know-how, and labor for infrastructure is also a crucial aspect of China's economic engagement with the CAR. This is something that has increased in importance since the early 2000s and culminated with the initiation of the BRI (Stronski & Ng, 2018). In Tajikistan and Kyrgyzstan, Beijing accounts for the majority of foreign direct investment (FDI). In Uzbekistan, China is ranked second after Russia. In Kazakhstan, China accounts for a smaller share of FDI, marginally less than Russia and substantially less than the Netherlands, Switzerland and the USA (National Bank of Kazakhstan, 2020; Samruk-Kazyna, 2018). In terms of the construction sector, China is the most dominant player. This is especially crucial in these states as they are severely lacking in the infrastructure needed to modernize and develop (Fengler & Valley, 2019). From 2005-2019, China undertook many construction projects across different sectors (American Enterprise Institute, 2020; CADGAT, 2019). Chinese investment and funding of infrastructure projects is mainly directed towards hard, rather than soft infrastructure.[8] As with trade, it is crucial to examine the contribution of inward FDI towards the GDP of these states. In all the CAR states, as of 2018, FDI contributed less than 6% of GDP.

---

[7] These figures are for 2018 except for Tajikistan's data. It is from 2017.
[8] Hard infrastructure general refers to physical infrastructure like ports, roads, buildings, airports, and railway lines, while soft infrastructure relates to institution building to ensure governance and maintenance of hard infrastructure.

Table 8 below summarizes inward FDI as a percentage of GDP in the 5 CAR states.

Table 8: Inward FDI as a Percentage of GDP in 2018 for Central Asian states

	FDI (% GDP)
Kazakhstan	0.12
Kyrgyzstan	0.6
Uzbekistan	1.2
Tajikistan	3
Turkmenistan	5

Source: (World Bank, 2020c)

Table 6 highlights that China is also a major source of foreign loans for the CAR states and that these Chinese loans take up a large chunk of these state's total external debt. Chinese lending activities in the developing world have raised concerns from both internal and external actors. This has resulted in accusations that China is dishing out loans to entangle these states into debt traps (Ameyaw-Brobbey, 2018; Cheng, 2018). However, for CAR states, particularly Uzbekistan, Kyrgyzstan, Tajikistan, and Turkmenistan, China is seen as a more reliable source of cheap funding, as Russia is financially incapable of providing such funds (Mitchell, 2014). It is only in Kazakhstan that China does not hold a significant share of foreign external debt, falling behind the Netherlands (30%), US (8%), and UK (13%), but ahead of Russia (6%). Chinese loans are crucial to these CAR states as "their governments rely on Chinese loans as an economic tool to boost local development. Regional infrastructure is inadequate and outdated and local funds are scarce" (Sim & Aminjonov, 2020). These loans also come with preconditions such as the involvement of Chinese companies, labor, and technology. When comparing Chinese loans to that of Western funders, these loans are more attractive due to their low interest rates and lack of preconditions of political, economic, and human rights reforms (Sim & Aminjonov, 2020). In research conducted by the Center for Global Development (CGD), it was found that Tajikistan and

Kyrgyzstan are most likely to experience debt distress (Hurley et al., 2019) exposing them to economic vulnerability to China.

China's Influence in Central Asia: A Cause for Concern for Russia?

Over the years, China and Russia have developed a strategic partnership (Xinhua, 2020a) and a friendship, with Xi Jinping describing Vladimir Putin as his 'best friend' and Vladimir Putin awarding China's ambassador to Russia, Li Hui, the Russian Order of Friendship. Much has been written about this relationship and its potential to blossom into a full-fledged alliance and whether or not it is sustainable. A crucial area that will either make or break this friendship is the CAR, which is Russia's traditional sphere of influence. This section discusses China's influence in the region as it relates to Russia's concerns.

Overall, the CAR has received a renewed interest in the study of power dynamics in the region, which has resulted in the conception of a so-called 'New Great Game' between the great powers that compete for a greater stake in the region. The most notable great powers are: China, Russia, the EU and the USA. The 'New Great Game' is shorthand to describe great power competition for 'influence, power, hegemony and profit' (Edwards, 2003, p. 83). Great power competition in the Central Asian theater is not new to the region. In the 1800s it was the centre British and Russian imperial maneuvering for control and influence, prompting Rudyard Kipling to label this competition as the 'Great Game'[9] (Hamm, 2013; Hauner, 1984). The analysis of this 'New Great Game, 'however, will be limited to the immediate great power neighbours of CAR states: China and Russia.

China's economic reach has penetrated deep into the CAR, with the

---

[9]   The difference between the original Great Game and the New Great Game is that former involved competition between two empires and the latter involves competition between more than two states. The original great game involved competing forms of imperialism, while the new great game hasa dynamic range of goals determined by neo-imperialism (Edwards, 2003)

majority of the region's states becoming highly economically dependent on China. This has encroached into Moscow's traditional sphere of influence (Jackson, 2016). Wigell & Landivar (2019) argue that this economic reach has credible potential to result in significant political influence in the long run. What is certain is that China's increasing economic engagement with the CAR has drastically changed the power dynamics in the region. These states are tilting more towards China to push forward with their economic development, making China an indispensable partner. In this context, Beijing strives to increase its influence at the expense of other powers in the region (Scobell et al., 2014). However, another argument that presents itself is that China has never explicitly expressed its desire to carve out a sphere of influence in the CAR. Beijing's attitude towards the region is simply to pursue its own interests in the region. If one frames this game as Russia and China's quest for influence in the region, there is a compelling argument that Russia simply cannot keep up with the pace at which China is extending its influence, as shown by the relative failure of Russia's Eurasian Economic Union (EEU) vis-à-vis the BRI (Stronski & Ng, 2018). This may frustrate Moscow in the future as both states "pursue great power aggrandizement and even neo-imperial policies there" (Blank, 2012). China is significantly more economically powerful than Russia and presents higher perceived opportunities to the CAR. As illustrated in the previous section, China has, over time, obtained a larger stake in CAR states' economies in terms of trade, investments, and loans. Thus, the economies of the CAR states are becoming more aligned with China rather than Russia. The BRI and its accompanying economic package present a challenge to Russia's influence in the region. China's latent economic dominance has resulted in Beijing's increased geo-economic influence (Beeson, 2018; Ferchen, 2016; Lain, 2018)

Geo-economics is used by China firstly to strengthen the economic base of CAR states and promote stability in the region, since this also helps secure China's national interests.[10] Secondly, the increase of China's diplomatic ties with the region increases the CAR states' propensity to side with China on a variety of issues, particularly in multilateral settings like the United Nations General Assembly. Lastly, China has cemented its place as the most important economic player in the region over the coming decades and become an indispensable partner, thus giving Beijing increased economic leverage to conduct power politics. In other words, China's economic expansion into the CAR is a geopolitical design insofar as the country tries to improve its prestige and power in the region while enhancing its economic security by diversifying its energy sources. The states in the CAR are also well aware of the asymmetrically negative consequences that might result from changes in China's economic policies towards them, primarily as a result of their economic dependence on China (Sharshenova & Crawford, 2017). This can potentially strengthen Beijing's political sphere of influence in the region, particularly with the context of the BRI (Wigell et al., 2019a). This is further exemplified by the notion that China is an ideal partner who provides generous trade, investment, and loan terms without trying to alter domestic issues (Olcott, 2013). Moreover, with China's rise, "Beijing and Moscow will be the region's principal economic, political, and security partners due to China's preeminent regional economic power and Russia's residual presence" (Rumer et al., 2016)

In a study conducted in Kazakhstan and Kyrgyzstan, the authors concluded that there is a general awareness that China's influence is on the rise while Russian influence is on a decline. This trend is expected to continue in the next decade, as China's influence is projected to gain supremacy (Chen & Jiménez-Tovar, 2017). Regarding the Uyghur situation, CAR states have ethnic ties with the Uyghur people but are reluctant to challenge China on the suppression of the Uyghur ethnic group.

---

[10] In this context, China's national interests is ensuring secure borders to curb the 'three evils' which are separatism, extremism and terrorism. Particularly in the Xinjiang region.' Additionally, economically supporting these states will also have positive economic effects on China.

This is largely due to the investments and loans that China provides to these states, which can be seen as 'hush money' (Mirovalev, 2020). China's infrastructure diplomacy in the CAR binds these economies to China and also expands China's influence in the region. This has propelled Moscow to play "catch-up" and increase its economic influence in the region through the creation of various multilateral security organizations like the Eurasian Economic Union (EEU) (Malashenski, 2013). Such analysis, however, considers only economic aspects of influence, ignoring the military/security and soft power aspects where Russia still dominates in the region.

On the other hand, up until recently, China and Russia have cooperated in the region instead of competing against each other for influence. This is due to both powers converging interests in the region, i.e. maintaining stability to curb extremism, terrorism and separatism. Both sides understand that they have more to gain geopolitically and geo-economically from cooperation than from competition (Stronski & Ng, 2018). Although cooperation seems to be the norm, it is expected that China's influence in the region will continue to spread. The tension between Moscow and Beijing may begin to escalate at some point, as great power relations tend to be unpredictable. In such situations, the CAR states would find themselves in a difficult position due to several factors. First, China-Russia cooperation is a form of control over the CAR states. Second, when China-Russia relations deteriorate, the CAR states may be caught in a situation of conflicting interests between the two world powers and struggle to attain their own personal interests. As such, the CAR states must perform a balancing act to extract as much as possible from their relations with two powers (Laruelle & Peyrouse, 2009).

Conclusion

The goal of this paper is to illustrate China's growing presence and influence in the CAR, through the lens of geo-economics. One shortcoming of this approach is that it relies solely on the examination of economic forms of power. There is no doubt that China has gained considerable influence in the region through economic instruments like trade, investment, loans, and aid. The CAR is an important node in the BRI, which has increased Beijing's interest in the region. As shown in this paper, the CAR states have become more dependent on China to push forward their own economic agendas. One can argue that this gives Beijing a certain level of leverage to foster asymmetric vulnerability interdependence. However, the geo-economics of China has not fully played out in the region due to China's interest in seeking to present itself as a friendly neighbour and its desire to maintain cordial relations with Russia. China is still operating on unstable grounds and their strategy is based on the premise that the exercise of geo-economics to secure its interests is a "long-game". China's influence is limited by Russia, a more crucial security and cultural partner to the CAR. Such a partnership is too long and deep to be displaced in the short-run. The "New Great Game" for influence in the CAR between the major powers will revolve around who has more to offer, particularly in the economic sphere of influence.

CHAPTER FOUR

NATIONALISM THROUGH FEAR: UZBEKISTAN

Ryan Michael Schweitzer

Introduction

For newly independent countries, it is imperative to solidify and differentiate their cultures and histories from colonial powers to create a unique national identity. This is especially true when independent nations fear foreign control. In turn, to protect the nation's chosen identity, a sense of nationalism is used to protect against perceived outside threats. Some scholars have argued that the Soviet Union collapsed due to a surge of nationalism in the various regions under Soviet control (Suny, 1993). However, this was not the case with Uzbekistan. There were no large nationalistic out-cries for an independent Uzbekistan, and in fact, Uzbek nationality was a product of Soviet engineering. Before the Soviet Union, various tribes with complex ethnic backgrounds hailing from the Turkic-Mongol empires were dispersed throughout the territory of the Central Asian region, but the region was not "Uzbek" as identified by any modern standards (Bell, 1999, p. 185).

Before the Soviet regime, Uzbekistan was composed of an array of ethnic tribes including Bukharians, Tartars and Tajiks. It was not until later in the Soviet Union era that "Uzbek" came to be considered as a nationality. This history demonstrates that Uzbek nationalism does not pre-date the Soviet Union era which some scholars use as a means to describe the rise of nationalism in the Central Asian region. Uzbeks did not become "Uzbeks" until much later, so there must be an explanation for the rise of nationalism in the region (Bell, 1999, p. 185).

Through this paper, it will become evident that the Uzbek ruling elite used, and still uses, Uzbek national identity to further encourage national independence and limit outside influence. After the fall of the Soviet Union and the creation of independent nations, a number of security threats became salient political and cultural topics. In the case of Uzbekistan, the rise of nationalism was a response to the perceived threat of Russian control. This threat continues to promote Uzbek nationalism today. This scholarly work is set to fill in the gap in the study of Uzbek nationalism and the trends that influenced the nation-building process under the former President Karimov's leadership.

Methodology

In conducting this research, historical data, publications, and speeches were examined. Additionally, first-person interviews with leading scholars were conducted before embarking upon research of historical sources to gauge the level of knowledge already understood. To understand the rise of Uzbek nationalism, several basic terms must be explained. Identity is a complex term, but when an individual identity or national identity is discussed in this paper, it will refer to how individuals choose and relate to origins, ethnicity, and language. Secondly, the word 'nation,' as used in this essay, will refer to what Snyder calls "a group of people who see themselves as distinct in these terms and who aspire to self-rule" (Snyder, 2000, p. 23). These definitions are indispensable in scrutinizing the trajectories and major developments in the establishment of Uzbek national identity.

Karimov's First Steps Towards Shaping Uzbek Identity

After the collapse of the Soviet Union, there were no governments or institutions dictating how to act, what to believe or how to protect individuals from outside threats. These security issues and threats, especially of foreign control—most notably from Russia—created the need for a strong identity amongst Uzbekistan's citizens. Former President Islam Karimov began to see the threat from Russia and, three months before the dissolution of the Soviet Union, on August 31st, 1991, declared that "Uzbek self-determination was realized" (Karimov, 1992). Since independence, Uzbekistan has seen a growing shift towards nationalism within its population through new policies regarding religion, economy, government and language. Through this process of self-determination and self-realization, Uzbekistan is moving away from its Soviet history and is instead embracing the resurgence (and creation) of its cultural identification. The Uzbek people's desire for autonomy and freedom from Russia provokes this process of self-discovery and identity creation.

The best way to realize this process is through the lens of de-Sovietization and de-Russification. After being a part of the Soviet Union for many years, Soviet history, culture, Russian language and Russian identity strongly pervaded the identities of many of Uzbekistan's citizens. However, with the collapse of the Soviet Union, none of these identity categories were relevant to an independent Uzbekistan or its people. The first step to building an independent state free from the control of Russia was to revise and re-brand the history of the Uzbek people.

Former President Islam Karimov started the revision of Uzbek identity by seeking to protect it while it was in the early stages of formation. He saw the need "to consolidate the fledgling state and imbue it with a secure national identity" in order to protect it from being lost in other, most likely Russian, identities (Bohr, 1998, p. 43). At all levels of the new Uzbekistan government, there was an aversion to and fear of deeper Russian integration. Consequently, the leaders of Uzbekistan believed that they needed "internal consolidation and sovereignty" to fend off Russian hegemony over the new nation (Bohr, 1998, p. 43). By creating a unique and strong identity, Uzbeks could establish a distinct identity from Russians.

The first step came in June, 1992 when Karimov ordered a "cleansing of Lenin's image from the streets and squares of Tashkent" (Bell, 1999, p. 201). For Karimov and other government actors, it was important that Uzbeks claimed a strong national attachment to their territory so that they could create a "national unifying policy" (Bohr, 1998, p. 21) that limits Russian influence. By choosing Uzbek history over Soviet history, Karimov and his administration not only demonstrated Uzbek solidarity within the country, but also were able to display their sovereignty in the face of perceived threats from Russia. This process of creating new historical meaning through de-Russification and re-naming of cultural spaces solidified power within the country. Uzbek officials realized the negative impact that former Soviet Union statues and history could have on the newly united Uzbek people. Therefore, they made the decision to get rid of the Lenin statues as "an obvious gesture towards reinventing Uzbek national identity...by casting Lenin out, Uzbek elites [created

Uzbek nationality]" (Bell, 1999, p. 201). In turn, they created an identity that Russians would find difficult negating and re-claiming.

After choosing to destroy the symbols of the Soviet Union to prevent Russian control, the next step for Uzbek solidarity was to effectively purge all reminders of the Soviet Union within society and to replace them with Uzbek identifiers. First, "Lenin Square" became "Independence Square." Then Karl Marx statutes were replaced with Timur, an Uzbek national historic hero. By using Timur, a respected and recognizable figure, Uzbeks were able to legitimize their power...[and also] ground the history of the Uzbek nation in a past that extends beyond the founding of the Uzbek Soviet Socialist Republic in 1925" (Bell, 1999, p. 203). By making Uzbek culture seemingly older than it was, and grounding it to a long-forgotten time, the Uzbek political elite met their objective of creating a shared mythological history; in turn, this action would increase solidarity and strength for the rest of the Uzbek nation. Additionally, it would signal to Russia that the Uzbeks had a history separate from Russian history, entitling the Uzbeks to self-government, without interference from Russia.

Finally, in the process of reclaiming history, President Karimov introduced Alisher Navoi as a "celebrated symbol of Uzbek culture," even though, "his works pre-date the emergence of an Uzbek nation" (Bell, 1999, p. 205). In doing so, President Karimov created a historical "golden age." These historical references are important because "they are rooted in a murky, distant past...[so that] Uzbek identity can be remolded to serve the purposes of...national state legislation" (Bell, 1999, p. 205-6). In other words, the Uzbek government was able to redefine what it means to be ethnically Uzbek and the culture that goes along with it. Uzbek political elites were then able to produce nationalistic rhetoric amongst the Uzbek population so that they could counter the old methods of Russian control. Moreover, this "murky past" (Bell, 1999, p. 205-6) prevents Russian influence in cultural identification, because there is no evidence to dispute the stories that Uzbeks claimed as 'historical.' In doing so, the Uzbeks sent a powerful message of their desire autonomy, while also pursuing domestic and foreign policies without Russian influence.

Russia as a Threat to the Formation of Uzbek Identity

Many see a democratic government and competitive economy as essential elements of a modern nation-state in the 21st century. However, the case of Uzbekistan shows that this transition is arduous to complete without consolidating national identity, defining the role of religion and establishing an independent foreign policy. These efforts were necessitated by the suppression of pre-Soviet cultural identity Many Uzbeks resented Russia for presuming its own Russian version of their collective history. The main reason for this resentment was because it portrayed Uzbeks as "backward peoples who had received support and enlightenment from the Russian 'elder brother'" (Critchlow, 1991, p. 119). Once Russia dominated the region, Uzbeks were forced to forget their histories or were taught that past achievements were successful because of Russia's help. For many Uzbeks, especially ones that were protective of their earlier collective history, the Soviet leaders made it illegal to promote Uzbek culture if it did not demonstrate Russia's help in creating that history. Especially for Uzbeks in the intelligentsia, this was alarming and unfair— this realization would eventually cause anti-Russian rebellions in the early 20th century. This resentment would last well beyond the collapse of the Soviet Union until the Uzbek intelligentsia were able to re-write their own history, including challenging narratives of the 'voluntary' nature of Uzbek annexation" (Critchlow, 1991, p. 130). Russians portrayed the annexation of Uzbekistan to the Soviet Union as voluntary, while Uzbeks perceived that the annexation of their territory was forced upon them. This contrast between the Russian perspective of voluntary regional annexation and the Uzbek perspective of forced annexation challenged Russia's narrative, rendering the Russian perspective inherently offensive. By rewriting history, Uzbeks realized their nationalism. Thus, it was resentment towards Russia and a fear of Russian dominance that was the driving force behind this nationalistic upheaval.

The perceived threat of and resentment towards Russia contributed to a revival of the Uzbek language, as well. Former President Karimov quickly denounced the use of the Russian language in government and industry insisting on Uzbek as the official language of Uzbekistan. This was a consequence of fears of Russian hegemony over jobs and culture in the region. Karimov could have easily used Russian to make his point, and because the majority of Uzbeks living in Uzbekistan knew Russian and they would have understood him. However, by choosing to use Uzbek, Karimov highlighted his favoring of Uzbeks over Russians. This promotion of the Uzbek language strengthened Uzbek nationalism, and was unique because it did not come from a desire to expand, or even to truly promote, ethnic ideas, but rather from a sense of fear regarding Russia.

As a newly independent state, Uzbekistan's officials were trying to maintain unity amongst its people and separation from the colonizer, Russia. To continue its independence efforts, it was important to connect with the Uzbek people and play on their resentment of Russia(ns). According to Kellner-Heinkele, language encourages independence and depends on it - a reciprocity process. In order for Uzbeks to maintain independence from Russia and collectively unite, a unifying factor was needed— the Uzbek language. As Critchlow points out, "In Uzbekistan, the national language emerged as an effective vehicle for opposition to Russification. It also became a potent force in consolidating nationalism" (Critchlow, 1991, p. 101). Although this emphasis on the importance of Uzbek diminished the role of the Russian language in public life and served as a rallying point for nationalism, it would also lead to security dilemmas for Uzbekistan and Russia.

During the Soviet Union, Russians (who spoke only Russian) lived in Uzbekistan for decades, especially concentrated in the capital, Tashkent. Russians moved to Uzbekistan during the Soviet Union and instantly "enjoyed a privileged situation" in terms of jobs, housing and status (Dollerup, 1998, p. 1). This favoritism was due largely to their knowledge of the Russian language. This fact would later cause resentment and a nationalistic uprising, as Uzbeks were historically unable to maintain job security or reach higher status due to their inability to speak Russian.

Tashkent is the center of business and politics within Uzbekistan, and much of the city's population has been Russian since the Soviet Union era (Rashid, 1994). Soviet Union leaders in Moscow were responsible for appointing all leadership within the Soviet Union, and they typically chose Russian natives or Uzbeks with strong Russian ties as the leaders during the Sovietization period. This process naturally excluded many Uzbeks, who did not know Russian at the time, from seeking government positions. Relations between Uzbeks and Russians were relatively harmonious at first. Eventually, however, "what rankled the Uzbeks was not the size of this influx [of Russians] but its level, the fact that the new arrivals occupied highly-rated jobs that were off-limits to the [Uzbek] locals" (Critchlow, 1991, p. 115). This resentment was towards "immigrant Russians, those who are seen as descending on the region to lord it over the natives and siphon off the best jobs" (Critchlow, 1991, p. 112). Since independence, Uzbeks do not have an issue with the few Russians "who consider the region to be their only home." Rather, Uzbeks fear Russians who view Russia as the motherland and would gladly see Uzbekistan fall under Russian control again (Critchlow, 1991, p. 112). This sentiment of fear is what seemingly sparked the Uzbek nationalism evident in Uzbekistan's governmental policies.

The solution to exiling Russians from prestigious government jobs was through "a renaissance of the Uzbek language" (Bohr, 1998, p. 33). Many Uzbeks saw the President Karimov's mandating of Uzbek as the official language "as perhaps the best means of not only widening its role in public life but also of redistributing cultural and political power in the republic" (Bohr, 1998, p. 33).

The emphasis on Uzbek is a sort of "purification [which] is frequently a defensive measurement against what is considered an external attack" (Kellner-Heinkele, 2001, p. 148). This process of emphasizing Uzbek language (in a way, an appeal to nationalism) created fear for the Russian minority living within the Uzbek territory.

Many Russians decided not to learn Uzbek. Only about 4.6 percent of Russians in Uzbekistan know the Uzbek vernacular (Bohr, 1998). This led to a mass exodus to Russia after the official working language change. The Russian government wished to be represented in Uzbekistan in terms of ethnic composition contributing to diversity, but the mono language policy resulted in Russians leaving. Upwards of 400,000 Russians have migrated back to Russia, citing language and lack of opportunity as their reason (Bohr, 1998). However, on migrating to Russia, "new arrivals have been known to wait months to receive housing, employment, and social services, particularly in the neglected rural areas of Russia where many have settled" (Bohr, 1998, p. 35). This situation creates instability within Russia's borders and results in Russians resenting the Russian system as well.

The retreat of Russians back to Russia has caused many political and social issues for the Russian government, raising security concerns. This has caused tensions between Uzbekistan and Russia, further fueling Uzbek fears of a hostile and vindictive Russia. Uzbeks seem to be uniting because they see Russian unity "as a danger" (Posen, 1993, p. 31). This 'Russian danger' is countered by Uzbek nationalism, which seeks to destroy Russian dominance of history and language in the region.

Another key language reformhas also recently been enacted—the changing of the Cyrillic script in favor of Latin script. In the early 90s, Uzbekistan sought to de-Russify their culture by switching to the Latin script. This decision was not taken because of the Uzbeks' rich literary tradition in Arabic and Latin alphabets. Instead, the push to a Latin-based writing system was motivated "by the political need to engage in a path different from that prescribed by the Soviet rulers" (Kellner-Heinkele, et al, 2001, p. 134). From a Russian perspective, this would seem to be a threat, because it indicates that one of its neighbors is aligning with the West. Switching to the Latin script would allow Uzbekistan to more readily adopt Western software and programming languages and compete with Russia in the arena of technology.

Finally, along with the changing of language and writing script come changes in the Uzbek school system. As Latin script becomes more important in Uzbek society, a greater importance is placed on learning and speaking English in the classroom. In the Soviet era, only Russian was spoken in the classroom. With the process of de-Russification, however, the role of the Russian language is being reduced in favor of more emphasis on English and other Western languages. As former President Karimov stated in many speeches, "students should leave school with the Uzbek language as a language of instruction experience while studying foreign languages" (Kellner-Heinkele, et al, 2001, p. 178). Therefore, instead of using Russian to teach foreign languages in the classroom, teachers instruct in Uzbek. This also contributes to straining Uzbek-Russian relations by reducing imports from Russia. Uzbeks are no longer buying Russian schoolbooks, and are instead producing their own Uzbek books domestically. By creating economic and trade tensions between the two countries, the security dilemma grows, further amplifying nationalist sentiment within Uzbekistan.

Once again, through the process of de-Russification, Uzbekistan is aligning itself with Western societies, leaving Russia behind. The de-Russification process started as resentment toward the Russian colonizers but continued out of fear of potential Russian imperialism and has become a unifying factor for nationalism in Uzbekistan. By aligning with the West, Uzbekistan can assure itself to have strong allies that would help prevent any possible hostile takeover (Lewis, 2016).

Ultimately, the easiest way to see the impact of this fear on the formation of Uzbek nationalism is by looking at the Uzbek government's foreign policy agenda. As Lake suggests, when groups "fear for their safety," they prepare for war (Lake, et al, 1996, p. 41). However, in the case of Uzbekistan, the Uzbeks do not seem to be preparing for a war, but are simply trying to maintain their sovereignty. This may explain why there has been little tension between Uzbeks and other minorities in the region (Drobizheva, et al, 1996). Nationalism in Uzbekistan is a result of vying for protection from Russian control, not from other ethnic groups.

As previously mentioned, there are thousands of Russians currently living within Uzbekistan's borders, and, because of this, Russia claims to have a reason to interfere for the security of its citizens—"a claim which Tashkent [Uzbek government officials] has resolutely rejected" (Bohr, 1998, p. 57). Russia's right to interfere for national security, Russia claims, even goes as far asprotecting "the USSR's old external borders from potential invaders" (Bohr, 1998, p. 57). This rhetoric is exactly what creates Uzbek fears of a hostile takeover from Russia and ignites Uzbek nationalism to maintain its own border and security.

This perceived danger of Russian foreign policy has led to protectionist Uzbek national and foreign policy. The most notable example of this is Uzbek officials "refusing to sign the Treaty for Defense of the CIS [Commonwealth of Independent States] External Borders in May 1995" (Bohr, 1998, p. 57). This treaty brought together the Central Asian countries and Russia after the collapse of the Soviet Union to achieve a smooth transition. Uzbekistan is the only Central Asian country which refuses to work with the CIS, citing fears of Russian control. In addition, "Uzbekistan uses virtually every possible opportunity to oppose Russian 'integrationist' proposals, appearing to view them as a smokescreen for a Russian hegemonistic agenda" (Bohr, 1998, p. 44). Such deep mistrust of the Russian agenda has created the frameworks for Uzbek nationalism and its foreign policy agenda.

As a response to these failed agreements, Uzbek nationalism soared and many Uzbeks claimed: "We are capable of reliably defending our 156-kilometer border with Afghanistan with our own forces and without the intervention of border troops from other countries, first and foremost from Russia" (Bohr, 1998, p. 58). By stating explicitly that Uzbekistan does not need Russia's ostensible help, Uzbeks have not only created a sense of nationalism as Hechter would describe (state-building) but have also created Posen's security dilemma (that Russia will perceive the Uzbek military as a threat to its own).

Foreign Policy and National Identity

Foreign policy and military policy generally go hand-in-hand. However, in this case, Uzbekistan is considered as an exception. The country's stance on military matters deepens the nationalistic rhetoric and the security dilemma with Russia. After independence from Russia, President Karimov realized "the need to consolidate the fledgling state and imbue it with a secure national identity" (Bohr, 1998, p. 43). In doing so, Karimov has created an "aversion to overarching structures and Russian proposals for deeper integration" (Bohr, 1998, p. 43). By unifying Uzbek solidarity, Karimov and the rest of the political elite ensure Uzbekistan's independence. With this in mind, nationalism in Uzbekistan is essentially an aversion to Russia simply out of security concerns. Uzbekistan's foreign and military policies ensure Russia cannot re-gain control in the area. The efforts employed in protecting against radical Islam are a clear example of this sentiment—"Rather than call for a Russian-led military alliance to counter the Taliban, [Uzbek officials] proposal for a multilateral initiative—that would include the United States as well as Russia—was in keeping with [their] general effort to curtail Russian influence in the region" (Bohr, 1998, p. 55).

Through the nationalistic trend, Uzbekistan and Western countries have become more closely aligned, and, in turn, Uzbekistan has become more protected against Russian hegemony. However, this creates another security dilemma for Uzbekistan. Russia still views Central Asian countries as falling within its sphere of influence and any divergence from Russian interests is a disruption to the status quo and a security threat. As a result, Russia is likely to try to counteract these nationalistic overtures to maintain some of its control over the region.

The reasoning behind these foreign and military policies also stems from scandals in the Soviet Union. In 1989, there were reports that Uzbek military recruits were being mistreated in the Soviet Army (Critchlow, 1991, p. 157). These allegations gained traction among the people and political elites and helped lay the foundation for an upsurge in nationalistic rhetoric. This was another defining moment for relations with Russia. No longer did Uzbeks desire control from Russia, nor did they trust any outside forces. These worries and perceived threats from Russia, whether based on fact or not, resulted in the nationalistic response.

Some scholars may view Uzbekistan's top-down nationalistic policies as the effort of political elites hoping to maintain their positions in government. While Uzbek nationalism may be a creation of political elites and the need of these elites to maintain their power, it is not the sole, or even the strongest, explanation. Nationalism is a highly volatile process and is a part of independence movements in many regions of the world. Uzbek nationalism was ultimately evoked not out of a desire to win independence, but a desire to keep its autonomy. The Soviet Union created cultural identities in Central Asia by force and once the Soviet Union collapsed, these shared, but partly idealized identities, needed to be redefined and protected from further Russian influence.

The state of Uzbekistan was going through major changes after the fall of the Soviet Union. To remain secure from Russia, the people relied on a shared identity and culture. This process of Uzbek unification created many outsiders in the region, most notably Russian minorities. Uzbeks feared not only Russian political influence, but also another takeover by Russian ideology. Thus, they sought to position Uzbek as a national standard in cultural, history, language, and foreign policy through governmental policies. President Karimov realized these security concerns and emphasized Uzbek in all aspects of society to defend against these perceived Russian threats. By reverting to Uzbek history and emphasizing the Uzbek language, Karimov and other political elites were able to instill a sense of security throughout the region while also creating a nationalistic society. In the aftermath of the rise of nationalism, Uzbeks created an Uzbek agenda in foreign policy, highlighting the need to "...oppose Russian 'integrationist' proposals..." (Bohr, 1998, p. 44). Uzbekistan was thus able to maintain its sovereignty through nationalistic means, and in the end, Uzbekistan became a "cultural center...for all Uzbeks" (Karimov, 1992, p. 15).

A New President, New Changes

The recent change of presidents in Uzbekistan created a fertile basis for further democratization of Uzbekistan. Newly elected President Shavkat Mirziyoyev began to develop the concept of the international politics of Uzbekistan, but also remained focused on internal affairs, state-building, and nation-building policies.

Karimov was known as a protective leader, and the Father of the Uzbeks. By contrast, Mirziyoyev appeals to the kindhearted sentiments of the Uzbeks. While Karimov was against Uzbeks working on low paid jobs in Russia, Mirziyoyev behaves differently. For instance, his reaction to a bus fire that killed 52 Uzbek labor migrants on their way to Russia emphasized that the immigrants were industrious workers, not traitors. "It's not for nothing… that these people are going through torment and suffering in foreign countries. These poor people too, after all, have their hopes before God, to feed their children and bring some money back to their fathers… They were so young… And all of them from Uzbekistan. We are so deeply saddened" (Putz, 2018). The two Presidents differ not only in their style of governing, but also in the sense of shaping national identity. With Mirziyoyev's leadership, the country is achieving its potential to empower civic nationalism and enhance state-society relations. Nation-building and state-building processes, however, are continuous processes. Particularly for Uzbekistan, clan identity is a sub-national factor that hinders the establishment of a unified national identity, although aggressive state policies are extensively deployed.

With the recent "opening" of Uzbekistan, there have been many countries willing and eager to extend help and investment. While President Mirziyoyev is eager to receive this support, he maintains careful control over all aspects of this "aid." China, with its Belt and Road Initiative is maintaining multi-million dollar investment projects inside Uzbekistan, including security equipment for "safe cities"; Russia is expanding its economic endeavors in gas and oil, and security measures through the sale of military equipment; South Korea is developing closer "soft power" ties through many language centers; and finally, the United States is investing in many new businesses and also attempting to make the political and civil society sectors more "democratic." Through these changes and investments, President Mirziyoyev has ensured that no one of these countries has too much influence or power over Uzbek culture and identity. In fact, the current Uzbek government is taking the same measures that former President Karimov took to preserve Uzbek identity. There is still an emphasis on the Uzbek language, including completely switching from the Cyrillic alphabet to the Latin alphabet; Uzbek music playing in all city center locations; new cultural centers in major Uzbek cities; and finally, ongoing efforts to get rid of the Soviet past by memorializing important "Uzbek" figures through statues and new street and building names. Such measures ensure that the Uzbek identity is protected, but they also ensure that other countries are not presenting a security threat by influencing or changing the Uzbek identity, society, or culture.

Conclusion

This article seeks to study the major developments and conceptions in the field of the national identity of the Uzbeks starting from the dissolution of the Soviet Union up until contemporary times. Following the dissolution of the Soviet Union, Uzbekistan has been struggling to shape its identity. Intertwining the state identity with the perceived identity existing among the Uzbek masses has been pursued as a means of defining national identity. Government promotion of the idea of 'Uzbekness' is ubiquitous at all levels of social life.

Uzbeks feared another takeover of Russian ideology, so sought to keep Uzbek identity as a national standard in cultural, history, language, and foreign policy through many governmental policies. Former President Karimov emphasized "Uzbekness," in all aspects of society as a response to these security concerns. However, the death of President Karimov in 2016 did not stop the Uzbek nationalization process.

The Uzbek policy of promoting national identity carries the risk of both \continuing of the Soviet-era reflex of eradicating diversity and encouraging the illusion that homogeneity exists where it does not. While many subcultures within Uzbekistan's borders have been induced to accept an official Uzbek national identity, that identity does not entirely reflect either their self-perception or their perception of their own culture. Current President Shavkat Mirziyoyev has continued to emphasize Uzbek identity formation while ensuring that outside countries cannot interfere. This displays a different approach to the nation-building process. As seen for the past few years, the Uzbek government has invited outside involvement, usually in the form of economic investments from different sources.

While the United States, Russia, South Korea, and China have all begun to involve themselves in Uzbek society, government, and business, no one of these countries is predominant in terms of influence. Each one has their own strengths and weaknesses in their relationship with Uzbekistan, and President Mirziyoyev has ensured Uzbek identity is always the deciding factor in societal, governmental, and entrepreneurial affairs. By protecting Uzbek interests from outside states and actors, the Uzbek government has ensured minimal interference in its collective identity formation. As a recently independent country, however, Uzbekistan still has a long way to go in solidifying its "Uzbek" identity. Until this process is advanced enough, the Uzbek identity will continue to be protected by the ruling elite from any and all outside forces.

Further studies on nationalism in Uzbekistan are recommended in order to expand on the impact security has on nation building and identity formation processes. For Uzbekistan, further studies of the enforcement of the Latin alphabet, foreign language learning, and other education trends should be examined to better understand the formation and definition of the modern Uzbek identity. A comparison of the impact of these measures in different Uzbek cities could yield a wide range of data that can contribute to an understanding of how linguistic modifications and foreign "soft power" influences in the fields of education, society, and politics affect the nature of nationalism in Uzbekistan.

CHAPTER FIVE

THE HISTORICAL AND GEOPOLITICAL CONTEXT OF TURKEY-CENTRAL ASIA RELATIONS

Halim Nezihoglu

Introduction

Central Asia has come to the fore in the agenda of world politics since the dissolution of the Soviet Union. Interest in the region from the great international powers and other regional powers has grown. The concept of the 'new great game' became popular among analysts to describe the rivalry between different players trying to take advantage of new opportunities created by the collapse of the Soviet Union. Central Asian states, situated in a great power-driven regional system, adopted multi-vector foreign policies as an overall foreign policy strategy. The Central Asian republics have sought to develop good relations and cooperation with different global and regional actors by balancing their diverse interests. One of the important players in the region has been Turkey, which has historical, cultural and linguistic relations with the region. However, high expectations about the progress of the relations between these historically connected countries have not been realized and remain limited. Although governments and leaders have changed in both Turkey and the Central Asian Republics since the collapse of the Soviet Union, the general framework and structure of the relations between them have remained largely unchanged.

Although preferences of leaders and governments influence foreign policy outcomes, the guidelines and contours of a country's foreign policy depend on historical-geopolitical background. Historical and geopolitical circumstances determine a country's position in its regional milieu and the unique distribution of power which constrain foreign policy options. The historical background and geopolitics of a country are closely interconnected and define policy makers' decisions as well as their foreign policy orientations. A country's geographical location, size, and regional environment all result from its history. Historical and geopolitical realities provide advantages or disadvantages; they motivate leaders or restrain their choices. Important geopolitical changes create new opportunities or threats which can be pursued by means of various foreign policy options.

During the Middle Ages, Central Asia played a central role in Eurasian political history. The region housed some of the largest Asian empires of pre-modern times including the Hun, Kokturk, Qarakhan, Seljuk, Mongol, Chagatai, Golden Horde, and Timurid Empires. Central Asia was also the heartland of Eurasian trade as the main trade routes of the ancient Silk Road passed through it. The region thus played a crucial role as a conduit for political, economic, commercial, cultural, and intellectual transfers between China and India on one side, and Europe, the Mediterranean world and Islamic civilization on the other (see Starr, 2013: 1-27). During this period, Central Asia maintained a dominant position in its relations with other empires around the region such as the Ottoman Empire, the Golden Horde, and the Delhi Sultanate of India. Although the core areas of the Ottoman Empire – Anatolia and the Balkans – are at the crossroads between Europe and Asia, and the Ottoman hinterland included the Black Sea region, the Caucasus, the Middle East and North Africa. Although Ottoman territory extended to the East, the Ottoman court developed a Western-oriented foreign policy outlook due to historical realities. These historical and geopolitical realities and their impact on the relations between Central Asia and the Ottoman Empire, the predecessor of modern Turkey, will be clarified in the following section.

Historical-Geopolitical Context of Ottoman-Central Asia Relations

From the mid-11th to the 14th-century, the Turks (first the Seljuk and then the Ottoman) migrated West thus leaving behind Central Asia, the seat of great nomadic dynamism, mobility, and innumerable invasions and wars. They advanced first in Byzantine territories in Asia minor and then in the Balkans and Eastern Europe until the late 16th-century. The great Seljuk Empire was born and centered in Central Asia. Seljuk Commander Alp Arslan's victory over the Byzantine army in Manzikert opened the doors of Anatolia to Oghuz tribesmen and the other Central Asian Turkic tribes (Starr, 2013: 384-386). The leaders of the later

Anatolian Seljuk state, which succeeded the previous Seljuk Empire that collapsed after the Mongol invasions, continued to view Central Asia as their ancestral homeland. Central Asia, as the base for the migrating Turkic tribes, provided military personnel for Seljuk Turks who, despite their high status as the ruling and military elite, were a demographic minority in Christian-majority Asia Minor. The founding fathers and the founding tribe who established the Ottoman Empire were from Central Asia, as were the other Turkic tribes who joined the empire. Central Asia kept its high position in the view of the Seljuk, and then the Ottoman, Turks until the conquest of Constantinople in the mid-15th century.

Timur, a Central Asian conqueror, enhanced the dominant position of the seat of the region by creating a large empire in Central Asia. Timur accomplished this by using Central Asia for a base for military campaigns in different directions and by his victories against the other empires present in Central Asia such as the Ottoman Empire, Golden Horde, and Delhi Sultanate of India. Timur occupied the strategic city of Sivas in Anatolia in 1400, then defeated the Ottoman army near Ankara in July 1402, taking Sultan Bayezid himself as a prisoner. Timur's army devastated much of the Ottoman lands in Anatolia, while the Balkans were largely spared. The Ottoman Empire's recovery dependent on embracing the Balkan region as its heartland After this great disaster, the Ottomans suffered from internal strife; a power struggle broke out between the sons of Sultan Bayezid. The chaotic battle for control of the empire continued until 1411. (Turnbull, 2003: 25-29; Manz, 1989: 73) During the battle of Ankara, non-Turkic soldiers in the Ottoman army who were originally from the Balkans remained loyal to the Sultan, while some Central Asian-originated Turkic soldiers aligned themselves towards Timur. The Turks were nomads who held tribalism and their freedoms in high esteem as opposed to royal order in a multi-ethnic, cosmopolitan empire. Thus, they preferred to revolt against authority and to pursue their own way by creating their own state.

For the Ottoman authorities, who had an imperial vision, keeping some of these nomadic Turkic tribes under their rule was more difficult than with other non-Turkic subjects. This experience along with sporadic Turkic tribal rebellions led the Ottoman ruling elite to be cautious and prudent in their strategies regarding Turkic tribes. The serious defeat at the hands of Timur was an enduring trauma for the Ottoman ruling elite and they subsequently avoided intruding into the messy affairs of the nomadic and warlike Central Asians.

Central Asia began to lose its dominant position after the Timur's era, while the Ottomans rose to a powerful status by the second half of the 15th century. The Ottoman Empire, which attained great power status until the 19th century, generally kept its face turned toward the West. While it unified the bulk of the Muslim world under its leadership by incorporating the Middle East and the North Africa under its rule, as a result of the above-mentioned psychology the Ottomans neither attempted to occupy Central Asia nor attempted to play a leadership role in the region during its six-century long history.

When the Russian occupation of Central Asia gained momentum in the 19th century, Central Asian khanates sent letters and envoys to Istanbul asking for help. However, the Ottomans could not provide any meaningful support. During this period, the Ottomans were experiencing steep decline and suffered from ever-weakening authority and military power. Because the empire was preoccupied with several problems, such as the separatist revolts and the repeated defeats in the military fronts, previous lack of interest by the Ottoman court toward Central Asia was replaced by a lack of capacity. Sultan Abdulhamid II, the last effective Ottoman Sultan, was only able to send a few clerics (Davutoğlu, 1997: 919: Kuru, 1999: 131, 132, 138; Saray, 1994: 5-25). Enver Pasha, who became a prominent leader of the Ottoman Empire after the powers of the sultan were limited by the Young Turk revolution in 1908, and who led the empire to join the First World War, lost his prestige and all his powers when the empire was defeated at the end of the war. In 1921, he went to Bukhara to lead the Central Asian Basmachi insurgents against the Bolsheviks. Though he gathered some insurgents and had some military success, he could not unite all the rebel leaders under his command. His brief successes were followed by heavy losses and defeats, and he was killed in 1922. Although he was an important political and military figure in the Ottoman Empire before and during the First World War, he was far from representing Turkey. His activities in Central Asia were not approved and supported by Mustafa Kemal and by the newly emerging Turkish parliament in Ankara that were busy with the Turkish war of independence (Yilmaz, 1999: 55-60).

Another state which originated in Central Asia, the Golden Horde, experienced disaster after Timur's attacks. While the Ottoman Empire recovered and continued to rise after its engagements with Timur, the Golden Horde did not. The capital city of Golden Horde's state, Saray, and other economic centers were destroyed; and the state began to decline gradually. The weakening of central authority led to struggles between different clans for the throne. Following two and a half centuries of dominance over the Russians, the Golden Horde domain divided into various khanates in the fifteenth century, including Astrakhan, Khazan, Crimea, Orda, Nogai, and Sibir. The decline of the Golden Horde and the struggles between the successor khanates created an opportunity for the Russians to initiate military campaigns and expansion to the east and southeast. They invaded Khazan in 1552, Astrakhan in 1556, and Volga and northern regions of the Caspian Sea, thus clearing access to the Caucasus, Kazakh steppes and Central Asia. The Ottoman Turks occupied the southern part of Crimea in 1475 and, afterwards, extended their suzerainty over the khanate. After the occupation of Kazan and Astrakhan by the Russians, the Ottoman grand vizier, Sokollu Mehmet Pasha, offered to dig a navigable canal from the Don to the Volga Rivers to achieve an access to the Caspian Sea for the Ottoman navy in order to stop the Russian advance. The project started in 1569 with the cooperation with the Crimean Tatars. However, it was abandoned as winter approached because the Sultan's and the Khan's courts did not share the far-sighted vizier's concerns about the coming danger of Russia's imperial advance (Soucek, 2000: 162, 163; Saray, 1982: 1, 2).

It took some time for this danger to manifest for the Ottomans and Central Asians. Russian tsars adopted expansionism, which started in the mid-16th century, as a stable state strategy in the following centuries. Russian advances were realized slowly but steadily, first in Siberia toward the Pacific in the 16th and 17th centuries, then in northern Kazakh steppes in the 18th century, and finally in Central Asia in the 19th century. Russian modernization in the 18th and 19th centuries also reinforced the expansion of the Russian empire. While Russia was rising, Central Asia was isolated from the innovation and modernization occurring in Europe. A stable Russian state pursuing a clear strategy with a well-organized and modernized army and state apparatus achieved supremacy and numerous military victories against Central Asia, which lacked unified strategic planning, and was divided into conflicting khanates and fighting leaders and tribes. The heyday of nomad-warriors was past, and the balance of military power was shifting to the detriment of the nomads owing to Russian supremacy in weapons technology. After European geographic discoveries across the Atlantic, Indian Ocean, and the Pacific, the Silk Road began to lose its importance in world trade. Economic depression, continuous political turmoil, population decline, and a lack of modernization took Central Asia from a central position to a peripheral one in terms of military power, political influence and socio-economic capacity. This process paved the way for the invasion of the region by Russia from the north and China from the southeast (Golden, 2011: 105, 115, 122-128). The Russians reached Tashkent in 1865, and their advance continued south until the last quarter of the 19th century. They occupied Merv in 1884 on one side, and on the other pushed south through the Pamirs to Kashmir in early the 1890s. The Pamir Boundary Commission, held in 1895, and the following Anglo-Russian convention, defined the southern borders of the Tsarist Russian Empire. (For the historical account of the Russian occupation of Central Asia see Allworth, 1994: 2-59, 131-150; Soucek, 2000: 195-200; Saray, 1982: 1-25)

Because of its geographic location, the rise of an imperial and expansionist Russia was bound to pose a geopolitical challenge to the Ottomans. The Russian and Ottoman Empires became historical rivals in geopolitical terms. They competed for supremacy in the regions where their imperial policies and interests clashed (Bağcı & Doganlar, 2009: 106). Reaching the limits of expansion in the south of Central Asia did not end Russian expansionist ambitions.

While some claim that Russia had a historic drive to achieve direct territorial access to warm waters and to occupy the Turkish Straits, these claims can be disputed (see Green, 1993). However, Tsarist Russia did attempt to enlarge its borders towards the Ottoman territories in different wars. The Crimean Khanate, a vassal state of the Ottoman Empire, faced Russian occupation in 1783. The 18th and 19th centuries were a period of decline for the Ottomans while the Russian empire was rising. The greed of the imperialist European and Russian powers was encroaching on Ottoman territory in the 19th century, a period in which the Ottoman empire was regarded as the 'sick man of Europe,' who was about to die and whose inheritance was to be partitioned. Russia was the main rival of the Ottoman Empire in the Balkans, the Black Sea, and the Caucasus. After the war of 1828-29, the Treaty of Edirne transferred sovereignty over the Caucasian coast of the Black Sea from the Ottomans to Russia. Russia also declared herself as the protector of the Orthodox Christian Ottoman subjects and the self-proclaimed heir of Byzantium, and kept a close eye on Slavic ethnic groups in the Ottoman Balkans. Russian narratives brought attention to holy places in Palestine, the Greek Church in Istanbul, and monasteries in order to press upon the Sublime Porte.

As it was rising to the status of a world power, Russia used the argument of Ottoman interference in Orthodox religious affairs as a pretext in its expansionist strategy and military campaigns against the Ottomans throughout the 19th century. Threatening statements by Russia against Istanbul culminated in 1853 and turned to ultimatums after the Russian tsar Nikolai signed an attack plan on the Turkish Straits. When the Sultan rejected Russian demands and its intervention in Ottoman internal affairs, Nikolai ordered the Russian army to invade the Ottoman principalities of Moldavia and Wallachia in the northern Balkans, which paid tribute to Istanbul (Badem, 2010: 60-87; Fairey, 2014: 131-157; Gerd, 2014: 193-214). The Russian move alarmed both Britain and France, who did not want Russia to rise to a more advantageous position in controlling strategic areas of the Ottomans to the detriment of their own interests. Anglo-French support for the Ottoman Empire against Russia in the Crimean War (1853-1856), which led to Russia's defeat, averted disaster from the Ottoman Empire and saved its territorial integrity.

Russia, however, continued to pursue a destabilization policy of supporting Slavic nations in the Balkans against the Ottomans in the following decades. It declared another war against Istanbul in 1877. In the war of 1877-78, the Russian army advanced into Ottoman territory in both the Balkans and Transcaucasia. While the Ottomans lost important cities in northeastern Anatolia, bordering on the Caucasus, the Russian army came close to Istanbul by occupying Edirne (Adrianople). The Ottoman Empire suffered from great territorial losses by the end of the war. Russia had won the war, but, British-Austrian diplomatic attempts to counterbalance Russian gains in the post-war peace treaty restored some of the Ottoman losses in the Balkans. On the other side, northeastern Anatolia remained under the Russian administration until 1918 (LeDonne, 1997: 138-144; Badem, 2014: 221, 222). It is possible that Russian attempts at expansionism in the Ottoman territories would have gone much further if the European great powers had not counterbalanced it. Russian ambitions over the Straits became apparent again during 1907-08 when Russian diplomacy pressed for a revision of the international status of the Straits. The Russian foreign minister, Sazanov, declared in 1913 that Russia's control over the Straits was essential for "a fleet-in-being strategy in the Mediterranean," which meant the deployment of a Russian fleet in the Straits as a deterrent force in the Mediterranean.

During its last decades, the Ottoman Empire developed an alliance with Germany. It joined the First World War with Germany when German ships carrying Turkish flags bombed Russian ships and ports in the Black Sea in 1914. After the war Britain, France, and Russia agreed on a partition plan of the Ottoman territories in the Sykes-Picot Agreement of 1916, and the Russian army further advanced in northeastern Anatolia by occupying some important cities. Meanwhile the divisions of the Ottoman army were fighting on different fronts throughout the Middle East (LeDonne, 1997: 144-146). At this time, another great event stopped further Russian advances in the Turkish territories; namely, the Bolshevik Revolution in 1917. The outbreak of the revolution led Russia to withdraw from the First World War. According to the Treaty of Brest-Litovsk, signed in 1918, the Bolshevik government of Russia ceded its provinces in northeastern Anatolia to the Ottoman Empire. Turkey and Russia signed the Treaty of Kars in 1921, which ultimately established their modern borders.

Following this era, the Soviet regime seemed to have abandoned the Tsarist Russian expansionism during the initial decades of consolidation of power. However, Stalin revived this strategy again after the Second World War. After defeating the Germans and bringing Eastern Europe under its control, the Soviet Union increased its pressure on Turkey by laying down territorial claims in eastern Anatolia and raising the issue of the Turkish Straits in 1945. The Soviet Minister of Foreign Affairs, Molotov, in meetings with the Turkish ambassador, declared that Kars and Ardahan, cities in eastern Anatolia, should be ceded to the Soviet Union by a revision of 1921 treaty and that the status of the Straits should be modified. Molotov notified the Turkish government about the Soviet intention to establish joint Soviet-Turkish control over the Bosphorus and Dardanelles and to create a Soviet military base in the Straits (Hasanli, 2011: 65-74). Turkish authorities regarded the pressure by the neighboring Soviet Union as a vital threat against Turkey's sovereignty and territorial integrity. Turkey sought an alliance with the US and Britain to resist against Soviet threats; and transitioned from a single-party regime to a multi-party democracy more palatable to the Western democratic world. Soviet expansion in Eastern Europe and the rise of communist regimes were considered by the US and Britain as a serious threat to the liberal-democratic world, thus marking the beginning of tensions between Stalin and the Western world and the Cold War era in world politics.

The Soviet threat, felt deeply by the Turkish ruling elite, played a crucial role in Turkey's decision to join the Western bloc and become a member of NATO in 1952. Soviet territorial claims were regarded in the western political circles as signs of Soviet expansionism in different regions. Turkey received great American economic and military aid throughout the Cold War era in accordance with the Truman doctrine and the containment policy, which aimed to support free peoples around the Soviet Union and prevent them from falling under communism as satellites in Moscow's orbit. Turkey's geopolitics gained a new and an important meaning for the Western world as a buffer zone against Soviet expansionism and a strategic area for US air bases. In conclusion, disregard for Central Asia in Western-oriented Ottoman foreign policy was replaced by a total isolation of the region after the decline and fall of the empire, along with persistent weakness in the face of the expansionist Russian empire and its successor, the Soviet Union.

Turkish Foreign Policy towards Central Asia

Mustafa Kemal Atatürk, the leader of new Turkey in the 1920s and 1930s, and his successors adopted a pacifist, inactive, and prudent foreign policy as a consequence of the trauma of large territorial losses in the Ottoman hinterland and the hard-won achievement of an independent state in Anatolia after a war of liberation. The painful memories of the First World War and the War of Independence, the loss of more than three million soldiers and civilians, along with millions of displaced people, prompted the ruling elite of the new Republic of Turkey to formulate a careful and non-assertive foreign policy, keeping distance from troublesome events, and pursuing a strategy of isolation and non-involvement. The new regime relinquished the past Ottoman and Islamic claims over the former Ottoman territories to satisfy the great powers of the era, such as Britain and France, and to avoid their hostility. Therefore, Turkey denounced any irredentist and revisionist goals (Kösebalaban, 2011: 53,

54), and avoided an adventurist foreign policy which would have been beyond the country's capacity. The westernized and secular ruling elite were very careful to avoid pan-Islamist and pan-Turkist tendencies in foreign policy. The main target of the foreign policy route of Turkey continued to be the West, much like its Ottoman predecessor (For more on the decades-long western orientation in Turkish foreign policy see Bozdağlıoğlu, 2003: 35-86). The main difference was that the Ottoman Empire was a great power up until the 19th century, and a proactive player until the end of the First World War. However, Turkey became a passive object in world politics driven by great powers, only reacting to external events rather than shaping them (Aydın, 2019: 367). Central Asia had already been absorbed by Tsarist Russia which evolved into the Soviet Union, a giant neighbor for Turkey, a great power, and one of the two superpowers of the Cold War era. It was impossible for the Turkish ruling elite to develop any interests in Soviet Central Asia while Turkey itself was anchored to the Western alliance, lacking the power and capacity to cope with the Soviet threat alone. So, several decades passed with no relations with Central Asia at all, which lacked independence and was isolated in the outer fringes of the Soviet space.

The collapse of the Soviet Union and the emergence of the newly-independent Central Asian republics during the transition from the Soviet system to a free market economy and democracy created new opportunities not only for great powers, but also several other regional powers. The region drew the attention of various players for its geopolitical importance, rich energy resources, underdeveloped areas ripe for investment, educational and cultural projects, and the other political, economic, and strategic factors. The region was very important for Turkey for the same reasons; however, Central Asia meant much more for Turkey due to some realities of Turkey and the psychology of Turkish people.

Firstly, the Kemalist regime based the new Turkish identity on ethnicity while trying to separate multi-ethnic Turkish society from its cosmopolitan Islamic and Ottoman background. In Ottoman society, ethnic identity was secondary. This new nation-building and identity formation policy involved a new state-centered historiography. State-sponsored historians and intelligentsia created new narratives in history books and a new discourse in education, national ceremonies, and public speeches which emphasized the ancestral roots of the Turks who came to Anatolia from Central Asia. The new generations who were educated and indoctrinated under this Turkish nationalist narrative and discourse internalized a Turkish nationalism with strong references to Central Asia. The emergence of the independent Central Asian republics created a new hope for the Turks to gain power again in cooperation with their ethnic brothers in Central Asia. Central Asians, meanwhile, did not identify themselves as Turk but developed different ethnic identities and affiliations in line with both their pre-Soviet history and the influence of Soviet policies.

These realities remained unknown by the Turkish public in early the 1990s. Turkish people perceived them as Turks and called them Central Asian Turks even after their independence. An emotional but unrealistic discourse became popular among the Turkish people, as they believed that a common Turkic world, divided by artificial boundaries, could be reunited. This idea was expressed by some Turkish statesmen as well. However, this vision remained symbolic at state level and could not be translated into concrete achievements. This emotional approach and sentimental enthusiasm gradually declined when the hard realities became more apparent (Bozdağlıoğlu, 2003: 96-102).

The collapse of the Soviet Union, therefore, radically changed the geopolitics of Turkey. The end of the Cold-War-era's static and bipolar world order opened new horizons for Turkey, which occupies a strategic geopolitical location as a bridge between dynamic regions. This geopolitical change Turkey's capacity to maneuver in different regions (Bağcı & Doganlar, 2009: 99-102). Central Asia provided alternative avenues of opportunity for Turkey, whose importance for the US in its containment policy against the Soviet Union seemed to be declining at the end of the Cold War era. Not long after, the rejection of Turkey's bid for full membership in the European Union, in spite of decades of efforts, disappointed Turkish rulers and public opinion. The Turkish ruling elite believed that Turkey should not miss the opportunities created in the post-Cold War era and should play an active role in the Caucasus and Central Asia. Turkish foreign policy, which used to be directed towards the West, gained a chance to start a new beginning as an important actor in the international arena. At the same time, Turkey provided a viable model for the CARs as a modern secular and democratic Muslim country. This model was more likely to be supported by Western powers which were fearful of rising extremism and fundamentalism in greater Central Asia, including Afghanistan, after the end of Soviet control. Thus, the post-Cold War era provided a set of circumstances that enabled Turkey to establish close relations with Central Asia after having had very limited relations for several centuries of the Ottoman era, and total isolation during the Soviet period. (see Fuller, 1993: 163-168; Gharabaghi, 1994: 115; Karpat, 1992/94: 105; Davutoğlu, 1997: 914)

The Turkish President of the era, Turgut Özal, aimed at increasing the regional role of Turkey on the international stage in accordance with his assertive foreign policy vision. His special interest in Central Asia contributed much to the rapid development of relations between Turkey and the region in the 1990s. Turkey became the first country to recognize the independence of the Central Asian republics and open embassies in their capitals. Özal brought with him large groups of businessmen in his official visits to these capitals. He enthusiastically supported both state-sponsored and private educational and cultural projects in the region. Özal's successor Süleyman Demirel spoke in some of his speeches about a Turkic world 'from the Adriatic Sea to the Great Wall of China'. Demirel emphasized Turkey's responsibilities, with its unique culture, geography and history, at the very center of the new geopolitics of Eurasia. He stated that Turkey should play an active role in the integration of these newly independent republics into the international society of states, and support them in their quest for an identity. The Turkish International Cooperation Agency (TICA) was established in 1992 to coordinate Turkish governmental assistance to the region. With daily flights between Istanbul and Central Asian capitals, both Turkish people and Central Asians began to pour into each other's countries. Tens of thousands of Central Asian students traveled to study at Turkish universities, as well as military and police academies. The Turkish government and private organizations opened numerous schools and universities in different Central Asian cities. Thus, Turkey became a significant actor in Central Asia, and developed its relations with the region proactively in numerous areas such as transportation, business and trade, investment and industry, education, culture, media, and other social relations. (Mütercimler, 1993, 206-228; Manisalı, 1992, 57-59; Frenchman, 1993: 21-23; Kuru, 1999: 142-144; Kösebalaban, 2011: 120-124; Aydın, 2004: 4, 5)

This momentum continued for most of the 1990s. However, the vigor and passion seen early in the 1990s began to fade away from the late 1990s onwards. Turkey's limited capacity, lack of strategic planning, and weakening political will due to instabilities in Turkish politics in the late 1990s and early 2000s created hindrances in its rising role in the region. Historical legacies and hard geopolitical realities of the region put restraints on the Turkish nationalist dream and dampened the public's emotional perception of the region. Subsequently, pragmatist approaches and prudent policies of Central Asian leaders, the revival of Russia's role after Putin, and rising involvement of the other players and rivals in the new great game placed constraints on Turkish activism in Central Asia. Central Asians, who fell under the Russian rule in the 19th century and then remained under Soviet authority for about seventy years, did not want another "big brother" after they gained their independence. Their desire to keep their sovereignty, establish relations with the other countries on an equal basis and to pursue their interests in a rationalist way was not in harmony with the Turkish nationalist approach.

Turkey, under the Erdoğan-led Justice and Development Party (JDP) and the minister of Foreign Affairs, Davutoğlu,began to pursue a proactive foreign policy during the second half of the 2000s and the first half of the 2010s (for some analyses of JDP-era proactive foreign policy see Öniş, 2010; Aras, 2009; Aras, 2014). Although Davutoğlu had a Eurasianist vision (Tüfekçi, 2012: 105-109), in addition to his neo-Ottomanism, and envisioned an expanded role for Turkey in its wider neighborhood with reference to Central Asia, Turkey's growing engagement on the international level was directed toward regions other than Central Asia. The 'Arab Spring' uprisings drew Turkey's attention towards the Middle East, and Central Asia was sidelined in Turkish foreign policy. The shift from a decades-long western-oriented focus to an eastern-oriented direction began slowly in Davutoğlu's era but became more pronounced in the personalized foreign policy of Turkey under Erdoğan in the second half of the 2010s (Aras, 2019: 3-6), but still could not build up the momentum of Central Asian-Turkish relations beyond what it had reached during the 1990s. During this period, Turkey grew closer to Russia, Iran, China, and some Middle Eastern countries, but not to Central Asia. A 'new' Turkey with rising authoritarianism and a rentier economy with decreasing levels of economic growth began to replace the previous Turkey, which was a candidate for the membership of the EU, close to the West, characterized by democratic values and a liberal and competitive economy with high levels of economic growth. This new Turkey, unable to provide an attractive model for the liberal progress of Central Asian countries or an alternative to the Russian-led state of affairs, aimed to keep the previous momentum of relations within certain limits that would be compatible with its new alliance with Russia. The rising role of Russia in the region thus ensures the maintenance of the historical and geopolitical status quo, which prevented Turkish-Central Asian relations from developing beyond established limits. By drawing closer to Russia and China, two great powers around the region, while growing increasingly distant from the liberal-democratic world and losing their support, Turkey has no option but to accept the status quo in Central Asia.

The Ottoman Empire adopted the expansion towards the west and the Islamization of Europe as the main building block of its foreign strategy. It turned to the East only when necessary in order to eliminate threats, such as the rise of Iranian Shia power, and to create a cohesive and stable Muslim world in the Middle East to consolidate its position against the West. Its successor, Turkey, because of the historical conditions of its birth after the collapse of the empire and its geopolitical circumstances and challenges, adopted both an internal socio-cultural westernization policy and a foreign strategy of western orientation for most of the 20th century. When Turkey recognized that European leaders did not welcome its attempts to be a member of the EU, it tried to balance its relations in Europe in the 1980s with interests in the Middle East. Economic liberalization during the 1980s fostered the rise of a business bourgeoisie and industrial production, and increased Turkey's need for new markets in the wider Middle East and Eurasia. Turkey did not miss the geopolitical opportunities created by the end of the Cold War era and expanded its role in different regions, including Central Asia. However, the euphoria of the 1990s was gradually replaced by a disillusionment due to limits of Turkey's capacity as well as other historical-geopolitical realities. The Middle East, rather than Central Asia, became the focus of JDP-period Turkish foreign policy activism became the Middle East rather than Central Asia. Turkey's expanded role in the Middle East in accordance with Davutoglu's 'strategic depth' was replaced by 'precious loneliness' when Turkey failed to achieve its goals in the Syrian crisis. (Aydın, 2019: 368-375)

Turkey reaped the benefits of the interim transition period of the early 1990s. However, after a time it became clear that Russia was back. Erdoğan's coalition with the authoritarian-minded and Eurasianist military bureaucracy after the corruption scandal of December 17-25, 2013, and the coup attempt of July-15, 2016 brought traditional Kemalist isolationist reflexes back in Turkish foreign policy. Almost all of the active and assertive foreign policy engagements were abandoned as the new regime prioritized the maintenance of its domestic authority. The new regime preferred a closed society under tight control to an open society which would have engagements in different regions requiring a proactive foreign policy. Thus, in spite of short-term fluctuations, Turkey was anchored again in its decades-long inactive foreign policy outlook in accordance with its - at best - middle-power position, vulnerable to the influences of great powers. Historically established geopolitical restraints as well as = Turkey's limited role in the great-power-driven regional and international system and status quo have dominated Turkish foreign policy to this day.

Foreign Policy of Central Asian States

The foreign policies of Central Asian states, on the other hand, cannot be defined in terms of ideology, emotions, or nostalgia. Central Asian republics pursue their interests in a pragmatic way according to their historical-geopolitical circumstances and with consideration to balances of power. The established status quo in the region in terms of the basic parameters of political systems and identities of the regimes and the leaders, which were inherited from the Soviet period, continues to a significant degree even today. Despite their independence, enduring Soviet legacies made it impossible to end dependence on Russia overnight. After independence the leaders of the Central Asian republics, almost all of whom were the first secretaries of the communist parties of their countries during the Soviet period, were well aware of the reality of Russia's dominant position in the region. Foreign policy options for the leaders are constrained not only by the conditions of the regional milieu and global setting but also by the historical, cultural, and geopolitical context, and the economic and military capacity of their countries. History, national identity, self/other perceptions, political culture, and geopolitical realities shape strategic mentalities and foreign policy impulses of the political leaders and foreign policy bureaucracies. Therefore, they did not share the emotional approaches of some Turkish leaders and nationalist sentiment of Turkish public opinion. As can be seen in the recent study of Amirbek and Aydin, Central Asian societies are also far from sharing the perception of the Turkish public opinion about a common Turkic world (Amirbek & Aydin, 2015: 22).

Different historical backgrounds shaped the respective national identities in Turkey and Central Asia. While the word 'Turk' referred to a common Turkic world, including Central Asian Turkic nations, in Turkish national conception because of Kemalist nationalist policies, Central Asian conceptions of nationality are the product of Stalin's 'nationalities' policy which divided the region into five principle nationalities who gained the status of Union Republic (Olcott, 2001: 14). Soviet Socialist Republics were demarcated as national units with clear boundaries and definite ethno-national affiliations under the Soviet central authority. Post-Soviet nationalisms were essentially the result of Stalin's conception of 'nation' in which the 'one nation - one state' principle predominated. Under the Soviet policy of nationalities, the national identity of each Central Asian republic was purified from previous references to Turkestan and to a common Turkic world in accordance with the Soviet 'divide and rule' strategy. The titular nation and the elite in each republic conceive their state as the nation-state of and for their distinct ethno-nation, distinct from the other Central Asian nations. Soviet ethno-politics emphasized the uniqueness and distinctiveness of the titular nation of each republic, and this legacy endured in post-Soviet national identity policies in Central Asia. (Bunce, 2005: 426-427; Goshulak, 2003: 494-498; Lapidus, 2002: 328; Slezkine, 1994: 413-452; Beissinger, 1997: 157-185). Because Soviet authorities perceived pan-Islamism and pan-Turkism as serious threats, they totally eliminated a common Turkish identity and replaced it with individual country-based national identities and nationalisms in Central Asian states. There is, therefore, no supporting base for Turkish dreams of a common Turkic world in the current socio-political realities of the region. As they attach great importance to their national sovereignty and distinct identities, the Central Asian republics are averse to coming under another supra-national political entity or another big brother (Aydın, 2004: 7). The leaders of the CAR are likely to maintain this Soviet-designed status quo in accordance with the requirements of national mobilization and the legitimacy of their existing national regimes and orders (Esenova, 2002: 12). 'Nationalism has a better chance of success than Pan movements in the political arena – as history has often demonstrated – thanks to its ability to generate stronger sentiments and deeper loyalties.' (Landau, 1995: 191). This historical-geopolitical context currently defines the foreign-policy identities and orientations of these republics. Their formulation of national identity, ideology, and foreign strategy is expected to be congruent with the master design and strategy of the historical-geopolitical overlords of the region because they lack an alternative identity, political will, and the power to radically change this status quo.

In the 1990s, some analysts and Turkish nationalists discussed the possibility of a reunification of Central Asian republics on the basis of historical Turkistan as a solution to problems of economic regionalization, trans-border conflicts and inter-ethnic strife (Gleason, 1993: 351). Reunification seemed to be an effective solution to minimize the negative side effects that may accompany the disintegration of the interdependent Soviet system. However, post-independence integration attempts did not emerge in Central Asia by the initiative of the republics themselves. Rather, they became members of regional organizations such as the Commonwealth of Independent States, Eurasian Economic Community, and the Eurasian Union which were created at a larger scale by Russia. Geographic proximity, shared Soviet-era traditions, a common language (Russian) and other common socio-economic features encouraged the development of regional integration with Russia. Before the collapse of the Soviet Union, the Soviet security umbrella had protected Central Asia from both external threats and internal (interethnic and inter-republic) conflicts. Because of entrenched habits and some mutual interests between the ruling elites, Russia has kept its leading place among the foreign policy priorities of the republics. However, these organizations could not achieve a level of integration like that of the EU because the republics lacked strong and stable political will for deeper integration. Leaders have been hesitant to give up any of their sovereignty to a higher mechanism, through which they might be vulnerable to the hegemony of Russia or of each other. (Nezihoglu and Sayin, 2013: 377-380). Their eagerness to maintain their national sovereignty, disagreements and border conflicts between each other leading to mutual distrust, Uzbekistan's "keep-away" policy from attempts for integration, and Turkmenistan's impartial policy and neutrality formed hindrances in the way of Central Asian integration projects (Amirbek & Aydin, 2015: 23). A Central Asian integration, however, designed by the Central Asian initiatives according to the Central Asian interests, has the potential to establish the region as a united and a greater entity in a stronger and more advantageous position against the interventions of great powers such as China or Russia. Therefore, these great powers are reluctant to see a Central Asia unified outside their leadership that would be less vulnerable to their influence. Iran is also likely to be opposed to the revival of a historically rival Turkic and Sunni world. The other global great powers such as the US are unlikely to support the rise of a Turkic world by the integration of Central Asia together with Turkey, which might attract Tajikistan, Afghanistan, and other countries in the Muslim world by leading to the rise of a Muslim power in world politics. Therefore, the current international conjuncture resulting from historical-geopolitical realities of the regional and international system seems to be the main systemic obstacle to the rise of an effectively unified Central Asia.

The industrial, technological, economic, and military capacity and power of a country define its position in the distribution and balance of power within a regional system. The abilities of countries to set goals and achieve their foreign policy objectives is proportional to their power position. Countries in a weak posture that are unable to end their dependency are likely to comply with great power policies until they are able to create a counter-balance by unifying with other smaller powers or aligning with some great powers against others. The enduring parameters of a regional system provide guiding principles and outlines for the foreign-policy options of a weak player within that system (Breuning, 2007: 149-156). To minimize the disadvantages and unfavorable circumstances of asymmetrical relations with the great power(s) in a regional system, weaker states prefer to diversify partners for cooperation and alternate allies instead of remaining loyal to only one power. While they avoid alarming the great power(s) of their region by threatening their strategic interests or entering a strategic alliance with other powers outside the region, they seek alternative outlets to decrease their dependency and create greater room for maneuvering. Central Asian countries avoid binding themselves to a single power. Instead, each republic prefers to diversify its foreign engagements to preserve its sovereignty (Bazarbayev and Zulpiharova, 2013: 104). Multi-vector foreign policy has appeared as the most rational foreign policy strategy for Central Asian states to attract a variety of actors in different issue-areas where they have needed alternative sources of assistance in order to mitigate the costs of dependency inherent in core-periphery relations. Since independence, the Central Asian republics have tried to develop their relations and cooperation with different global and regional actors, though Russia has maintained its dominant role in their strategic orientation. While they were trying to diversify partners with a pragmatic and market-oriented rationale in order to pursue their interests, they sought to balance the diverse interests of various players and avoided becoming dependent on a single power. All these historical-geopolitical realities set the boundaries of the relations between Central Asia and Turkey.

Conclusion

In accordance with neorealist or structural realist arguments, structural parameters of an international or regional system define behaviors of the units of the system. Distribution of national capabilities in a system creates systemic restraints on the foreign policies of the actors interacting in the system. The position of an actor in a system defines the contours of its foreign policy in proportion to its relative power. Weaker states in a great power-driven regional system can pursue their foreign policy objectives within limited confines without violating guiding principles of the regional structural establishment. The fact that weaker states lack capabilities to act independently leads to asymmetrical patterns of relations with the great powers of the regional system, and creates dependency. Central Asia, which once held a central position and was a dominant military power in world politics, fell under the rule of two expanding powers in the 18th and 19th centuries. Russia, expanding from the northwest, occupied Central Asia while China, expanding from the southeast, invaded historical eastern Turkestan, Xinjiang. Transition from a central position to a peripheral one in the imperial designs of two rising giants by the loss of military power and independence created a new but enduring geopolitical system in the region. From the Cold War era to the post-Cold War era, the name of Russian power changed from the Soviet Union to Russia or the Russian Federation. However, Russia's status as a great power has not changed. Both Russia, as the former overlord of the region and a military great power, and China, as a military, financial-economic, and industrial-technological giant, surrounding Central Asia, have been further increasing their influence in the region in recent years.

Turkey seemed to be the closest partner for the newly independent republics s early in the 1990s. There were high expectations, especially on the Turkish side, regarding the emergence of a Turkic world. However, enduring historical-geopolitical legacies and its limited capacity ultimately made Turkey no more than one of the several players with which Central Asian states have established relations without alienating Russia. Putin revived the leading role of Russia in the "near abroad" and, accordingly, gradually integrated Central Asian economies under the Eurasian Economic Union and Customs Union so that Russian manufactured goods began to dominate the regional market. Decades-long Russian domination, territorial proximity, its military operational capacity in Eurasia and Central Asia, and its role as a guarantor against security challenges such as border conflicts and ethnic tensions put Russia in a more advantageous position than other players. Central Asian leaders learned from the Georgian and Ukrainian crises in which there was no immediate military response by Western powers to Russian military operations in its traditional zone of influence. While Russia is trying to bring the countries in her "near abroad" under its hegemony again, China is also increasing its influence in the region through commercial expansionism and assertive projects such as the BRI (the Belt and Road

Initiative). Through the BRI, China is investing billions of dollars in the Central Asia and developing the economy of the region as well as increasing trade ties and transportation and energy infrastructure It is not realistic to expect either of the great powers dominating the geopolitics of Central Asia to abandon the region to their own initiatives or to the influence of the other powers. These geopolitical twin giants regard the rise of influence of the other powers in the region as detrimental to their strategic interests and encroaching on their zone of influence. Any vital threat to the historical status quo in the region is likely to be opposed by these powers.

The historical-geopolitical realities of Central Asia have created a regional context that limits room for both Turkey and the Central Asian republics to maneuver. Only a radical change and a tectonic shift in this historical establishment and geopolitical context might allow them to go beyond the limits. Moreover, a foreign policy assertiveness and activism beyond these limits would require a strong political will at the state level in these countries as well. However, there are no such signs of such a will at either the state or societal level in Central Asian countries because of the enduring Soviet socio-political and socio-cultural legacies. Post-Soviet political regimes in Central Asia seem to be comfortable in the persistent authoritarianism of the Russo-China-led regional system. Turkey, on the other side, also lacks such a political will, as its top priority in the past decade became the consolidation of an authoritarian regime. If Turkey continues on the same authoritarian path, steering away from liberal democracy and the West, it is unlikely to be able to provide an alternative model or exit from the established regional status quo. A rising Turkish role and increased activism in Central Asia with its limited power and capability is likely to bring Turkey into confrontation with Russia without any likelihood of success. Neither Turkey nor the Central Asian republics can change this status quo without a democratic political and liberal economic transformation, as well as a strong alliance with the Western democratic world. Central Asian countries currently lack signs of such a transformation. Furthermore, the U.S. and the EU have failed to develop a coherent joint strategy towards Central Asia to give effective support for such a transformation and to provide the region with the assistance needed to exit from this regional status quo.

CHAPTER SIX

CROSS-BORDER STUDENT MIGRATION FROM, TO AND WITHIN CENTRAL ASIA: PUSH AND PULL FACTORS

Alexey Fominykh

Introduction

S tudy abroad is a part of the larger phenomenon of international education, which can be studied through the prism of different disciplines including education itself, economics, political science, intercultural communication, psychology and sociology.
Cross-border student migration is the most substantial part of international education and an integral part of global human migration flows.
In 2017, there were over 5.3 million international students, up from 2
million in 2000. As UNESCO's Institute of Statistics notes, more than
half of these were enrolled in educational programmes in six countries: the United States of America, the United Kingdom, Australia,
France, Germany and the Russian Federation (2019). Prominent send-
ing countries of international students include China, India, Germany,
South Korea, Nigeria, France, Saudi Arabia and, notably, several Central Asian countries.

In the wider context of international relations, higher education plays
an integral role in shaping a nation's soft power, defined as "the ability to
get what you want through attraction rather than through coercion or pay-
ments" (Nye, 2005, p.11). Educational exchanges are effective vehicles of
public diplomacy and international development aid programmes as they
are often sponsored and coordinated by governments. This is especially
true in the case of short-term exchange programmes that involve younger
participants who are considered future leaders of their respective countries. As Joseph S. Nye rightly noted, "Because exchanges affect elites, one
or two key contacts may have a major political effect" (Nye, 2005, p.14).
Another key aspect of the sector is the booming global market for higher
education, in which universities compete to attract international students.
An increasing number of countries have introduced scholarships and established exchange programmes to facilitate cross-border student mobility. Universities and governments also consider exchange programmes as
great tools to promote their image internationally and raise awareness of
their culture, language, and politics, as well as expanding their recognition
and elevating their reputation. Central Asia is fortunate enough to be the

subject of interest of numerous international actors and as such is a recipient of opportunities provided by higher education mobility agencies such as Russia's Rossotrudnichestvo, the EU's Erasmus+, the American EducationUSA and Fulbright Program, China's Confucius Institute, as well as Turkey's scholarships, Indian governmental scholarships, Pakistan's HEC and many others.

The region has seen rapid growth in the number of students attending higher education since the end of the Soviet period, particularly in Kazakhstan and Kyrgyzstan. In Uzbekistan and Tajikistan, on the contrary, the governments tried to salvage the situation by improving weak secondary education performance, and did not consider tertiary education as the priority. As a result, in the latter two countries, which also demonstrated the highest birth rates among the post-Soviet states, domestic tertiary enrolment remains markedly low, and national universities have not kept pace with the growing demand for higher education (Brunner & Tillett, 2007: pp. 30-33, 37-38). According to the UIS (2019b), the number of nationals of Central Asian countries studying abroad has experienced steady growth from 67,300 in 2003 to 156,600 in 2012 and 197,055 in 2019.

International education and, more specifically, study abroad, have received a great deal of coverage in academic literature, particularly on the topic of human and labor migration from Central Asia. However, there are not many publications examining trends in cross-border student migration in this particular region. For the purposes of this paper, a comprehensive analytical review of the role of Russia and Kazakhstan in the Eurasian migration system conducted by Ryazantsev & Korneev (2014) was particularly useful, as it considers student mobility as an integral and important part of migration flow in the post-Soviet space. Also worthy of note are works devoted to educational reforms in the post-Soviet transition period by Anderson and Heyneman (2005), for instance, and also by Brunner and Tillett (2007), the latter being an extensive analytical report prepared for The World Bank. Additionally, there are some interesting pieces focused on the *Bolashak* national scholarship program of Kazakhstan by Nurbek et al. (2014), Sagintaeva & Jumankulov (2015), and Del Sordi (2017).

The Russian Federation attracts more mobile students from Central Asia than any other destination; besides, Russian is the widespread language of communication, education and media throughout the region. It is for this reason that this chapter also utilises academic publications in the Russian language, reflecting the Russian perspective, as well as approaches from the region, especially Kazakhstan. The topic of student migration is presented in a comprehensive study supported by the Eurasia Heritage Foundation (Gavrilov et al., 2012). Various aspects of international mobility from Central Asia to Russian universities are covered by Mitin (2010), Poletaev (2012), Alexeeva (2012), Shneyder (2019). Most of the listed Russian authors consider cross-border student mobility and recruitment of international students as a tool of internationalization of Russian universities by engagement in the global tertiary education market. Practical issues, such as course design, language programmes, accommodation, cultural adaptation and legal status of international students are also covered. Works by Dementyeva (2008), Bulatova and Glukhov (2019) provide good examples of perspectives on recruiting, teaching and assisting international students in Russian universities. Student migration from Kazakhstan to Russia, given its larger scale, is the focus of Rakisheva and Poletaev (2011), who analyze the cross-border student mobility between the two countries as a part of the Russian-led Eurasian economic integration.

This paper is intended to analyze outward student migration from, in and between post-Soviet Central Asian Republics. Two research questions are at work here:

1. What are the most prominent destinations to study abroad for the Central Asian mobile students?

2. What are the pull and push factors beyond cross-border student migration from, to and within the region?

The research is based mostly on data from open sources such as annual country reports on the flow of tertiary-level students, which are collected and published by the UNESCO Institute of Statistics (UIS) (see Tables 1-3). The UIS is still the most comprehensive database on this subject, with global coverage including Central Asia. However, some numbers are indirect estimates or nonexistent, as in the case of Turkmenistan. The Migration Portal managed and developed by International Organization for Migration (IOM) also contains valuable data on internationally mobile students. Other statistics on mobile students, such as reports from the national ministries of higher education, were also used as auxiliary sources. For example, the Russian Ministry of Science and Higher Education issues annual statistical bulletins on international students containing information on their countries of origin, source of tuition (self-paid or sponsored by the Russian government), academic profile, mode of study (full-time or extramural), and distribution throughout the Russian regions and universities.

International education has no universally agreed upon definition in academic literature. This paper defines international education as "the informal, non-formal, and formal educational relationships among peoples of various nation-states", without focusing on global issues that transcend national boundaries, otherwise necessary for a more complete definition (Gutek, 1993, p.33). In modern literature, the term "international education" is concurrently used along with "internationalization (of higher education)", and variations like "borderless education", "transnational education", and "cross-border education". According to Knight (2003), internationalization at the national, sectoral, and institutional levels is defined as "the process of integrating an international, intercultural, or global dimension into the purpose, functions or delivery of postsecondary education" (p. 2). In practice, the six major components of internationalization of higher education are: a) international student recruitment b) student and scholar mobility; c) research and knowledge exchange and technical assistance; d) marketing and expansion of university campuses and branches abroad; e) internationalization of campus curricula; and f) virtual transnational internationalization (like MOOCs) (Khorasandi Taskoh, 2014, pp. 24-25).

"International students" refers to foreign nationals who left their country of origin and moved to another country for the purpose of study. This definition is borrowed from the glossary adopted by the Organisation for Economic Cooperation and Development, which also defines international students as "students who are not permanent or usual residents of their country of study or alternatively as students who obtained their prior education in a different country" (OECD, 2012, p. 371). In 2015 the UNESCO Institute of Statistics (UIS), OECD and EUROSTAT, the European Union's statistical office, gave a more precise definition of "internationally mobile students" as those who are enrolled for a tertiary degree (or higher), therefore the length of stay is typically more than one year, and up to 7 years (UNESCO Institute of Statistics, 2015; Migration Portal, 2017). International students generally hold a non-resident visa status (sometimes called a student visa) to pursue a tertiary degree (or higher) in the destination country. These individuals are also called "degree-mobile students," to emphasize the fact that they would be granted a foreign degree, and to distinguish them from "credit-mobile students" on short exchange or study-abroad trips (Migration Portal, 2017).

Key Statistics

The UIS data collection provides an assessment of current trends in cross-border student mobility in Central Asia. For this paper, the selected parameters for observation are the numbers of nationals of Central Asian countries going to study abroad, and the most prominent countries of their destination (Table 9); numbers of internationally mobile students coming to central Asia with academic purposes and their distribution between the five hosting countries (Table 10); a comparison of several indicators showing each country's share in the global student migration flow, number of tertiary students from the country studying abroad and percentage of international students hosted within each country (Table 11). These figures show the degree of involvement of each nation in the global student migration and the level of internationalization of regional universities.

Table 9: Top 10 Study Abroad Destinations for Students from Countries of Central Asia (2019)

No.	Kazakhstan	Kyrgyzstan	Tajikistan	Turkmenistan	Uzbekistan
1.	Russia (65,237)	Russia (5,523)	Russia (14,204)	Russia (17,457)	Russia (20,862)
2.	Kyrgyzstan (3,290)	Turkey (2,032)	Kyrgyzstan (1,856)	Turkey (10,418)	Kazakhstan (9,641)
3.	Turkey (2,015)	Kazakhstan (1,117)	Turkey (692)	Belarus (7,434)	Ukraine (1,872)
4.	USA (1,707)	Germany (477)	Kazakhstan (563)	Ukraine (3,679)	South Korea (1,716)
5.	Czech Republic (1,648)	Saudi Arabia (359)	Belarus (478)	Kazakhstan (1,378)	Latvia (1,025)
6.	United Kingdom (1,436)	South Korea (195)	Saudi Arabia (397)	Tajikistan (869)	Kyrgyzstan (882)
7.	Malaysia (808)	USA (195)	Ukraine (207)	Uzbekistan (246)	Turkey (736)
8.	Germany (750)	Tajikistan (129)	USA (202)	USA (233)	Germany (651)
9.	South Korea (659)	Malaysia (124)	Egypt (167)	Azerbaijan (226)	USA (495)
10.	Poland (649)	Jordan (103)	Poland (164)	Malaysia (213)	Japan (384)

Data analysis: A Russia-centric Student Migration System?

As is evident from Table 9, the most popular destination to study abroad for students throughout Central Asia is the Russian Federation, possibly due to geographic proximity, economic interdependence, developed transportation infrastructure inherited from the Soviet Union and the persistent presence of the Russian language as a medium of communication in all five republics, apart from Turkmenistan.

Table 10: Top 10 Countries of Origin of International Students in Central Asia Countries (2019)

No.	Kazakhstan	Kyrgyzstan	Tajikistan	Turkmenistan	Uzbekistan
1.	Uzbekistan (9,641)	India (6,828)	Turkmenistan (869)	no data	Turkmenistan (246)
2.	India (3,719)	Kazakhstan (3,290)	India (573)	no data	Russia (174)
3.	Turkmenistan (2,699)	Tajikistan (1,856)	Afghanistan (256)	no data	Kazakhstan (108)
4.	Russia(1,511)	Russia (1,535)	Kazakhstan (177)	no data	Kyrgystan (36)
5.	China (1,472)	Uzbekistan (882)	Kyrgyzstan (129)	no data	Tajikistan (20)
6.	Kyrgyzstan (1,117)	Turkey (624)	Russia (111)	no data	Ukraine (14)
7.	Mongolia (612)	Pakistan (579)	Korea, DPR (35)	no data	Armenia (7)
8.	Tajikistan (563)	China (273)	Uzbekistan (35)	no data	Azerbaijan (6)
9.	Afghanistan (427)	Afghanistan (169)	Iran (25)	no data	no data
10.	Turkey (257)	Turkmenistan (51)	Turkey (7)	no data	no data

Table 11: Indicators of International Student Migration to and from Central Asian Countries (2019)

Indicators	KZ	KG	TJ	TM	UZ
Students abroad:					
Total number of students from the country studying abroad	84,681	11,399	19,762	46,223	34,990
Percentage of the global number of students studying abroad	1,6	0,2	0,4	0,9	0,7
Outbound mobility ratio (total number of tertiary students from the country studying abroad, expressed as a percentage of total tertiary enrolment of that country)	13,5	4,9	7,5	-	12,4
Gross outbound enrolment ratio (total number of tertiary students from the country studying abroad, expressed as a percentage of tertiary age in that country)	6,8	2,1	2,3	-	1,1
Students hosted:					
Total number of students from abroad hosted	22,728	16,534	2,238	-	700
Total number of international students hosted, expressed as a percentage of the global number of mobile students	0,4	0,3	0,0	-	0,0
Inbound mobility rate (total number of tertiary students from abroad studying in the country, expressed as a percentage of total tertiary enrolment of that country	3,3	7,6	0,8	-	0,2

Indeed, nationals from the former USSR now make up more than a half of the total number of international students (about 53 %), the majority of which represent students from Central Asian countries. In the 2016/2017 academic year, the Russian Federal Ministry of Higher

Education and Science reported on 122,508 citizens of post-Soviet states (including Transnistria, Abkhazia and South Ossetia), of whom 90,560 (or 73,9%) came from Central Asia (Ministry of Science and Higher Education of the Russian Federation, 2018, pp. 168-173). The UIS figures on tertiary student migration generally exceed the data presented in the Russian ministerial statistics. This is partially due to the fact that the enrollment of foreign nationals in part-time degree programmes is counted separately. In the same period 83,869 international students took part-time courses in Russia, of whom 96% (80,505) hailed from post-Soviet countries. Among this subgroup, Central Asian mobile students constituted about 63% (51,065) (Ministry of Science and Higher Education of the Russian Federation, 2018, pp. 306-310).

Considering this data, it is difficult to avoid the conclusion that the student migration flow from Central Asia to Russia naturally converges with the stream of labor migration. The decisive factor, in this case, is demography. Russian birth rates had significantly reduced the number of high school graduates by the early 1990s, causing competition for applicants among higher education institutions. Hence, universities were forced to become more open internationally and to recruit more students from abroad (Dementyeva, 2008, p. 40; Ryazantsev & Korneev, 2017).

One of the most important, but often untold, motivations to study in Russian universities is the use of academic mobility as a channel for permanent immigration, particularly by ethnic Russians from Central Asia. Half of the eight million or more ethnic Russians from the former Soviet Republics between 1990 and 2003 were from Uzbekistan, Turkmenistan, Tajikistan, Kyrgyzstan and Kazakhstan, as these countries housed more than one third of the Russian diaspora (Peyrouse, 2008). According to the Federal Law No. 99 of 1999, students from newly independent states generally received the designation 'Russian compatriots' (*sootechestvenniki*). A 'compatriot' is, in Russian terms, 'any citizen of the former Soviet Union, even if he or she, or their forebears, never lived in the RSFSR (now the Russian Federation)' (Zhuravsky & Vyhovanets,

2013). Article 17 of this Law set out measures designed to defend the rights of compatriots in the areas of culture, language, religion and education. For migrants from the former Soviet republics, their constitutional right (on a competitive basis) to receive free higher education was and remains a strong incentive as it offers an opportunity to become naturalized citizens of the Russian Federation. Hence, foreign nationals able to prove their compatriot status (a relatively simple task) could claim a right of admission equal to that of a Russian citizen, including enrolment in tuition-free university programmes. For the most part, an ethnic Russian migrant student will achieve Russian citizenship after graduation and therefore cease to be a foreigner.

Overlapping cross-border student migration and permanent immigration to Russia is a common phenomenon in the case of Kazakhstan. The majority of ethnic Russians from Central Asia wishing to study in Russia aimed to stay there for permanent residence; many mobile students consider naturalization after graduation 'a natural choice' (Gavrilov et al., 2012). Russian universities are also preferred by 53 % of interviewees of non-Kazakh ethnicity, while 90 % of ethnic Kazakhs would choose any other study abroad destination except Russia (Rakisheva and Poletaev, 2011; Poletaev, 2012). Kazakhstan's reputation as the biggest "supplier" of foreign students to Russian universities (more than 65,000 in 2019) has been reported with alarm by the country's media, who often blame Russia for a brain drain and depopulation of its adjacent territories (Gareeva, 2018).

Russian governmental support for universities and their proactive marketing policies contribute to the pull factors of incoming cross-border student migration. Since 2003, Russia has been distributing quotas for tuition-free university education for foreign applicants subsidized by governmental scholarships. This quota was fixed at 7,000 students from 2003-2007, and grew to 10,000 in 2008-2012. In 2013 the annual quota for foreign students was increased to 15,000, resulting in significant growth in the number of international students (predominantly from Post-Soviet countries) in Russian universities. Students were recruited not only in "traditional" hubs for international education like Moscow, Saint-Petersburg, Novosibirsk and Voronezh, but even in small and medium-sized institutions throughout the country. A number of provincial universities have taken international students exclusively from Central Asia, the majority of whom speak Russian well. The Russian government discussed further increases to subsidize 20,000 scholarships per annum by 2019, but the Western sanctions imposed in 2014 and economic difficulties have resulted in the deferral of these programs (Chernykh & Kiseleva, 2015). Despite these limits, the total share of international students from the Central Asian Republics on Russian campuses reached 39,4% in the academic year of 2016/2017, followed by 25% from the Asia-Pacific region (predominantly China, India and Vietnam), which supplied more international students globally than any other region (Ministry of Science and Higher Education of the Russian Federation, 2018, pp.168-173). Such figures imply that Russia regards Central Asia as their priority international market and employs vigorous outreach in this region.

Russia's strong advantages include geographic proximity, the common cultural legacy of the Russian empire and Soviet Union and the Russian language, which is still among the main means of local communication. Furthermore, Russian higher education is generally more affordable than fee-based programmes in North America, Europe or the Asia-Pacific.

Established in 2008, the Federal Agency for the Commonwealth of Independent States, Compatriots Living Abroad and International Humanitarian Cooperation *(Rossotrudnichestvo)* has linked Russian universities with foreign policy and, therefore, placed higher education programmes into the context of Russia's public diplomacy and development aid. Operating under the auspices of the Ministry of Foreign Affairs, the agency gave Russian universities greater ability to promote themselves abroad using a network of Russian Centres of Science and Culture (RCSC). Generally operating at Russian diplomatic missions, the RCSC provides language courses, libraries and support offices for ethnic Russian communities and NGOs. They also organize presentations and exhibitions on opportunities to study in Russia for the local public. Although a few of the wealthier Russian universities choose to engage recruits on their own and organize exhibitions at more expensive and prestigious international higher education fairs, the RCSC events might be the only way that many smaller institutions can afford to represent themselves. RCSC also provides their premises as testing centers for many Russian universities. This practice is not tolerated in some countries, however, particularly in Turkmenistan and Kazakhstan (REGNUM News, 2018).

Russia continues its ambitions to extend the RCSC's global network to 100 countries in order to support pro-Russian NGOs and promote Russian-language studies and cultural diplomacy initiatives (Kosachev, 2012). The Russian government is also attempting to restore ties with Soviet and Russian university alumni around the world. In 2020, the Global Alumni Alliance of Soviet/Russian Academic Institutions acted as an umbrella for 73 country associations (Vsemirnaya, 2020).

Some Russian universities have also established regional branches in Central Asia in line with Russia's foreign policy guidelines. For instance, Lomonosov Moscow State University has opened branches in Nur-Sultan, Tashkent and Dushanbe. Also worthy of note is the network of joint Russian (Slavonic) universities that operate in Dushanbe and Bishkek under bilateral intergovernmental agreements under the joint jurisdiction of the Russian Federation and the host country.

In summary, the Russian Federation is the centre of gravity for migrants in the post-Soviet space, including internationally mobile students. As Ryazantsev and Korneev note, a sustainable migration subsystem has formed between Russia, Kazakhstan and the Central Asian countries. "It is characterized by large-scale migration flows and sustainable geographic direction. It is from the Central Asian states that the main outflow of migrants to permanent residence has been taking place lately and they currently provide Russian and Kazakh industries with migrant workers and Russian universities with students" (p. 15). Embedded in public diplomacy and development aid initiatives, higher education programmes and governmental scholarships aim to strengthen Russia's influence in Central Asia and promote long-term regional projects for Moscow-led Eurasian economic integration.

Data Analysis: (Not so) Minor Actors

As the data in Table 1 suggests, many routes of cross-border student migration in the post-Soviet area exist due to inertia. For example, some major mobile student flows go to the former Soviet republics like Belarus (#3 for students from Turkmenistan, # 5 for Tajikistan) and Ukraine (#3 for Uzbekistan, #4 for Turkmenistan). In fact, these trends reflect a legacy of sustainable student mobility networks within the USSR. Belarus and Ukraine, which exist in similar economic and demographic situations as Russia, also pursue active marketing in Central Asia, offering affordable study programmes in Russian. The two countries' universities have become the most serious competitors to Russian universities. In Belarus, Russian is one of the two official languages and the dominant language of higher education instruction (Zakon, 1990). In Ukraine, Russian is the language of instruction in higher education "on choice" (Ukrainian International Education Council, 2018). After the collapse of the Soviet Union in 1991, many international education actors came to the newly independent Central Asian states to explore the region's emerging market with a total population of more than 82 million. Turkey (#2 for students from Kyrgyzstan and Turkmenistan, #3 for those from Kazakhstan and Tajikistan), has also expanded its educational and Turkish language programmes in the former USSR under the motto of the 'brotherhood of Turkic nations' (Azeri, Kazakhs, Kyrgyz, Turkmens, and Uzbeks). Conversion from the Cyrillic to Latin alphabet in Turkmenistan, and (partly) in Uzbekistan and Kazakhstan was one of the visible signs of independence and manifestation of the pan-Turkic solidarity. Since 1991, with governmental or private funds, Turkey has founded a number of joint higher education institutions in the region, such as Ala-Too International University in Bishkek or Suleyman Demirel University in Almaty. Turkey has also developed its own governmental scholarship programmes (e.g. Türkiye Burslari and TÜBİTAK), which have gained recognition in Central Asian countries.

The United States has also started to pay much attention to the development of educational exchanges within their public diplomacy with post-Soviet states. Apart from various US Department of State programmes (Fulbright, Freedom Support Act, IREX UGRAD, etc.), numerous American Corners and EducationUSA advising centres started to provide guidance on admission to American universities and colleges in almost every country of Central Asia. The US educational presence is now obvious in the Bishkek-based American University of Central Asia (AUCA) and International University of Kyrgyzstan (operated jointly with San Francisco State University) as well as in a private Kazakh-American university in Almaty.

Other minor international education players in Central Asia include the United Kingdom with its establishment of the Kazakh-British Technical University in Almaty and Westminster International University in Tashkent, as well as Germany with its network of DAAD country offices, regional offices of foundations sponsored by German political parties (Friedrich Ebert, Konrad Adenauer, Rosa Luxemburg), and joint academic institutions like German-Kazakh University in Almaty. China sponsors its network of Confucius Institute centres throughout the region (Confucius Institute, 2020). Other East Asian actors are also active, including South Korea (#4 study abroad destination for students from Uzbekistan, #6 for Kyrgyzstan, #9 for Kazakhstan) and Malaysia (#7 for Kazakhstan, #9 for Kyrgyzstan, #10 for Turkmenistan). South Korean Inha University and Singapore's branch of the Management Development Institute are operating in Tashkent. Tajikistan and Kyrgyzstan have many nationals studying in the Middle East, particularly in Saudi Arabia and Egypt where many of them pursue Islamic education.

One of the major pull factors directing the flows of internationally mobile students was the increasing popularity of English along with a decreased use of the Russian language during the process of nation building in post-Soviet Central Asia. Indeed, good command of the English language opens possibilities for migration and work in international businesses or NGOs with foreign ties. Knowledge of English is also needed for prestigious educational opportunities inside the region, such as the American University of Central Asia (Bishkek), the newly established Nazarbayev University (Astana) and the three campuses of the Aga Khan supported University of Central Asia (in Khorog, Tajikistan, Naryn, Kyrgyzstan and Tekeli, Kazakhstan). In Kazakhstan - which is at the forefront of the introduction of multilingualism as a tool of modernization and global communication - the government has set a goal for 20% of the country's population to have a mastery of English by 2020 (Fierman, 2012, pp. 1098-1099).

In this regard, special consideration should be given to Kazakhstan's national Bolashak ("The Future") scholarship. The aim of establishing the programme in 1993 was to invest in human capital development and ensure that this investment creates a long-lasting impact on the country's development (Sagintaeva and Jumakulov, 2015). According to statistics by Nurbek et. al., the majority of more than 10,000 Bolashak grantees study in English-speaking countries (39,5% in the UK, 25% in the United States) while only 8,4% Bolashak scholars go to Russia (2014, p. 48). The programme enforces a Kazakh language entry test, which, as a rule, prevents applicants of non-Kazakh ethnicity from using this opportunity to study abroad.

It is quite interesting to observe such strong cross-border educational migration within the Central Asian region. For example, students go to Kazakhstan from Kyrgyzstan and Uzbekistan and to Kyrgyzstan from Tajikistan. Some of these linkages are successful due to a Soviet era legacy coupled with the limited availability of high quality institutions providing education for specific programmes; interethnic connections, geographic proximity and affordability also have an influence. Against this general backdrop, Kyrgyzstan prevails as the most attractive study abroad destination for internationally mobile students within Central Asia, with an inbound mobility rate of 7,6 compared to 3,3 in Kazakhstan (see Table 11). The reasons for this may include the country's openness for international players who came to explore the national market of higher education in the post-Soviet period. Hence, Kyrgyzstan might re-evaluate the capabilities of its economy by transforming itself into a regional hub for quality international education. However, intra-regional cross-border mobility also carries some political risks. For example, on February 7, 2020, the Uzbek Education Ministry offered an opportunity for students in Kazakhstan, Kyrgyzstan, and Tajikistan to submit applications to transfer to an Uzbek university with minimal paperwork and waived the requirement of entry exams. This decision caused chaos in many universities in Kazakhstan, Tajikistan and Kyrgyzstan, which host about 25,000 Uzbek students. Authorities in all these countries did not welcome such a sudden decision, which, in their opinion, violates many administrative and academic rules of a host country, and significantly reduces revenues from tuition fees (Najibullah, 2020).

Conclusion

The emergence of new international actors put an end to the previous monopoly of national educational systems in Central Asia, which retained significant elements from the old Soviet educational structures, and was, therefore, tied to the Russian academic tradition. However, due to economic, political and cultural interdependence, Russia remains the number one study abroad destination for the growing population of internationally mobile students from Central Asia. The Russian Federation, in turn, supports this cross-border student migration through governmental scholarships or tuition free admission quotas and various public diplomacy and development aid initiatives. Nationals of Kyrgyzstan, Tajikistan, Turkmenistan and Uzbekistan form a strong flow of student migration to Russia, which more or less coincides with the labor migration flows. This is not the case, however, with incoming student mobility from Kazakhstan, which brings many ethnic Russians and other students of non-Kazakh ethnicity seeking naturalization as Russian citizens.

Central Asian countries support, or at least do not hinder, outgoing cross-border student migration, as most of them cannot provide universal access to quality and affordable national higher education. In Kazakhstan, with its more favorable economic situation, the government considers studying abroad an important tool for the nation's modernization and, potentially, Westernization, for further engagement in the global economy. This does not apply, however, to Russia, as the exodus of young people threatens the economic, demographic and societal sustainability of Kazakhstan. The topic of cross-border student mobility remains politically loaded. The most recent examples are the securitization of recruiting activities by Russian universities in Kazakhstan or Uzbekistan's decision to ease the return of its nationals studying in neighboring Central Asian states.

To attract students from Central Asia, international actors are adopting a range of policy incentives like national and private scholarships, sponsored quotas for enrollment, tuition waivers and various outreach activities from education fairs and language contests to the establishment of new universities and branches in the region. Bearing in mind the dynamics of demography and economic growth in the region, as well as the ever-tightening geopolitical rivalry between Russia, China, and the West in Eurasia, the five post-Soviet republics of Central Asia are becoming a fast-growing higher education market and is likely to remain a growing source of international students for the coming decades.

CHAPTER SEVEN

UZBEKISTAN JOINING THE EURASIAN
ECONOMIC UNION: IMPLICATIONS FOR
CENTRAL ASIA'S REGIONAL BALANCE

Fabrizio Vielmini

Introduction

In 2019, Uzbekistan's prospects of joining the Eurasian Economic Union (EAEU) became a top priority in the country's foreign policy agenda. The theme of Uzbek inclusion in the EAEU is hotly debated both in Uzbekistan and among experts on post-Soviet Central Asia. This paper presents an external view of the debate and assesses the implications of this development for Central Asia.

The paper first explores how the opportunity to join the EAEU is perceived within Uzbekistan versus the concrete economic advantages of membership. The paper argues that Uzbekistan's accession should be viewed with a holistic and long-term perspective rather than purely in terms of economic reasons. After 25 years of self-imposed isolation, renewed connectivity between Uzbekistan and the EAEU countries entails several implications and potentialities. The EAEU is regarded as the main framework for advancing regional integration in Central Asia. To explain this, the paper analyzes the possibility of accession against the background of the foreign policy doctrine elaborated by Uzbekistan after independence. As a consequence of the chosen posture regional integration stalled because its neighbours feared Uzbekistan would control the process.

To overcome these obstacles, this paper considers the EAEU as a phenomenon of new regionalism (Söderbaum & Shaw, 2003), a complex process that goes beyond economic interests to encompass culture, politics and security to establish an autonomous path of development which softens the impacts of both Western neo-liberal globalization and Chinese economic expansion. This proposed union does not exclude other architectures of cooperation, particularly those put in place by the European Union as a "Greater Eurasian Partnership". Although it was adversely affected by the geopolitical effects of the crisis in Ukraine, the EAEU still has the potential to provide a framework for a wider and more inclusive regional initiative to combine Russian and Chinese influence with the EU's regional agendas.

The paper is based on both primary and secondary sources, including interviews with senior Uzbek experts and a review of relevant materials published on the subject.

Uzbekistan's Foreign Policy Trajectory and Its Impact on Regional Integration

Since independence, a central tenet of Uzbek foreign policy has been to affirm a special responsibility to lead Central Asian integration, acting as the aggregating core of the five post-Soviet republics (Tolipov, 2019). Although this idea was treated as a national historical mission, its implementation was at odds with other policy initiatives. Namely, Karimov's Uzbekistan adopted a national ideology assigning an absolute value to the country's "eternal independence" (*mustaqilik*) (Romashov, 2016).

Tashkent approached regional integration in Central Asia as a continuation of the historical leadership exerted by Uzbek political formations, from the khanates to the special role of the Uzbek SSR during the Soviet era. In this context, other Central Asian states resisted Uzbek pretensions, leading to a number of stalemates and flashpoints in regional relations during the three decades since independence. One reflection of this situation was the disbanding of the Central Asian Cooperation Organization (CACO) in 2005 and the consequent merger with the Eurasian Economic Community (EurasEC), the EAEU's predecessor (Weitz, 2018). This development marked the demise of the autonomous regional integration process. In the following years, Uzbekistan's erratic politics reached a point where Russian and Kazakh integration projects had to be planned so as to make detours around Uzbekistan's borders.

All of this changed in 2016, when, after the death of Islam Karimov, President Mirziyoev directed Uzbek foreign policy in a more pragmatic direction based on mutual understanding with its neighbours. The new political line opened a period of eventful change for Central Asia where the core of the region ceased acting as an obstacle to regional connectivity and again began to assume its natural role as a hub of Central Asian relations.

The situation called for a resumption of the processes of regional integration. In 2018 and 2019, Uzbekistan strived to re-animate regional integration by facilitating the organization of the first two meetings of all the Central Asian leaders in thirteen years. At the same time, it is evident that in spite the enthusiasm elicited by the summits, Central Asian integration continues to face hurdles. For instance, the second follow-up summit, held in Tashkent in November 2019, took a long delay before coming to fruition. During the summit, the leaders took precautions to make clear that their gatherings are primarily consultative in nature, and "not directed against someone's interests," with no new regional organization foreseen to emerge as a result (Makszimov, 2019).

This is representative of a constant in the modern history of Central Asia in which regional relations are shaped by external powers. Accordingly, as with the EurasEC, the EAEU could be a framework where Central Asian integration takes place. This also reflects Russia's will to remain entrenched in regional processes and an awareness among regional leaders that any attempt to exclude Moscow will have unpleasant consequences, since Russia will then use the existing differences between the five states to advance its interests.

Factors Pushing Uzbekistan towards the EAEU

Uzbekistan's EAEU access is evaluated by national experts primarily in terms of its implications for the national economy. Tashkent expects that the EUEA will fit Uzbek plans to reinforce export-oriented sectors of the national economy. Access to EAEU membership will be instrumental in removing trade barriers and expanding the presence of Uzbek exports (such as automobiles and textiles) in Russian and other EAEU markets by reducing transport costs and streamlining border crossing procedures (Nyematov, 2020). Given that Uzbekistan is a land locked country, easing the cross-border flow of goods is essential to improving the country's role in international trade.

Uzbekistan can also benefit from several preferential free trade agreements which the EAEU has signed with several countries such as

Serbia, Israel, Iran, Singapore, Vietnam, China, Cuba, Egypt and Thailand. This can lead to still more opportunities for Uzbek exports. Additional benefits are expected in the area of energy security. Since the EAEU is developing a "Single Hydrocarbons Market" (Mukhtarov, 2014), Uzbekistan can expect fee reductions due to the large amounts of fuel it imports from Russia and Kazakhstan.

Tashkent also expects that its EAEU membership will increase foreign investment. Such investments are expected from both from inside the bloc (especially infrastructure investments by the Eurasian Development Bank and Russian banks such as VTB, Gazprombank and VEB) and externally from the side of economic players interested in the country as a platform for operating in the markets of other EAEU countries (Karavayev, 2019).

The issue of labor migration also stands high in the debate. Uzbekistan has the largest population of migrant workers in the Union countries, as high as three million by some estimates.[11] Accession to the EAEU can also dissolve several administrative hurdles that migrants currently face. This also has the potential to yield consistent economic returns in terms of remittances.

Regional Significance of the EAEU's Expansion to Uzbekistan

The third most populous post-Soviet country, Uzbekistan is projected to soon become the second largest nation in Eurasia. As a result of the entrance of Uzbekistan into the EAEU, the Central Asian component of the organization would be decidedly reinforced. Adding Uzbekistan's 33 million citizens and its developed economy to the current EAEU population of 190 million, Uzbekistan's membership will contribute to moderating the EAEU's internal imbalance, where Russia accounts for 85% of the organization's GDP and population. Due to this imbalance, the trade flows within the EAEU have a centripetal character: Russia acts as

---

[11]   At least other 2-2,6 million Uzbek labor migrants live mostly in Russia. Paramonov 2020, "The Russian Foreign Policy toward Central Asia in Economic, Security and Social Spheres: a View from Uzbekistan", Post-soviet studies, 3 (2), https://e46c205d-83c7-4e8c-bb4b-8df266fbea81.filesusr.com/ugd/0206eb_493d778031134245a9ba835d-fb611b34.pdf

a center around which the economies of the four other members gravitate (with the exception of Kazakhstan, with its large energy exchanges
with Western countries and China).

Figure 4: Economic Ties Between EAEU Members in 2017[12]

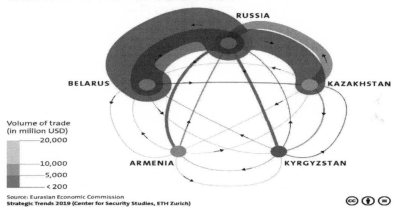

Economic Ties Between EAEU Members in 2017

Volume of trade (in million USD)
- 20,000
- 10,000
- 5,000
- < 200

Source: Eurasian Economic Commission
Strategic Trends 2019 (Center for Security Studies, ETH Zurich)

Source: Eurasian Economic Commission; first published in: Perović, Jeronim (2019). Russia's Eurasian Strategy; Thompson, Jack, Thränert, Oliver. Strategic Trends 2019. Key Developments in Global Affairs, Zürich,
45–63, here: 53; Adapted by the Russian Analytical Digest, No. 247, 17
February 2020, p.9

The entry of Uzbekistan will shift this balance, intensifying intra-regional ties and balancing Moscow's outsized influence. The Central
Asian component of the EAEU is projected to further grow given that
Tajikistan is expected to join after Uzbekistan. In this way, Uzbekistan's
EAEU accession could create a second Central Asian center, thus balancing Russian "Great Power" ambitions. This will be the case especially
if Uzbekistan works in tandem with Kazakhstan, the second EAEU power, which also is sensitive about any threat to its national sovereignty (In-

---

12   The image illustrates the meaning of the passage ("trade flows within the EAEU have a
     centripetal character: Russia acts as a center around which the economies of the four
     other members gravitate"). Exchanges are currently centered on Russia, and the addition
     of Uzbekistan's economy will reinforce flows across CA

deo, 2019). Membership in the EAEU, with its multilateral institutions regulating the functioning of the organization, may enable Kazakhstan and Uzbekistan (as well as Kyrgyzstan and subsequently Tajikistan) to balance their dependence on Moscow and contain Russia as part of a rules-based organization (Stronski & Sokolsky, 2020). In this conjuncture, Uzbekistan's importance is even more pronounced as a result of the beginning of a succession of power in Kazakhstan which can be expected to limit Astana's role in regional processes for the years to come.

Although the economic dimension is constantly portrayed as a priority, it is evident that the EAEU's primary raison d'etre is geopolitical. The EAEU is backed by Russia as an instrument to structure a regional security system which shapes the geopolitical order within the post-Soviet space. Russia also seeks to strengthen the EAEU as part of its strategy of positioning itself as one of the poles shaping the international order on the world stage. At the same time, Moscow has demonstrated that it is interested in controlling its neighbors' domestic politics. Russia's priority is to ensure that its neighbors do not align with other regional power blocs to work against its strategic interests (Perović, 2018). This Russian agenda can lead to problems in Central Asian relations with Western partners. On the other hand, the experience of Kazakhstan and Armenia in concluding an *ad hoc* association agreement with the EU demonstrated that there is no incompatibility between EAEU membership and structured relations with the EU and other global players active in the Central Asian sphere. Similar considerations apply with regards to Uzbekistan's access to the WTO. Apart from Belarus, all current EAEU members are also part of the WTO. Uzbekistan can simultaneously approach both organizations (WTO and EAEU) through selective negotiation openness and reanimation of traditional preferential trade agreements. The country would thus be following modern regionalism processes around the world, where regional integration is compatible with non-discriminatory trade practices and openness to external players.

The EAEU is a phenomenon of new regionalism, not only as an adaptive response to the challenges in the field of economics and security, but also as a new way to "go global," affecting the cultural and political aspects of the societies involved. Uzbekistan, like all other Eurasian states, is economically vulnerable compared to the mature capitalist economies of Western nations and the fast-growing markets in East Asia. Accordingly, Central Asian states cannot risk adopting unconditionally liberal models of economic freedom, as this would expose them to the turbulences of global trade and finance. As observed by Molchanov (2018, 506), the EAEU is set to provide answers to these challenges through the "resuscitation of mutually beneficial ties of the late Soviet era and the state-guided developmentalism of a market variety." For disadvantaged states like Kyrgyzstan and Tajikistan, the EAEU may serve as the "legalization" of their economic dependence on Russia.

Uzbekistan's consideration of EAEU membership, a major shift in the foreign policy line followed by Tashkent since independence, should be interpreted in light of the crisis of the US-centered globalization model in the last decade. With the diminution of US influence in the region and the launch of the Belt and Road Initiative (BRI), China has emerged as an alternative driver of globalization in Central Asia. While the additional investments brought by BRI were certainly welcome in the region, increasing Chinese clout in regional affairs raises concerns regarding Beijing's growing influence. One can expect that Uzbekistan's membership in the EAEU will enhance the organization's capacity to balance the Chinese presence, as well as making it more compatible with Central Asian interests. Although there are certain areas that the two projects clash - the first being based on enhanced regionalism, the second on open, cross-border free trade - China understands the importance of the EAEU for Russia. At the same time, the EAEU provides a legal and technological platform for ensuring connectivity within a homogeneous economic space based on coherent principles and minimal internal barriers. This is also in China's interests, which can use this space as a bridge between the Asia-Pacific region, Europe and the Middle East.[13] Uzbeki-

---

[13]   Jing Shuiyu and Zhong Nan, "China Signs Trade Deal with Eurasian Economic Union," *China Daily*, May 18, 2018, http://www.chinadaily.com.cn/a/201805/18/WS5afe4aaba3103f6866ee941b.html

stan, as the crossroads of Central Asia, fits quite well into this concept of Greater Eurasian cooperation.

The China-Kyrgyzstan-Uzbekistan (CKU) railway project, a crucial infrastructure link for regional connectivity to change Central Asia's interaction with other regions of Eurasia, will be a crucial test of this model. Though the project has been under discussion for over 20 years, it has faced some stumbling blocks, including Kyrgyzstan's fears that if the project is implemented, the country will become financially vulnerable to China and be at risk of seeing an increase of internal division between the northern and southern regions. Russia and Kazakhstan are also wary about the possible negative consequences of the CKU project. Kazakhstan expects that the new line will create strong competition to its current dominance of East-West rail transport from China. Russia sees the project as a potential blow to its position in the region as a whole (Peacenexus, 2019).

Against these negative scenarios, the EAEU can provide a framework for developing China-Uzbekistan railway connections in parallel with a North-South connection linking the Russian-Kazakhstani network with the line from China. As a result, Kyrgyzstan will not be left dependent on China while Russia and Kazakhstan will have concrete interests in developing the CKU project with its potential for increased connectivity in the direction of Iran and the Persian Gulf countries.

The CKU's fate underlines the centrality of geopolitical considerations in shaping regional developments. The creation of transport corridors requires regional stability and security, which establishing a solid framework of relations between the Central Asian republics. Within the region, state fragility in Kyrgyzstan and Tajikistan remains a major challenge for the future, exposing Uzbekistan and the rest of Eurasia to threats of uncontrolled migration, drug-trafficking and spreading insurgencies. Bad management of looming geopolitical, demographic, ecological and other processes inside the region may create waves thst reverberate on the western edges of the continent.

These considerations call for a framework that at once softens regional imbalances between the countries of the region and also provides security guarantees to underpin the process of Central Asian integration. This is the mission of the Collective Security Treaty Organization (CSTO), the main post-Soviet security bloc, whose membership (which was suspended unilaterally by Uzbekistan in 2012) overlaps with that of the EAEU. An EAEU-CSTO compact reinforced by Uzbekistan stands as a promising framework for exerting a positive influence on Afghanistan's future. Tashkent's diplomatic efforts in the talks for the future of Afghanistan would complement Moscow and Astana in creating momentum to find solutions involving all the parties of the Afghan conflict. Against this background, the EAEU appears to be a necessary framework to keep Central Asia together and create infrastructure for stability and development.

Though it receives less attention the influence that Uzbekistan's EAEU membership may have on the socio-cultural environment in the region is, in the authors view, of equal importance. The ongoing transformations in Uzbekistan and other Central Asian societies have sustained momentum, and their implications in the medium to long term are far from predictable. This is true particularly with regard to the impact that further Islamisation may have for Uzbekistan's future. Within the framework of cultural globalization, a "free-floating" interaction with the international parties may push the country to gravitate towards Islamic confessionalism, a model that will have serious repercussions if applied in the context of the country's diversity (Abdullaev, 2005). An anchorage to the EAEU vector represents a balancing factor against this risk and a way to solve the problem of maintaining a common cultural space and linguistic understanding between the region's countries. For Russia, as well as for the Central Asian states, it is important to overcome certain processes that led to mutual cultural exclusion in the past. These processes have not only complicated the social adaptation of labour migrants, but also caused deep cultural upheavals and conflicts both among the masses and the elite at all levels of societies in the post-Soviet states. In the long run, these factors are also important for reducing the potential for destructive social protest, which remains high in Uzbekistan and in the region. Preserving the Russian speaking culture during the process of nation-building will maintain norms and cultural values that form bridges between different internal constituencies, as well as the connection of the large Russian diaspora with their Motherland, an important factor for the future stability of Uzbekistan's society (Molchanov 2015).

This is even more important since migration links are expected to continue expanding in the coming decades as they help to solve Russia's and Central Asia's opposing demographic problems, with an aging and decreasing number of population leading to a labor shortage for the former, and overpopulation for the latter.

Demographic interconnectedness between Russia and Central Asia also drives cooperation in science and education. This is set to be another important driver in Uzbekistan's approach to the EAEU. Due to demographic pressure, the Uzbek educational system faces serious challenges in maintaining its human capital at the levels inherited from the socialist system. Since there is high demand in Uzbekistan for opportunities for its constantly growing student population, the EAEU framework can fill an important gap. Russian, and to some extent Kazakh, academic systems already provide places for Uzbek students, including via university branches opened in Uzbekistan.

The Difficult but Necessary Road Ahead

The issue of Uzbekistan's accession to the EAEU is very complex and controversial, and the road ahead will be a long one. In 2020, Uzbekistan expects to attain observer status in the union.

At the same time, the accession will not be a fast process and may take years. A formal pledge for admission does not automatically lead to actual membership. Having entered the CIS Free Trade Zone in 2015, the Uzbek government agreed to adopt several harmonization measures before 2020, such as the gradual reduction of protective tariffs and excise taxes on a range of goods. As of the end of 2019, only a few had been implemented. EAEU measures could very well see similar results.

In this way, the government could grant Moscow the prestige of its formal membership in the bloc, while in practice, a number of licensing, import quotas, and other restrictions on imports could be left in place, as the country may not be ready for the associated shocks. This would be a temporary solution, while policy-making bodies continue to thoroughly assess the pros and cons of full membership. The same is happening in Tajikistan, where this "studying" phase has been underway for several years already.

Over this period, the pace at which various trends within the EAEU develop will determine Uzbekistan's decision. If the norms and regulations established will boost the economies of member countries, then Uzbekistan will be encouraged to become a member so as to maintain relations with its neighbors and partners. Among the factors preventing a full-fledged accession is widespread internal resistance. Even if convinced that the EAEU path is the right one for the country, Uzbek elites will have to work to change the ideological bases that have informed the country's position in the international arena. Indeed, in the formal foreign policy strategy document adopted to date, Tashkent pledged to never join any external block (Tolipov, 2012). After 30 years of official propaganda at different levels, a strong national ideology of self-reliance and absolute independence has penetrated all spheres of Uzbek life (Fazendeiro, 2017). This mindset presents major challenges to any potential commitment to integration.

Of no less importance for the future potential forUzbekistan's EAEU accession is the kind of leadership that Russia will be able to exert in steering the aforementioned processes. Many of the EAEU cooperation measures are only partially implemented, often because of ambiguities in implementation from the Russian side since Russia is the largest member of the Union. This could lead to derailing agreed upon EAEU rules, as the recent crisis in the relations between Russia and Belarus and renewed trade skirmishes between Kazakhstan and Kyrgyzstan exemplified (Amrebayev, 2020).[14] Overall, with its capitalist character, the current Russian political regime lacks a real developmental vision, contributing to a distortion of the rules that the EAEU is supposed to guarantee. Similar problems exist on Kazakhstan's side, with whom there is a legacy of competition that makes it difficult to establish the proposed tandem for balancing. EAEU development is also adversely affected by the enduring geopolitical confrontation between Russia and the West over the crisis in Ukraine and the associated neo-imperial narrative which this rivalry feeds among certain Russian political forces (Shagina, 2020). In this context, Russia appears satisfied with the EAEU for its symbolic value rather than its practical implications.

Conclusions

Almost thirty years after the end of the USSR, the whole of Central Asia maintains strong links to the Russian space. The EAEU is an objectively post-imperial structure allowing the management of the whole spectrum of persisting interconnections with the former imperial center. The nature of economic dependence and geopolitical configurations make the integration structures necessary. The new political course of Uzbekistan presents great opportunities to change things for the better in and around Central Asia. Since it is breaking from its previous course of isolation, the country is again finding its natural role as the fulcrum and core of the whole region. However, Uzbekistan's regional environment will remain an extremely difficult one due to the amount of security problems linked to Afghanistan and the challenges of growing Chinese influence in the region.

The EAEU stands out as a platform which will make it possible to attain collective solutions to complex tasks for a new regionalist agenda. It may also establish a resilient environment in Central Asia able to shape

---

[14]   During the Kyrgyz presidential election of October 2017, Bishkek accused Astana of meddling in the electoral process. As a result, Kazakhstan imposed reinforced security measures at border crossings, which resulted in severe hindrances for the flow of goods and persons between the two countries. In 2020 Kyrgyzstan appealed to the WTO against Kazakhstan alleging violations of the EAEU agreement.

the massive inflows of Chinese infrastructures and capitals in a direction more suited to local needs. The EAEU was originally developed as a tool in which the public sector serves as an engine of economic growth. The EAEU has a future if it can fulfill this mission after the geopolitical turbulence of the Ukrainian crisis is overcome. In this perspective, the new position of Uzbekistan, as it reconfigures the whole network of relationships crossing Central Asia, represents a unique opportunity to work towards such a partnership.

CHAPTER EIGHT

"CONNECTIVITY" FOR ECONOMIC SUSTAINABILITY: INDIA'S MARCH TOWARDS EURASIA

Anirban Chatterjee

Introduction

The importance of connectivity in an era of economic interdependence is especially pertinent for India, one of the fastest growing, yet energy deficient, economies. As a result, the country is increasing its engagement with neighboring regions, and Eurasia in particular. In an effort to expedite its market diversification strategy and reduce its dependence on traditional sources in the West, India, together with Russia and Iran, has launched the International North-South Transport Corridor (INSTC). This corridor aims to substantially reduce travel time, cost, ease of access to Eurasian markets, and ultimately extend to European markets as well. India's strategic interest in the Eurasian region stems from its increasing need for economic growth and energy cooperation, leading the country to enhance efforts towards connectivity. India's growing presence in the region is also buttressed by the fact that India has become a full member in the Shanghai Cooperation Organization (SCO), and is in negotiations with the Eurasian Economic Union (EAEU) as part of the process to sign a Free Trade Agreement (FTA). India perceives China's Belt and Road Initiative (BRI) with skepticism, and is consequently pushing for the speedy operationalization of INSTC and other Indian-led connectivity initiatives.

Against this backdrop, this paper will be dealing with the following research questions: How do India's objectives for INSTC overlap or compete with those of China's BRI? How does Eurasia, as a region, present opportunities for India to fulfill its geo-strategic interests? How does India's membership in the SCO and cooperation with the EAEU give it a firm foothold in the region to further bolster the prospects of connectivity with the region?

Although the issue of connectivity has received considerable attention over the last decade, the economic, strategic, political and cultural significance of connectivity projects have been discussed since the disintegration of the Soviet Union. After the collapse of the USSR, attempts to initiate a host of projects appeared with the intention to resuscitate the ancient Silk Road in Eurasia. Despite having distinct geo-cultural privileges, India was not a part of these connectivity initiatives in Eurasia at the time. India's recent endeavors to bolster connectivity initiatives with Eurasia have had a strong cultural mooring, besides pursuing economic and commercial exigencies.

The geo-strategic significance of Eurasia has been highlighted by many scholars since the days of Harold MacKinder, a British academic, who in his seminal article entitled "The Geographical Pivot of History," published in 1904, says, "Who rules East Europe commands the Heartland; Who rules the Heartland commands the World-Island; Who rules the World-Island commands the world" (MacKinder, 1904). Much later, Zbigniew Brzezinski, a former American National Security Advisor, defined Eurasia as a "chessboard" where the competition for geo-political supremacy is played out. He argues "[A] power that dominates Eurasia would control two of the world's three most advanced and economically productive regions." (Brzezinski, 1997: 31)

Following the adoption of liberalization and the free market economy model in the 1990s, India's economy witnessed considerable growth in the first decade and a half of the twenty-first century. As a result, there is a huge demand for energy to meet its domestic requirements. Eurasia, with its vast geographical landmass, contains a number of countries with rich energy deposits, and offers India an opportunity to fulfill its energy requirements. Beyond trade and commerce, a cultural and historical legacy also links India to the region. Buddhism spread from India to Central Asia, China, Tibet, and Afghanistan via these routes and Sufism came to India from Central Asia through the silk routes (MEA, 2018). India's growing bilateral relations with countries in the Eurasian region is a point to the convergence of these interests.

SCO, EAEU, and India–Central Asia Dialogue: Mechanisms to Expand Regional Cooperation

India's strategic interests in Eurasia and the need for increasing economic and energy cooperation with the region require it to bolster engagement with Eurasian countries. India's growing visibility in the region is evidenced by the fact that India became a full member in the Shanghai Cooperation Organization (SCO) at the Astana Summit of 2017. The Russia-initiated EAEU is another such regional organization comprised of five countries which provides further opportunities for India to enhance trade and economic interactions with the Eurasian region. Full membership in the SCO enables India to become more visible in Eurasian affairs, rather than being a mere fence sitter in the happenings of a region that is strategically important for India (Roy, 2017). India's elevation from observer status is politically significant as India's prime minister, rather than the external affairs minister, can now take part in SCO summits. It is also significant from a security perspective as India can now become an important player in the regional security architecture to combat terrorism and forces of extremism emanating from Afghanistan and the surrounding countries. India's growing counter-terrorism cooperation and strategic partnership with many of the member countries is a sign of this shift. The SCO is an effective multilateral forum through which India can further push its "Connect Central Asia Policy" and "Extended Neighborhood Policy." Prime Minister Narendra Modi's meetings with his Central Asian counterparts on the sidelines of the last two SCO summits—2018 in Qingdao and 2019 in Bishkek—in addition to bilateral exchanges between India and Central Asian countries in the recent past exemplify this trend. During the Qingdao summit, Prime Minister Modi highlighted the importance of connectivity between the member states.

The lack of direct connectivity remains an obstacle to forging energy ties between India and the hydrocarbon-rich areas of Central Asia. However, there are differing perceptions and opposing positions between countries such as China, India and Pakistan in terms of connectivity. India sincerely values its participation in the Ashgabat Agreement between Iran, Oman, Turkmenistan and Uzbekistan, which led to its presence at the Chabahar Port in Iran as part of INSTC. While Pakistan extends its cooperation with China by way of the China–Pakistan Economic Corridor (CPEC), India has expressed its displeasure about the BRI, while other member countries of the SCO are willing to be a part of it. The Chinese President, Xi Jinping, at the Qingdao SCO summit, proposed conducting feasibility studies for signing FTAs with the member countries, and even floated the idea of setting up a development bank. The EAEU has even signed non-preferential trade and economic cooperation deals with China, and is currently negotiating a bid to connect the EAEU with the BRI. India has also been discussing with the EAEU to sign an FTA (Kapoor, 2019). To avoid missed opportunities in the race to gain a strategic foothold in and economic benefit from the region, it remains imperative for India to articulate its standing in the region in a more robust way.

The EAEU has a market of approximately 183 million people, 14 per cent of the world's farmland, an area of over 20 million sq. kms and a combined gross domestic product of over $1.9 trillion. The union already signed trade deals with Association for South East Asian Nations (ASEAN) member countries including Vietnam in 2015, and most recently with Singapore in 2019, and is currently negotiating deals with Cambodia, Thailand, the Philippines, Indonesia, and Brunei (Simes, 2020). In the wake of its foreign minister's visit to New Delhi in January 2020, Russia pushed for India's entry into the EAEU, which according to Russia will extend the possibilities of third country partnerships in the Central Asia–Eurasian region (Roy Chaudhury, 2020a).

Signing an FTA will streamline business travel, promoting the ease of doing business and resolving issues regarding consular services. It will also embolden the EAEU–India strategic partnership. The Joint Feasibility Study Group, in its 2017 report, highlighted that the potential increase in trade between EAEU and India may be as high as $37–62 billion. The report also mentioned that the potential growth in exports from the EAEU to India could be an additional $23–38 billion, with $14–24 billion exports originating from India to the EAEU (FICCI, 2017). India is one of the top twenty trade partners of the EAEU, occupying the fifteenth position in terms of exports from the EAEU and the eighteenth position in terms of imports to the EAEU. From 2016 to 2017, the trade turnover between India and the EAEU jumped by 23 per cent from US $ 8.8 billion to US $ 10.8 billion. Trade witnessed a similar growth trajectory in 2018 as well. The trade balance of the EAEU with India is positive (Roy Chaudhury, 2018). However, it is necessary for both the sides to augment the volume of trade to realize the full potential of the engagement in a more meaningful way.

One significant development in India's foreign policy towards Eurasia, and Central Asia in particular, under Narendra Modi, is the materialization of the First India–Central Asia Dialogue attended by foreign ministers held in Samarkand, Uzbekistan from 12–13 January 2019. It was the first time that the foreign ministers of five Central Asian countries along with India's External Affairs Minister joined in the deliberations, along with Afghanistan's foreign minister. The platform has existed since 2012, however, when it was first floated by then Minister of State for External Affairs of India, E. Ahamed, in Bishkek. Although stability and peace in Afghanistan were the mainstay of the dialogue, building connectivity by constructing regional and international transport corridors through joint ventures were also discussed (MEA, 2019).

Prime Minister Modi's visit to five Central Asian countries in 2015 paved the way for a much deeper engagement between Central Asia and India. The India–Central Asia Dialogue at the level of foreign ministers is the logical extension of India's "Connect Central Asia Policy" - mooted in 2012 when the Congress-led United Progressive Alliance was in power - and the outcome of Modi's "Extended Neighborhood Policy." The fact that the foreign ministers of five Central Asian countries along with the Afghan foreign minister participated in the First India–Central Asia Dialogue, an India-led initiative, is indicative of a realization among all participants of the potential for mutually beneficial relationships by organizing and institutionalizing relations between the participating countries. The proposal by India's then Foreign Minister, the late Sushma Swaraj, to set up the India–Central Asia Business Council and the India–Central Asia Development Group in order to bolster cooperation is a testimony to that (Karle, 2019). The next India–Central Asia Dialogue is scheduled to take place in New Delhi in 2020, which points to the conclusion that the participating countries will continue to sustain and strengthen their relationship.

A cursory glance at some of the recent high-level bilateral visits between Central Asian and Indian officials and the agreements inked thereafter may help readers to understand the scenario in a holistic manner:

Table 12: High-level Bilateral Visits Between Central Asian and Indian Officials

	Who visited	Country	Agreements Signed	Year
1	Prime Minister of India	Kazakhstan	1) Defense and military technology 2) Railways 3) Uranium supply to India 4) Sports 5) Transfer of sentenced prisoners	2015
2	Prime Minister of India	Uzbekistan	1) Joint Working Group on Counter Terrorism 2) Uranium supply to India 3) Uzbekistan–India Joint Working Group on Counter-terrorism	2015
3	Prime Minister of India	Kyrgyzstan	1) Agreement of Defense Cooperation 2) MoU and Cooperation in the field of Elections 3) Culture	2015

4	Prime Minister of India	Turkmenistan	1) MoU on supply of chemical products 2) Program of Cooperation in Science and Technology 3) MoU on Cooperation in the Field of Tourism 4) Defense Agreement	2015
5	Prime Minister of India	Tajikistan	1) Exchange of Note Verbale (NV) on setting up of Computer Labs in 37 schools in Tajikistan	2015
6	President of India	Tajikistan	1)MoU on "Cooperation on Peaceful Use of Space Technology for Development" 2)MoU for Renewable Energy Cooperation	2018
7	External Affairs Minister, India	Uzbekistan	1) India– Central Asia Dialogue inauguration	2019
8	President of Tajikistan	India	1) Agreement to prevent financing of terrorism and money laundering	2016
9	President of Kyrgyzstan	India	1) MoU for youth exchange programs 2) MoU on agriculture and food security	2016
10	President of Uzbekistan	India	1) MoU on Tourism, Agriculture and Allied Sectors, Health and Medical Sciences, Pharmaceutical Industry, Science, Technology and Innovation, Military Education	2018
11	President of Uzbekistan	India	1) Agreement on importing uranium from Uzbekistan 2) MoU on Cooperation between Gujarat and the Andijan region of Uzbekistan	2019

12	D e f e n s e Minister of India	Uzbekistan	1) Military Medicine 2) Military Education	2019
13	Uzbekistan's Internal Affairs Minister	India	1) Security Cooperation 2) Counter Terrorism 3) Human Trafficking	2019

Source: Ministry of External Affairs, Government of India.

A quick glimpse of the trade figures between Central Asian countries and India in recent years may also shed some light on the trade trajectory.

Table 13: The Figures of Trade between India and Central Asian countries from 2015–2016 to 2018–2019 (Value in US $ Millions)

	(2015-2016)		(2016-2017)		(2017-2018)		(2018-2019)	
Country	Imports	Exports	Imports	Exports	Imports	Exports	Imports	Exports
Kyrgyzstan	1.79	25.11	1.48	30.44	30.94	28.59	2.59	30.02
Tajikistan	9.98	22.26	21.82	20.44	50.29	23.94	4.24	22.28
Turkmenistan	46.97	68.53	21.32	57.60	26.15	54.31	20.63	45.64
Uzbekistan	55.86	96.64	45.26	108.97	101.67	132.72	126.73	201.41
Kazakhstan	352.93	151.91	521.29	120.88	907.43	125.37	708.78	143.13
Total	467.53	364.45	610.88	338.33	1116.49	364.93	862.97	442.48

Source: Export Import Data Bank, Department of Commerce, Government of India

Even though Central Asia and India have no serious problem areas in their political and diplomatic engagement, trade turnover between the two is still below the potential, which can be inferred from the table above. However, India is able to extend its line of credit and Buyers Credit etc., which will facilitate more business between Central Asia and India. The India-Central Asia Business Council, originally proposed by the former foreign minister of India, has been supported by top industrial/business bodies in both Central Asia and India as a way to increase the possibilities for business development.

International North–South Transport Corridor (INSTC)

For India, the INSTC is a gateway to greater investment and trade connections with Central Asia, Eurasia and even Eastern Europe. This holds great significance for India's Foreign Trade Policy (2015–2020). In September 2000, Russia, India and Iran decided to increase connectivity with the landlocked countries of Central Asia by establishing transportation networks between the corridor's member states through the INSTC. The INSTC links South Asia and Eastern Europe along the north-south axis through rail, road, and water transport linkages in landlocked areas (Zafar, 2016). This multimodal trade transport corridor aims to connect Mumbai with the Chabahar and Bandar Abbas ports of Iran, which in turn will be linked with Baku, Moscow and countries in Central and Eastern Europe via the Caspian Sea. This will also be cost-effective for India as it will shorten the distance to transport goods to Central Asia and Eurasia in comparison to the present route, which traverses the Suez Canal and Western European countries. It will significantly reduce the transportation costs of goods from India to Eurasia.

The INSTC presents geostrategic opportunities for India to establish its relevance in the Eurasian region. Modi's statement at the Ufa Summit in 2015 is a testimony to India's growing interest and desire to become a player in the region, which can be summarized by his speech, "As we look forward, we would lend our support to improving trans-

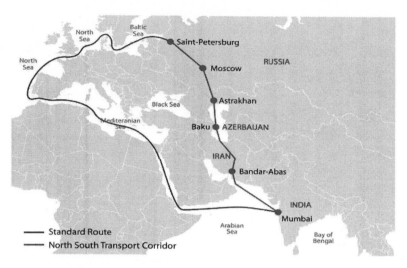

Map 1: International North South Transportation Corridor
Source: Alena Repkina

portation and communication networks in the region. We can create a vast network of physical and digital connectivity that extends from Eurasia's northern corner to Asia's southern shores. The International North South Transportation Corridor is a step in that direction" (Roy, 2015).

India has invested considerably in projects such as the INSTC in the last five years. The INSTC got a fillip after India joined the Customs Convention on International Transport of Goods Under Cover of TIR Carnets. This has facilitated the smooth transport of cargos which recorded a surge from a paltry 28,000 tons in 2017 to 287,000 tons in 2018, an estimated jump of around 963 per cent. The volume of cargo transportation was expected to reach around 600,000 tons in 2019 (Sen, 2019). On seeing these developments, Kazakhstan's ambassador to India, Bulat Sarsenbayev, said in February 2019, "Our trade is going but the potential is much more. Chabahar and Bandar Abbas are part of one project in reality. Chabahar will be completed, they [Kazakhstan] will construct a railway from Chabahar to the Iranian railway network; it will later go to Turkmenistan and Kazakhstan" (ANI, 2019). To increase bilateral trade and augment cooperation with the Central Asian region, both Uzbekistan and India agreed to initiate a joint feasibility study to expedite the process of signing a Preferential Trade Agreement (PTA). This was dis-

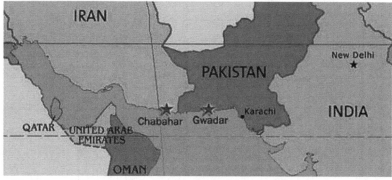

Map 2: Chabahar Port and Gwadar Port
Source: Outlook India

cussed during a meeting between the Uzbek Foreign Minister, Abdulaziz Kamilov, and Indian Foreign Minister, S. Jaishankar, during his visit to India in January 2020 (Roy Chaudhury, 2020). During his ministerial address at the prestigious Raisina Dialogue in New Delhi, the Uzbek foreign minister stated, "... New Delhi is associated among the countries of the region not with competition for regional leadership, but as an example of mutually beneficial and respectful cooperation. From of old, India's role in our region has always been constructive and in-demand one" (Roy Chaudhury, 2020).

Various Projects of the INSTC

Because the INSTC is a multimodal connectivity network, this section is divided into three subsections to highlight its economic viability and importance, mainly from India's perspective. The following details (*a*) projects already operational, (*b*) projects under process, and (*c*) proposed projects.

Already Operational Projects

The Iran-Turkmenistan-Kazakhstan (ITK) railway line is considered one of the most important links among the rail lines within the scope of the INSTC. Turkmenistan concluded a multilateral agreement with Iran and Kazakhstan in 2007 to construct the new North-South ITK railway line which connects Turkmenistan in the north with Uzen in Kazakhstan and with Gorgon in Iran in the south. The total length of the railway stretch is 912.5 kms, 700.5 kms of which are in Turkmenistan itself. This railway line was completed and became operational in 2014, serving as a link to the INSTC. Besides the ITK rail link, Turkmenistan-Afghanistan-Tajikistan (TAT) is another rail-line project of note. Turkmenistan completed the construction of the Atamyrat-Imamnazar part of the TAT and opened the railway link with Afghanistan on 28 November 2016. The Tajikistan-Afghanistan segment of the project has yet to be completed. The entire project was scheduled to be finished by 2018 (Abbasova, 2015). India has also been instrumental in building a 218-km road connection between Delaram and Zaranj in Afghanistan as an alternative route to transport goods to Afghanistan via Iran. The total cost of the highway project, 600 crore Indian Rupees (approximately 82 million USD), was borne by India and the road has been operational since 2009 (Kaul, 2009). Almost a decade later, Afghanistan constructed the Zaranj–Chabahar route to transport goods to India via the Chabahar port, thus bypassing Pakistan. Afghanistan in its largest year ever for foreign exports, is estimated to have exported goods worth $740 million to India in 2018. An estimated 15,000 tons of wheat reached Afghani-

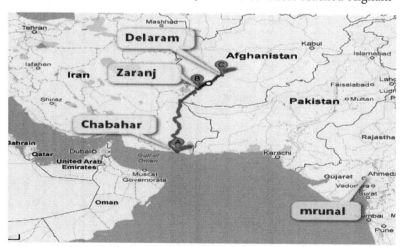

Map 3: Delaram-Zaranj-Chabahar Highway

stan from India in 2017 via the Chabahar trade route (Panda, 2019). In addition to the construction of Delaram–Zaranj highway, India has also financed the construction of major port facilities at Chabahar.

Projects under Development

An agreement was signed in 2003 between India and Iran to develop the Chabahar Port as part of the INSTC. However, it did not materialize as Iran was reeling under economic sanctions at the time. India concluded another Memorandum of Understanding (MoU) with Iran in May 2015 to develop the port with an investment estimated at US $85 million. The purpose was to construct a container terminal and a multipurpose cargo terminal in the Chabahar Port. The Chabahar Port is important for India in gaining access to landlocked Afghanistan and the energy-rich Central Asian region by bypassing Pakistan. The port is equipped according to modern standards and will become Iran's first deep-water port (Kalsotra, 2015a). In the future, Turkmenistan and Uzbekistan are also likely to become members of the INSTC. This will give Central Asian countries further access to the Gulf of Oman and the Arabian Sea. It will also help India to obtain gas from Turkmenistan and uranium from Uzbekistan via the Chabahar Port (Kalsotra, 2015b). The first dry run of the route was held in August 2014 by the Federation of Freight Forwarders Association in India (FFFAI). The report on the trial highlighted, "The proposed INSTC route via Bandar Abbas in Iran to Russia and Commonwealth of Independent States (CIS) destinations in transit through Iran, could be the best route with optimal transit/cost for Indian exporters/importers" (Sood and Bhaskar, 2017).

The Union Cabinet of the Indian government, in its March 2016 meeting, chaired by Prime Minister Modi, decided to take part in the Ashgabat Agreement, which was initially signed by five countries, namely Uzbekistan, Turkmenistan, Iran, Oman and Qatar on 25 April 2011. The Ashgabat Agreement is poised to build the shortest possible corridor/route to facilitate trade between Central Asia and Iranian and Omani ports (Gulati, 2015). At present, Qatar is no longer a member of this agreement as it withdrew in 2013, and Kazakhstan became a member in 2015. The Ashgabat Agreement seeks to establish rail connectivity through Kazakhstan, Uzbekistan, Turkmenistan and Iran. It improves India's prospects to make use of the functioning transit and transport corridor to augment commercial deliberations and bolster trade with the Eurasian region (The Hindu, 2017). Talks on this subject are ongoing between both sides. The Ashgabat Agreement entails greater opportunities for India to instrumentalize Chabahar as an important gateway and one of the shortest land routes to Central Asia. This move would also validate and expedite India's endeavors to increase connectivity by means of the INSTC. It will further deepen India's bilateral relations with the member countries, especially Turkmenistan, which has some of the largest gas reserves in the world (The Hindu, 2017). Kazakhstan is also in the process of augmenting its non-oil exports by up to 50 per cent by 2025, which will be beneficial for India to procure energy wealth from Central Asia to boost its manufacturing sector (Stobdan, 2018). This holds immense potential to greatly increase trade between India and Central Asia. It is only through increased transport connectivity that the full potential of economic engagement between India and Central Asia can be realized.

The connectivity aspect of the corridor was the focal point of discussions with Turkmenistan during the visit of India's then Foreign Minister, the late Sushma Swaraj, to Ashgabat in April 2015, and got a fillip when Prime Minister Narendra Modi himself visited Turkmenistan in July 2015 (Gulati, 2015). For India, Turkmenistan is an important regional and continental transit and transport hub. In this context, the construction of the Afghanistan-Turkmenistan-Azerbaijan-Georgia-Turkey transportation corridor, also known as the Lapis Lazuli transport corridor, which connects landlocked Afghanistan with Turkey via Turkmenistan, Azerbaijan, and Georgia up to Europe, is essential. The completion of the corridor will facilitate trade between the member countries and increase access to the world markets and increase inter-regional cooperation (Hasanov, 2017). The draft agreement of the corridor was signed by the concerned countries during the ministerial meeting of the

7th Regional Economic Cooperation Conference on Afghanistan in Ashgabat on 17 November 2017 (Afghan Voice Agency, 2019). The corridor was inaugurated in 2018 and the total cost of the project is approximately US $2 billion (Afghan Voice Agency, 2019). While appreciating the relevance of the transport corridor at the inaugural ceremony in Herat, Afghan President Ashraf Ghani noted, "[I]t makes Afghanistan not only the gateway to the Indian subcontinent, but once again the gateway to the Caucasus, Central Asia and Europe" (Khan, 2018). This transport corridor connects with the Middle Corridor Project of Turkey and other regional connectivity initiatives as well, such as the Five Nations Railway Corridor (Khan, 2018). The ITK is a major route under the Ashgabat Agreement, and it has been made a part of the INSTC. Therefore, it is believed that the Ashgabat Agreement and the INSTC will be synchronized to bolster connectivity (Stobdan, 2018).

Proposed Projects

To access transnational multimodal connectivity, India ratified the Transport Internationaux Routiers or International Road Transports (TIR) Convention. India will be the 71st country to sign the international transit system. This is aimed at integrating India with Myanmar,

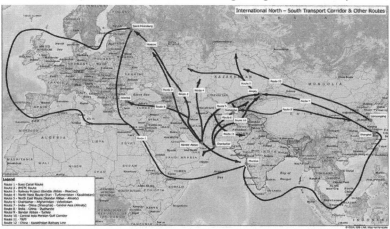

Map 4: Various Proposed INSTC Routes
Source: The Institute for Defense Studies and Analyses

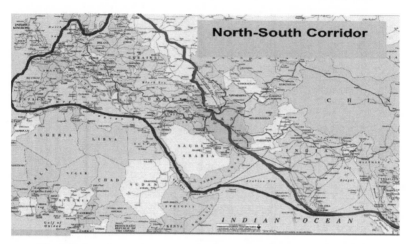

Map 5: Qazvin-Rasht-Astara Railway Link as Part of the INSTC
Source: Railway Pro Communication Platform, www.railwaypro.com

Thailand, Bangladesh, Nepal and Bhutan on the eastern front, while also enabling India to seamlessly move goods through the INSTC via the Chabahar Port in Iran on the western front in order to to gain access to landlocked Afghanistan and the energy-rich Eurasian region (Sood, 2017). India's endeavor to set up the Trans-Asian Railway (TAR) route was presented in the first week of March 2017. A meeting between the chief executives of the respective railways of India, Iran, Bangladesh, Pakistan, and Turkey was held in March 2017 to activate the Dhaka - Kolkata - Delhi - Amritsar - Lahore -Islamabad - Zahedaan - Tehran - Istanbul TAR route1. During his budget speech in February 2017, the then Finance Minister, the late Shri Arun Jaitley, underscored India's interest in developing a multimodal transport strategy involving highways, waterways and railways. He also highlighted the importance of a viable multimodal transportation network for a competitive economy (Sood, 2017)

At present, Iran and Azerbaijan are constructing the Qazvin-Rasht-Astara railway route, which is projected for completion in the near future, as part of the INSTC (Azernews, 2016). Once these routes become available, it will give India leverage in the Eurasian region to augment trade and economic cooperation with these countries while also providing access to the markets of adjoining countries. The first trial run between the Qazvin and Rasht stretch was initiated in November 2018. The stretch between Rasht and Astara is yet to be completed (Mammadova, 2018). The 164-km-long Qazvin and Rasht railway line, part of the Rasht-Astara project, will connect the Azerbaijani and Iranian railway networks. Upon the completion of the entire project, an estimated 10 million tons of goods and 4 million passengers will be transported via the railway line annually (Railwaypro, 2018).

The INSTC as an Alternative to the BRI? The Indian Perception of and Response to the BRI

The INSTC was conceived well before China's ambitious Belt and Road Initiative (BRI). The BRI aims to connect Asia and Africa with Europe through a network of multifarious transportation corridors which will are set to transform the geopolitics and geo-economics of the Eurasian region (Sachdeva and Vergeron, 2018). The Indian perception about the BRI must be understood in the context of the strained bilateral relationship between India and China, and the launching of the BRI as a unilateral exercise - as opposed to the INSTC which is multilateral in nature. Indian skepticism arises from the fact that the BRI, as a Chinese initiative, is poised to advance the geopolitical interests of China in India's neighborhood and in the Indian Ocean Region at the expense of Indian geo-political interests. As a consequence, the INSTC and other connectivity initiatives received a renewed impetus in the Indian narrative.

India's main opposition to the BRI is twofold. The first point of opposition pertains to the China–Pakistan Economic Corridor (CPEC) which passes through disputed territory. The second relates to the lack of transparency in the funding of projects. The growing China–Pakistan bonhomie, Chinese investments in Pakistan and the question of territorial sovereignty over Pakistan-Occupied Kashmir are some of the issues of concern for India. As with the First Belt and Road Forum (BRF), India did not participate in the Second Belt and Road Forum held in Beijing

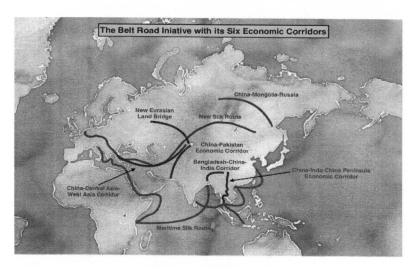

Map 6: Belt and Road Initiative
Source: The Wire

from 25–27 April 2019, in which forty countries participated (Hashmi, 2019).

There are two main dimensions as far as the BRI is concerned: one is geopolitical and the other is developmental. The geopolitical implications and sovereignty issue have largely overshadowed the developmental aspects of the BRI in the Indian perception. This cynicism and skepticism will be multiplied in the aftermath of the ongoing border tussle between India and China over the Galwan valley in Eastern Ladakh. India's presence in the Eurasian region, its membership in the SCO and BRICS and its growing engagement with the EAEU countries have done little to allay its apprehensions about the BRI. Although some analysts have advocated limited participation in the BRI by India, the Indian government is instead pursuing its own regional connectivity projects through the INSTC and similar initiatives.

India's Response to the BRI

The ever-increasing naval presence of China in the Indian Ocean region (IOR), which is economically significant for India and the surrounding littoral countries, is a matter of concern for India. India has a coastline that stretches for 7,500 kms with 1,200 outlying islands. It also has 13 major ports and an exclusive economic zone of 2.4 million square miles. Of its total exports, 90 percent are transported by sea. 10–15 percent of the country's population lives along the coastline, and around 14 million people are employed by the fishing and aquaculture industry. 80 per cent of India's oil imports are dependent on sea transport routes. Out of India's total annual foreign trade, 68 percent by value and 95 percent by volume moves through the Indian Ocean (Ahmad, 2018).

China also has core interests in the Indian Ocean, as 80 per cent of its oil imports and 90 per cent of its foreign trade sail through the sea. To ensure hassle-free maritime movement, China must ensure that the Straits of Malacca and Hormuz, which are among the most strategically important shipping lanes in the world, function smoothly and without disruption from piratical incursion or obstruction from regional powers. Chinese economic activities, such as the building pipelines and ports, as well as its navy presence, are seen by India as an intrinsic part of the BRI. Chinese commentator's description of such posturing as peaceful, cooperative and inclusive have done little to assuage India's concerns. Gopal Suri, a maritime security specialist, is among those who view China's heavy investment in the construction and development of ports in the Indian Ocean littoral states, namely Sri Lanka, Myanmar, Bangladesh, Pakistan, and the countries of East Africa, along with its first-ever naval base in Djibouti, in the Horn of Africa, as clear evidence of China's ambition to establish along term presence in the Indian Ocean Region (Ahmad, 2018). Against this backdrop, India's foreign policy has been updated to highlight the importance of maritime safety and security by augmenting its bilateral relationship with the island countries located in the IOR in recent years. This has led to the acceleration of the domestic ship-building industry as well as research and development into upgraded naval capabilities.

In order to minimize its concern over the Gwadar port on the southern coast of Pakistan, India has increased its presence in Chabahar just 80 kms away from Gwadar, in addition to bolstering cooperation with Oman by using the strategically important Omani ports along the coastline of the Indian Ocean. As a response to the Chinese naval presence in the IOR, India has also undertaken increasing maritime cooperation with a host of regional and extra-regional naval powers. New Delhi will be constructing a deep-sea port at Sabang in Indonesia besides increasing its presence in the Andaman and Nicobar Islands.

India is contemplating an invitation to Australia to participate in the 24th trilateral Malabar naval exercise in the Bay of Bengal after the monsoon season ends in 2020. Discussions regarding the invitation have already been initiated (Pandit, 2020). The Malabar naval exercise began in 1992 as a bilateral exercise between India and the United States and included Japan as a permanent member only in 2015. The participation of Australia will make the Quadrilateral Security Dialogue (QUAD) countries come together after a thirteen-year hiatus to take part in the joint naval exercise on the high seas. China vehemently opposed the 2007 Indo-US Malabar exercise in the Bay of Bengal when it sought to expand its reach by including Singapore, Australia and Japan. India has also agreed to upgrade the QUAD dialogue from the level of joint secretaries to foreign ministers once Australia joins. The growing India–Australia bilateral defense cooperation was visible when both the sides conducted their biggest ever naval exercise in April 2019 which is known as "AusIndEx" at the Visakhapatnam coast along the Bay of Bengal (Pandit, 2020).

As a response to the growing Chinese clout in the region, India stresses the Look East Policy. The aim of this policy is to enhance connectivity and increase cooperation between India and its eastern neighbors, including the ASEAN countries. India has been working on a slew of connectivity projects like the Kaladan transport project, which aims to connect the North East region of India with other parts of the country via Myanmar and the Bay of Bengal. India, Thailand, and Myanmar are building a 1,400-km-long highway to link Moreh, located in Manipur state in the NorthEast of India, to the Mae Sot district in western Thailand through Myanmar. Two sections of the India-Myanmar-Thailand

Trilateral Highway are being constructed with Indian assistance (Borah, 2019).

India and Japan have come closer to each other to augment co-operation at various levels. The International Cooperation Agency of Japan will provide the required financial assistance to construct India's longest bridge of around 20 kms in the North East region over the Brahmaputra river. At the international level, Japan and India will work in collaboration with the Sri Lankan Port Authority to develop the East Container Terminal at the Colombo Port. Bangladesh and India are also negotiating to materialize a slew of projects, namely the building of the Titas bridge, the Bhairab bridge and the construction of the Akhaura–Agartala rail network. Bangladesh has been offered around US $8 billion by India for this project by way of multiple credit lines (Borah, 2019).

Conclusion

In an era of global economic interconnectedness, economic interests between nations converge. In such a situation, connectivity contributes to the growth and sustainability of the respective countries' economies. The INSTC and plans for other transcontinental corridors exist in such a context. The progress in recent years is a case in point. The INSTC, coupled with other connectivity initiatives, entail greater possibilities to deepen engagement between member countries. India must remain committed to augment cooperation with friendly Central Asian countries in its venture to Eurasia. The Central Asian region, which is considered India's extended neighborhood, holds the key for India to attain the full potential of connectivity. The relationship between India and Central Asian states is currently positive and needs to be strengthened further for the mutual benefit of both sides

The issue of engagement between India and Central Asia is becoming more prominent as the possibility for regional integration gains currency. The swearing-in of the new Uzbek President Shavkat Mirziyoyev in 2016 following the death of erstwhile President Islam Karimov heralded a new political scenario in the region. His quest to solve bilateral issues with neighboring countries through a policy of "zero problems" is significant for regional integration. The reciprocation of other Central Asian countries to this policy and the resultant initiatives are a positive development. The resolution of vexing issues between Central Asian countries themselves is an opportunity for India, which enjoys goodwill in the region, to deepen its engagement. The INSTC is fraught with certain challenges but it has the potential to become an economic artery for its member countries to accelerate their development and increase engagement with the greater Eurasian region. India's growing presence in the region through the Ashgabat Agreement will smoothen the integration process envisaged under the rubric of the EAEU and the SCO in more concrete ways. However, the utility of the connectivity initiatives and the fullest potential of connectivity will depend to a large extent on how the post-COVID global order unfolds and the behavior of states in the post-pandemic world.

CONCLUSION

THE GEO-POLITICAL NEXUS IN CENTRAL ASIA

Kashif Hasan Khan and Halil Koch

The eight papers gathered in this book highlight the current attitudes of the major powers towards Central Asia from different perspectives. Their focus highlights post-Soviet scenarios, considering recent drastic changes in the equation of international relations in general and, more particularly, in the CAR. Evidently, all the authors included in this book believe that Central Asia is not only a region that may lead to conflict between the major powers, but that also plays a pivotal role in de-escalating tensions through negotiations. At the same time, the region seems to be making a noticeable progress toward more democratic and open societies based on free markets, the rule of law and respect for human rights. There are four unified aspects that outline the core development of the five countries of Central Asia: leadership succession, economic challenges, corruption and poor governance in the form of political repression. As mentioned in the introduction, the contributors touch upon crucial factors such as security challenges; historical relations with other major powers; immigration of labor and students; the rise of nationalism; the energy sector and the BRI in their respective chapters.

In the context of a "soft power approach", the book argues that since the independence of Central Asian states, the US made an attempt to fill the gap left by the dissolution of the Soviet Union by taking on the role of the "international security manager" whereas Turkey, the European Union, India, Iran and Japan tried to expand their sphere of influence into Central Asia through "soft power". However, due to the natural richness of the region, countries such as the United States, China, Iran, India, Turkey and the European powers were in a hurry to benefit from the abundant hydro-carbon resources in the region – gas in Turkmenistan; oil, gas and huge uranium reserves in Kazakhstan; uranium and gas in Uzbekistan; and hydropower potential in Tajikistan and Kyrgyzstan

– and the new market links they could provide. Turkmenistan has the fourth largest gas reserves in the world. According to British Petroleum (BP), Turkmenistan has nearly 18 trillion cubic meters of gas.o put this into perspective, it is enough to fulfill the European Union's gas needs for 30 years.

Pursuing a soft power approach, China has extended huge loans to Turkmenistan to develop its gas fields and construct a pipeline linking them to China. This means Turkmenistan will not get all the profits for the gas that they send to China since an unknown percentage will go toward paying off the loans. It is still unknown how much this will be, but it certainly cuts into the amount of money that Turkmenistan will receive. Since the early days after Turkmenistan's independence, the government has provided an allotment of water, electricity and gas to the public at no charge. However, because of a deteriorating economic situation these benefits are to be canceled. The people of Turkmenistan have to pay these expenses now, and many people are unemployed. The government has imposed travel restrictions to keep people in the country, and this applies especially to men forty and younger. In the past, many travelled to Turkey to seek a livelihood in the light of past historical and cultural connections (see Halim's chapter for details). Turkmenistan has a border with Iran, but Turkmen-Iranian relations are limited in terms of trade.

Throughout most of the 20th century, Central Asia was rarely if ever the subject of neighboring states' disputes. However, after radical Russian economic reforms led to the destruction of the former Soviet Union's economic complex, a political and economic vacuum emerged in the heart of Eurasia.

According to the World Bank, Kyrgyzstan's GDP per capita in 2017 was $1,220 USD. Kyrgyzstan now suffers in terms of foreign trade due to its large debts to China. Balancing their budget remains a struggle, as the country takes on Chinese and Russian loans that go toward different projects. Besides gold, there are no other substantial industries in Kyrgyzstan. The Kyrgyz state is highly dependent on agriculture, and is also one of the most remittance-dependent countries in the world. Some 35 percent of the Kyrgyz GDP comes from remittances from migrant labor, most of whom work in Russia. Consequently, Kyrgyzstan depends heavily on the condition of the Russian economy(Khan, K.H, 2020). Kyrgyzstan's external debt to China is 41% of its total external debt. Tajikistan is only slightly less dependent on remittances. About 30 percent of the Tajik GDP comes from remittances, also primarily from migrant laborers in Russia. As such, Tajikistan is also dependent on the Russian economy. Tajikistan foreign debt to China is even greater than Kyrgyzstan's, with more than half of Tajikistan's total external debt belonging to their East Asian neighbor.

Corruption is a challenge for both Tajikistan and Kyrgyzstan. However, Tajik corruption is different from that of Kyrgyzstan as it is much more diffused. Kyrgyzstan is able to maintain its democracy to some extent, and at the least maintains a higher degree of stability relative to other Central Asian republics. The degree of corruption in Tajikistan has seen ebbs and flows over the years since independence due to political revolutions, the last of which happened through a presidential election. Power in Tajikistan is consolidated in the hands of President Rahman and his relatives. Almost every major industry, of which there are few, belong almost exclusively to one or more of Rahman's family members.

Big Powers: USA Vis-à-vis China and Russia

American and European development agencies claim that their assistance has improved healthcare, education and promoted human rights, helping to alleviate the region's socioeconomic tensions and prepare the CAR to participate in a more globalized economy. China claims that its financial assistance has improved the infrastructure and developed several industries and lead to the construction of a number of factories. Russia claims to maintain the political and military stability in the region. Other powers take credit for improving international education through local universities and the resulting labor migration from Central Asia (see Fominykh's chapter). Tola Amusan (see Chapter Three) writes that the "New Great Game" (discussed in the introduction) between the major powers will revolve around who has more to offer, particularly in the economic sphere. Therefore, based on this theory, China will continue to play a dominant role, as has been the case in the region since the 1990's.

In Chapter One, Aizada points out that Chinese President Xi Jinping proposed to "join hands in building a Silk Road Economic Belt (SREB) with innovative cooperation" in 2013, thus offering the Chinese view of Eurasianism. Many researchers believe that Eurasianism is a new "Great Game" between the Eastern and Western powers vying for influence. Fabrizio Vielmini (see Chapter Seven) argues that as a "Greater Eurasian Partnership", the EAEU can provide a framework for a wider and more inclusive regional initiative to combine Russian and Chinese influence, further linking them with the EU regional agendas. Amusan further writes (see Chapter Three) that over the years, both China and Russia have developed a strategic partnership. Much has been written about this relationship, debating whether such a situation is sustainable and if it has the potential to blossom into a full-fledged alliance. A crucial area that can either make or break this friendship is Central Asia itself, which is Russia's traditional sphere of influence. Tola writes that China has undoubtedly gained considerable influence in the region through trade, investment, loans and aid. Tola further mentions that China is still operating on shaky grounds, however, and that the exercise of geo-economics is intended to pursue the 'long-game'. China's influence is limited by Russia, who remains a more important security partner and has a stronger cultural link to the CAR states. This partnership is too deeply rooted to be displaced in the short-run.

The CAR states have become more dependent on China mainly to push forward their economic agendas. One can argue that this gives Beijing a certain level of leverage and fosters asymmetric vulnerability interdependence. However, geo-economics favouring China have not fully played out in the region, as China seeks to present itself as a friendly neighbour so as to not startle Moscow. Chinese companies are also spending on Public Relation Initiatives (PRI) to improve their image in the region. They have burned through billions of dollars to extend soft influence in the region, however it has battled to win the hearts and psyches of the general population.

The Central Asia republics have been quick to respond by shutting down anti-China protests across the region and generally silencing those who criticize China. Often, the aims of Central Asian regimes and government interests are disconnected from those of their citizens. China is admittedly a source of investment infrastructure for the CAR and helps to modernize their economies at a crucial time. However, there is evidence which confirms that China conducts its economic relations in the region in a non-transparent manner, increasing the likelihood of local corruption and making the government more receptive to Chinese investments. Lere Amusan (see Chapter Two) takes the discussion to another level when he argues that China identifies itself as a developing country and that its future and interests align with that of other developing countries. For this reason, the 21st century has seen China prioritize developing countries, including those of the CAR, in its overall foreign policy, particularly within a multilateral framework. Unlike the West, China does not enforce conditions of political reform in exchange for cooperation and this dynamic serves Russian interests, as well. China's involvement in the CAR is not out of altruism, but a means to further their own economic and political stability in the region. Without the support of Central Asian states, Beijing may not have a lasting solution to its challenges regarding domestic terrorism. Such concerns also underpin Chinese economic engagement with the CAR states. This relationship benefits China economically by securing access to alternative sources of energy and natural resources, as well as additional markets for Chinese products and opportunities for the expansion of Chinese companies.

On the other hand, Russia is pursuing its own vision of interconnectivity, especially with the Eurasian Economic Union, to standardize legal norms, taxes and duties between participating nations. While the Russian vision focuses on military and political stability that allows for greater connectivity with the region, the United States seeks to discourage Central Asian states from pursuing close relations with China and Russia. However, since the collapse of Russia's relationship with the West over the Ukraine crisis, the Sino-Russian strategic partnership has become more concrete. Russia and China are also blamed for sharing a common desire to challenge the principles of the Western-dominated international system. The balance of competition and cooperation is most evident in Central Asia, the Russian Far East and the Arctic. Engagement in these theaters has tested Russia's and China's abilities to manage their differences and translate the rhetoric of partnership into tangible gains, which the USA perceives as a threat. The 'New Cold War' between the USA and China over the last few years, and very recently COVID-19 pandemic, has escalated these tensions.

There is a slogan in China that promotes "a community of common destiny". It is understood that China, as an authoritarian state, is looking to create a new post-Western world order. However, according to many scholars (Roberts, 2015, Xing, 2010, Sorensen, 2016, Steward, 2013), there is another threat to the Western world order, also known as the liberal world order, which does not come from China or Russia or even from a so-called authoritarian jurisdiction. Rather, it comes from within the liberal order itself in the form of three key issues. The first is the failure of Western democracies to live up to the principles of a liberal rules-based international order. The United States in particular has been a serial rule breaker. American exceptionalism has encouraged other great powers to take a similar approach to their international relations. Second, the sheer incompetence and ineptitude of Western policymaking is highlighted by failed wars in Iraq, Afghanistan, Libya and the indecision regarding Syria. Western actions are not only regarded in much of the non-western world as morally illegitimate, but they have also exposed the limits of Western power. Thirdly, the unsoundness of Western economic institutions and policies. The 2008 global financial crisis undermined the West's moral and political credibility as well as the assumption that the West is the ideal to which other countries must strive. Western financial institutions have been slow to bounce back from the crisis in a sustainable way. Western decision makers must address the incoherence between the rhetoric of liberal values and aspirations and the dismal realities of narrow nationalism. They must demonstrate, not just to others, but to their own populations, that they uphold the principles of liberal democracy, confronting xenophobia, and maintaining social and economic justice and the rule of law.

Identity crisis is one of the most debated topics in the postcolonial period. Volumes are filled with theories,, discussions and critical analyses covering post colonialism. Central Asians are no exception to this trend. Ryan discusses (see Chapter Four) this phenomena, describing how when Russia overwhelmed the region during the Soviet period, narratives were forced upon the Uzbeks that maintained that the success of previous endeavors was due to Russia's assistance. Some Uzbeks, particularly those who were defensive of their history, perceived that Soviet leadership proscribed expressions of Uzbek culture and argued against narratives of Russia's assistance in making that history. This conflict between the Russian viewpoint of intentional territorial addition and the Uzbek viewpoint of constrained extension tested Russia's story, which was typically seen as hostile. By modifying history, the patriotism of the Uzbek public and Uzbek national identity was amplified. Nonetheless, it was a direct result of disdain towards Russia and a dread of Russian predominance that drove this change.

Even though it seems that China, Russia, and the West all share a common goal of promoting regional stability in Central Asia, their approaches to the problem differ. Nonetheless their efforts need not be at odds with one another. As a result of rising Uzbek nationalism, Uzbekistan and Western countries have become closer aligned, and this in turn protects Uzbekistan against Russian hegemony, but, it creates another security dilemma for Uzbekistan (see Chapter Four). Russia, for its part, still views Central Asian countries within its sphere of influence, and any detraction from Russian interests is seen as a security threat and a disruption to the status quo. Russia is thus more likely to try to counteract these nationalistic overtures in order to maintain some of its control over the region.

Small Powers in the Region

The US, China and Russia are the three great powers who have most impact in the region. However, one can also argue that against the backdrop of this Great Game, a 'small game' emerges in Central Asia in two ways. Firstly, relatively small powers like India, Japan, the EU and South Korea have their respective interests and policies for Central Asia though they are unlikely to compete with the big three. In the second sense, the small game also means that regional countries are vying for influence and have not yet begun to cooperate on the regional level. Hence, there is ample room for India, the EU and Japan to align and coordinate in their policies towards Central Asia.

The EU issued its Central Asia strategy in 2007, which was replaced by a new strategy in 2019. The core priorities include sustainable economic development, human rights, connectivity, environmental protection, transport and energy links. The EU adopted its Central Asia strategy in 2019 in Bishkek, while India announced its Connect Central Asia policy in Bishkek in 2013. Though China may have taken the spotlight over the idea of reviving the Silk Road through its enormous BRI ventures, the European Union was equally instrumental in resuscitating the Silk Road through its Transport Corridor Europe-Caucasus-Asia (TRACECA) activity, dispatched in 1993. In 2018, The EU also published its strategy to connect Europe and Asia which highlights sustainability, reducing carbon emissions, enhancing transparency and public consultation and reducing the debt-burden on partner states. The EU also emphasizes digital connectivity and people to people links in its Central Asia policy.

It should be mentioned that within the EU, Germany has been particularly active in engaging the Central Asian countries, both through the EU platform and also bilaterally. Germany is the only EU member to have embassies in all the five Central Asian countries. Hence, according to the European Union's new EU-Central Asia Strategy, the CAR is an overlooked region, but one that is gradually becoming more important for the European Union. The EU has steadily intensified diplomatic relations with the region, while simultaneously ramping up development aid, trade and investment, above all in Kazakhstan.

The EU-Central Asia Strategy is interfering in various dimensions of the politics between the CAR and the major powers, and ultimately the course taken by CAR states will revolve around who has more to offer, particularly in the economic sphere. CAR states are seeking to increase and improve relations with other powers such as the European Union that could lead to strengthen the nexus and land-linkage between Asia and Europe. According to the EU Strategy outline, the EU remains Central Asia's biggest economic partner, accounting for 30% of the region's total trade. China's trade with Central Asia has grown tenfold since 2000, and it has invested an estimated US$25 billion in the region since the announcement of BRI in 2013, but it remains second to the EU in terms of trade, with a 20% share of the total, followed by Russia in third place with slightly under 20%. While the EU is a highly important economic partner for Central Asia, it is hardly perceived as a major actor and is much less visible. The previous Strategy for Central Asia, adopted in 2007, was intensely scrutinized for its broad character and lack of responsiveness to local needs. Central Asia has traditionally received a lower priority from the EU given the greater interests and more urgent developments in its immediate neighbourhood, but this fact is gradually changing. During the next decades, EU-Central Asia relations will depend on the interests and developments in both regions and other external factors, like the Chinese or Russian roles in Central Asia. Several internal challenges with a significant probability to impact external relations exist both in the EU and Central Asia. On the part of the EU, its lack of cohesion, the heterogeneity of its member states and their external engagement priorities will be major factors determining its role towards other regions.

The other small player in the region is Japan. It mainly interacts with the Central Asian republics on three levels: diplomatic/political communications, trade and investment, and development assistance.

Current trade trends, investments, and Japan's Official Development Assistance (ODA) assistance to Central Asian countries reveal that the region is not yet a major factor in shaping Japan's foreign policy, but this does not prevent Japan from pursuing public diplomacy in the region. The region's two largest, most populous, and resource-rich countries - Kazakhstan and Uzbekistan - account for the majority of Japan's direct investment and ODA in Central Asia. Interestingly, judging by figures from the Ministry of Foreign Affairs of the Republic of Uzbekistan in 2018, Japan's ODA in Uzbekistan was higher than reported by the Ministry of Foreign Affairs of Japan.

As the other important country in the region, India, discussed in Chapter Eight, plays an equally pivotal role in the region. India trains Central Asians in areas like IT, rural development, agriculture, and banking. Tajikistan is one of the largest beneficiaries of India's ITEC program, with 200 spots per year. Two private universities from India, Amity and Sharda, have opened campuses in Uzbekistan. This supports the Uzbek education sector, but also further strengthens people-to-people links between India and Uzbekistan. Central Asia has a lot of potential to play a part in India's energy security, but given the connectivity issues, the energy ties have been subpar (Please see Anirban's chapter for more details). Moreover, like the other small players, India is also operating in the region mostly through soft power approaches and military training operations.

This book has dealt with different perspectives on the CAR states that explore how they are managing relations with the big and small powers in the region. Its diversified approach is intended to contribute to strengthening relations with growing powers that may eventually improve the geo-politics and geo-economics of the region, since despite positive trends in the five Central Asian republics, gaps in the economic development, trade vectors, external political and economic engagements, social development rate, rule of law, and other factors could alienate some countries from others.

REFERENCES

Introduction

Burles, M. (1999). Chinese Policy Toward Russia and the Central Asian Republics. Santa Monica, CA: RAND Corporation. Retrieved June 10, 2020 https://www.rand.org/pubs/monograph_reports/MR1045.html. Also available in print form.

D 'Souza, H. (2015). Central Asia: The Great Game or the Great Gain? Retrieved June 5, 2020, https://www.pgurus.com/central-asi-a-the-great-game-or-the-great-gain/

Papkova I & D, G. (2011) The Russian Orthodox Church and Russian Politics: Editors "Introduction", Russian Politics and Law, Vol. 49, No. 1, January–February, pp. 3–7.

Romanowski, M. (2017). (Rep.) Central Asia, Russia, AND China: U.S. Policy at Eurasia's Core. German Marshall Fund of the United States. Retrieved June 10, 2020, from https://www.gmfus.org/publications/central-asia-russia-and-china-us-policy-eurasi-as-core

Roman Kozhevnikov B. (2011) Tajikistan (Reuters) retrieved August 5, https://www.reuters.com/article/us-tajikistan-china-land/ta-jik-land-deal-extends-chinas-reach-in-central-asia-idUSTRE-72O1RP20110325

Soliev, N. (2019). CENTRAL ASIA: Kazakhstan, Kyrgyzstan, Tajikistan, Turkmenistan, Uzbekistan. *Counter Terrorist Trends and Analyses, 11*(1), 65-70. Retrieved July 14, 2020, from www.jstor.org/stable/26568579

Stronski, P., & Ng, N. (2018). (Rep.). Carnegie Endowment for International Peace. Retrieved July 19, 2020, from www.jstor.org/stable/resrep16975

Khan, K. H., & Kuszewska, A. (2020). The Significance of India's (Re) connectivity Strategy in Central Asia: An Introduction. In K. H. Khan (Ed.), *The Strategy of (Re) connectivity: Revisiting India's Multifaceted Relations with Central Asia.* New Delhi, India: KW Publishers.

Khan, K. H. (2020a). An Introduction. In K. H. Khan (Ed.), *Central Asia and India: Emerging Extended Neighbourhood.* New Delhi, India: New Century Publication

Chapter 1

Arbatova, N. (2019). Three Faces of Russia's Neo-Eurasianism. *Survival,* 61(6), 7-24. https://doi.org/10.1080/00396338.2019.1688562.

Baitabarova, A. (2018). Unpacking Sino-Central Asian Engagement Along the New Silk Road: A Case Study of Kazakhstan. *Journal of Contemporary East Asia Studies,* 7(2), 149-173.

Bassin, M. Glebov S. Laruelle M. (Eds.) (2015). *Between Europe and Asia: The Origins, Theories, and Legacies of Russian Eurasianism.* University of Pittsburgh Press.

Baruah, D. (2018). India's Answer to the Belt and Road: A Road Map for South Asia. Carnegie Endowment for International Peace. https://carnegieendowment.org/files/WP_Darshana_Baruah_Belt_Road_FINAL.pdf .

Brattberg, E. & Soula, E. (2018). Europe's Emerging Approach to China's Belt and Road Initiative, Carnegie Endowment for International Peace. https://carnegieendowment.org/2018/10/19/europe-s-emerging-approach-to-china-s-belt-and-road-initiative-pub-77536.

European Bank for Reconstruction and Development. (2012, July 10). Trade within the Russia-Kazakhstan-Belarus Customs Union: Early Evidence. http://www.ebrdblog.com/wordpress/2012/07/trade-within-the-russia-kazakhstan-belarus-customs-union-early-evidence/ .

European Commission. (2015). Investment Plan for Europe Goes Global: China Announces its Contribution to #investEU [Press Release]. https://ec.europa.eu/commission/presscorner/detail/en/IP_15_5723.

Guo, X. (2018). China's Belt and Road Initiative (BRI) and Turkey's Middle Corridor: "Win-Win Cooperation?" https://www.mei.edu/publications/chinas-belt-and-road-initiative-bri-and-turkeys-middle-corridor-win-win-cooperation

Harper, T. (2019). China's Eurasia: The Belt and Road Initiative and the Creation of a New Eurasian Power. The Chinese Journal of Global Governance, 5, 99-121. doi:10.1163/23525207-12340039.

Hemmings, J. (2013, May 13). *Hedging: The Real US Policy Towards China?* The Diplomat. https://thediplomat.com/2013/05/hedging-the-real-u-s-policy-towards-china/

Kamdar, B. (2019, May 9). What to Make of India's Absence from the Second Belt and Road Forum? The Diplomat. https://thediplomat.com/2019/05/what-to-make-of-indias-absence-from-the-second-belt-and-road-forum/

Kang, D. (2007). *China Rising: Peace, Power, and Order in East Asia.* Columbia University Press.

Kapital (2015). "Nurly Zhol I Noviy Shelkoviy Put Otkryvaiut Vozmozhnosti Dlya RK I KNR" ('Bright Road' and 'New Silk Road' are to Open New Opportunities for Kazakhstan and China), September 1, 2015, Kapital (Center for Business Matters) http://kapital.kz/economic/43285/nurly-zhol-i-novyj-shelkovyj-put-otkryvayut-vozmozhnosti-dlya-rk-i-knr.html

Kassenova, N. (2017). China's Silk Road and Kazakhstan's Bright Path: Linking Dreams of Prosperity. *Asia Policy*, 24, 110-116. https://doi.org/10.1353/asp.2017.0028

Kavalski, E. (2019, March 29). *China's "16+1" Is Dead? Long Live the "17+1"*, The Diplomat. https://thediplomat.com/2019/03/chinas-161-is-dead-long-live-the-171/

Kazinform (2015, September 17). *Nurly zhol Yavlyaetsya Perspektivnoi Chast'iu Poyasa Noviy Shelkoviy Put'*, https://www.inform.kz/ru/prezident-rk-nurly-zhol-yavlyaetsya-perspektivnoy-chast-yu-poyasa-novyy-velikiy-shelkovyy-put_a2819249

Kembayev, Zh. (2018). Development of China-Kazakhstan Cooperation. *Problems of Post-Communism*, 1-13.

Koga, K. (2018). The Concept of "Hedging" Revisited: The Case of Japan's Foreign Policy Strategy in East Asia's Power Shift. *International Studies Review*, 20(4), 633-660.

Korolev, A. (2016) Systemic Balancing and Regional Hedging: China-Russia relations, *Chinese Journal of International Politics*, 9(4), 375-397.

Laruelle, M. (2008). *Russian Eurasianism: An Ideology of Empire*. Woodrow Wilson Center Press.

Ministry of Foreign Affairs of the PRC. (2013, September 7) President Xi Jinping Delivers Important Speech and Proposes to Build a Silk Road Economic Belt with Central Asian Countries. https://www.fmprc.gov.cn/mfa_eng/topics_665678/xjpfwzysiesgjtfhshzzfh_665686/t1076334.shtml.

Mohan, G. (2018). Europe's Response to the Belt and Road Initiative [Policy brief]. The German Marshall Fund of the United States. https://www.gmfus.org/publications/europes-response-belt-and-road-initiative.

Nazarbayev, N. (1997, October) Poslanie Prezidenta Respubliki Kazakhstan N.A. Nazarbaeva narodu Kazakhstana «Procvetanie, bezopasnost' i uluchshenie blagosostoyaniya vsekh kazakhstancev», Dolgosrochnaya strategiya razvitiya Kazakhstana "Kazakhstan – 2030", [Presidential Address to the People of Kazakhstan, Flourishing, Security and Prosperity for all Kazakh Citizens, Long-term Development Strategy Kazakhstan-2030], http://www.akorda.kz/

Rolland, N. (2019). A China-Russia Condominium over Eurasia. *Survival*, 61(1), 7-22.

Runde, D. (2015, June 29). "Kazakhstan: The Buckle in One Belt One Road" http://www.forbes.com/sites/danielrunde/2015/06/29/kazakhstan-buckle-one-belt-one-road/.

Wohlforth, W. (2004). Revisiting Balance of Power Theory in Central Eurasia, in *Balance of Power Revisited: Theory and Practice in the 21st Century,* eds. T. V. Paul and James Wirtz (Palo Alto, Calif.: Stanford University Press, 2004), pp 214-238.

Chapter 2

Amanbayeva, A. (2009). The Collision of Islam and Terrorism in Central Asia. *Asian Journal*

of Criminology, 4(2), 165-186. https://link.springer.com/article/10.1007/s11417-009-9072-9

Amusan, L. (2017). Politics of Biopiracy: An Adventure into Hoodia/Xhoba Patenting in Southern Africa. *African Journal of Traditional, Complementary and Alternative Medicines,* 14(1), pp. 103-109.

Amusan, L. & Adeyeye, A.I. (2014). Nigeria: A Rogue State in the Wake of Umar Farouk

Abdulmutallab's Terror Adventure? *Mediterranean Journal of social sciences,* 5(23), pp. 1866-1874.

Amusan, L. Adeyeye, A.I. & Oyewole, S. (2019). Women as Agents of Terror: Women

Resources and Gender Discourse in Terrorism and Insurgency, *Politikon,* 46(3), pp. 345-359.

Amusan, L. & Oyewole, S. (2016). Iran's National Interests and the Geo-Strategic Imperative.

Geopolitica, 5(2), pp. 209-226.

BBC. (2018, October 12). *Xinjiang territory profile.* Retrieved from https://www.bbc.com/news/world-asia-pacific-16860974#:~:-text=Its%20full%20name%20is%20the,scale%20immigra-tion%20of%20Han%20Chinese.

Bellasio, J., Hofman, J., Ward, A., Nederveen, F., Knack, A., Meranto, A. S., & Hoorens, S. (2018). *Counterterrorism evaluation: Taking stock and looking ahead.* California: RAND Corporation.

Borkoev, B. (2013). The problem of terrorism in Central Asia and coun-tering terrorism in Kyrgyzstan. In O. Tanrisever, *Afghanistan and Central Asia: NATO's Role in Regional Security Since 9/11* (pp. 72-79). Amsterdam: IOS Press.

Byman, D., & Saber, I. (2019). *Is China prepared for global terrorism? Xin-jiang and beyong.* Washington, D.C.: Brookings Institute.

Castets, R. (2003, September-October). The Uyghurs in Xinjiang – The Malaise Grows. *China perspective, 49,* 1-22. Retrieved from https://www.researchgate.net/publication/30445718_The_Uy-ghurs_in_Xinjiang_-_The_Malaise_Grows

Cheng, X. (2010). Separatism, Extremism And Terrorism: Challenge To Central Asia's Security. *Himalayan and Central Asian Studies, 14*(4), 44-55. Retrieved from http://www.himalayanresearch.org/journal-2010.html

Chin, J., & Bürge, C. (2017, December 19). Twelve Days in Xinjiang: How China's

Surveillance State Overwhelms Daily Life. *Wall Street Journal.* Ret-rieved from https://www.wsj.com/articles/twelve-days-in-xinjiang-how-chinas-surveillance-state-overwhelms-daily-life-1513700355

Chung, C. P. (2002). China's "War on Terror": September 11 and Uighur Separatism. *Foreign*

Affairs, 81(4), 8-12. Foreign Affairs, 81(4), 8-12. doi:10.2307/20033235.

Clarke, M. (2018). China's 'War on Terrorism' Confronting the Dilem-mas of the 'Internal–

External' Security Nexus. In M. Clarke, *Terrorism and Counter-Terrorism in China: Domestic and Foreign Policy Dimensions* (pp. 17-38). New York: Oxford University Press.

Clarke, M. (2018). Terrorism and Counter-Terrorism in China. In M. Clarke, *Terrorism and Counter-Terrorism in China: Domestic and Foreign Policy Dimensions* (pp. 1-17). New York: Oxford University Press.

Clarke, M. (2019, March 27). Counterterrorism yearbook 2019: China. *The Strategist: Counterterrorism yearbook 2019*. Retrieved from https://www.aspistrategist.org.au/counterterrorism-yearbook-2019-china/

de Haas, M. (2016). War Games of the Shanghai Cooperation Organization and the Collective Security Treaty Organization: Drills on the Move! *The Journal of Slavic Military, 29*(3), 378-406. https://doi.org/10.1080/13518046.2016.1200383https://www.tandfonline.com/doi/full/10.1080/13518046.2016.1200383

Dillon, M. (2014). *Xinjiang and the Expansion of Chinese Communist Power: Kashgar in the Early twentieth century.* New York: Routledge.

Dirks, E., & Cook, S. (2019, October 21). *China's Surveillance State Has Tens of Millions of New Targets. Foreign Policy.* Retrieved from https://foreignpolicy.com/2019/10/21/china-xinjiang-surveillance-state-police-targets/

Duffield, J. (2007). What Are International Institutions? *International Studies Review, 9*(1), 1-22. Retrieved from www.jstor.org/stable/4621775

European Parliament. (2015). *The Shanghai Cooperation Organisation.* Brassels : European Union. Retrieved from https://www.europarl.europa.eu/RegData/etudes/BRIE/2015/564368/EPRS_BRI(2015)564368_EN.pdf

Feng, E. (2018, August 5). Crackdown in Xinjiang: Where have all the people gone? *Financial Times*. Retrieved from https://www.ft.com/content/ac0ffb2e-8b36-11e8-b18d-0181731a0340.

Feng, E. (2018, March 13). Security spending ramped up in China's restive Xinjiang region. *Financial Times*. Retrieved from https://www.ft.com/content/aa4465aa-2349-11e8-ae48-60d3531b7d11: 2018

Frankel, J. (2017). Islamisation and Sinicisation: Inversions, Reversions And Alternate Versions Of Islam In China. In A. C. Peacock, *Islamisation: Comparative Perspectives from History* (pp. 495-514). Edinburgh: Edinburgh University Press.

Greitens, S., Lee, M., & Yazici, E. (2019). Counterterrorism and Preventive Repression:

China's Changing Strategy in Xinjiang. *International Security, 44*(3), 9–47. Retrieved from https://www.belfercenter.org/publication/counterterrorism-and-preventive-repression-chinas-changing-strategy-xinjiang

Guang, P. (2004). China's anti-terror strategy and China's role in global anti-terror cooperation. Asia *Europe Journal, 2*, 523–532. Retrieved from https://link.springer.com/article/10.1007/s10308-004-0115-7

Heywood, A. (2011). *Global politics.* New York: Palgrave Macmillan

Human Rights Watch. (2018, September 9). "Eradicating Ideological Viruses" China's Campaign of Repression Against Xinjiang's Muslims. *Human Rights Watch*. Retrieved from https://www.hrw.org/report/2018/09/09/eradicating-ideological-viruses/chinas-campaign-repression-against-xinjiangs

Human Rights Watch. (2019, May 1). China's Algorithms of Repression: Reverse Engineering a Xinjiang Police Mass Surveillance App. *Human Rights Watch*. Retrieved from https://www.hrw.org/report/2019/05/01/chinas-algorithms-repression/reverse-engineering-xinjiang-police-mass-surveillance

Information Office of the State Council. (2019). *China's national defense in the new era*. Beijing: Foreign Languages Press Co. Ltd.

Information Office of the State Council. (2002, December 9). *White Paper on China's National Defense in 2002 Paper* . Retrieved from http://english.people.com.cn/features/ndpaper2002/nd.html

Institute for Economics & Peace. (2016). *Global Terrorist Index 2016.* Sydney: Institute for economics and peace. Retrieved from https://reliefweb.int/report/world/global-peace-index-2016

Institute for economics and peace. (2017). *Global terrorism index 2017.* Sydney: Institute for economics and peace. Retrieved from https://reliefweb.int/report/world/global-terrorism-index-2017

Institute for economics and peace. (2019). *Global Terrorism Index.* Sydney: Institute for economics and peace. Retrieved from http://visionofhumanity.org/indexes/terrorism-index/

Jackson, R., & Sorensen, G. (2013). *Introduction to international relations: Theories and approaches* (5 ed.). Oxford: Oxford University Press.

Jin , W., & Dehang, K. (2019). Counter-Terrorism Cooperation Between China and Central Asia States in the Shanghai Cooperation Organisation. *China Quarterly of International Strategic Studies,* 5(1), 65–79. DOI: 10.1142/S2377740019500027

Keohane, R. (2012). Twenty Years of Institutional. *International Relations* , 26(2), 125–138. https://doi.org/10.1177/0047117812438451

Lain, S. (2016). Strategies for countering terrorism and extremism in Central Asia. *Asian Affairs, 47*(3), 386–405. Retrieved from https://www.tandfonline.com/doi/full/10.1080/03068374.2016.1225899

Leibold, J., & Zenz, A. (2016, December 23). Beijing's Eyes and Ears Grow Sharper in Xinjiang: The 24-7 Patrols of China's "Convenience Police". *Foreign Affairs*. Retrieved https://www.foreignaffairs.com/articles/china/2016-12-23/beijings-eyes-and-ears-grow-sharper-xinjiang

Lennox, C., & Short, D. (2016). Introduction. In C. Lennox and D. Short, *Handbook of*

Indigenous Peoples' Rights (pp, 1-10). Abingdon, UK and New York, USA: Routledge.

Lewis, D. (2014). Crime, terror and the state in Central Asia. *Global Crime, 15*(3-4), 337-356. Doi:10.1080/17440572.2014.927764

Liu, A., & Peters, K. (2017). The Hanification of Xinjiang, China: The Economic Effects of

the Great Leap West. *Studies in Ethnicity and Nationalism, 17*(2), 265-280. https://doi.org/10.1111/sena.12233

Mahmut, D. (2019). Controlling religious knowledge and education for countering religious extremism: case study of the Uyghur Muslims in China. *Forum for International Research in Education, 5*(1), 22-43. Retrieved from https://eric.ed.gov/?id=EJ1207558

Maizland, L. (2019, November 25). China's Repression of Uighurs in Xinjiang. *Council on Foreign Relations.* Retrieved from https://www.cfr.org/backgrounder/chinas-repression-uighurs-xinjiang

Mansbach, R., & Rafferty, K. (2008). *Introduction to global politics.* New York: Routledge

Meyer, P. (2016). *China's de-extremization of Uyghurs in Xinjiang.* New America. https://www.newamerica.org/international-security/policy-papers/china-de-extremization-uyghurs-xinjiang

Murphy, D. (2017). *China's Approach.* Washington, D.C. : United States Institute of Peace.

Office of the United Nations High Commissioner for Human Rights. (2008). *Human Rights, Terrorism and Counter-terrorism.* Geneva: United Nations. Retrieved from https://www.refworld.org/docid/48733ebc2.html

Omelicheva , M. (2009). Convergence of Counterterrorism Policies: A Case Study of Kyrgyzstan and Central Asia. *Studies in Conflict & Terrorism,* 32(10), 893-908. https://doi.org/10.1080/10576100903182518

Omelicheva, M. (2007). Combating Terrorism in Central Asia: Explaining Differences in States' Responses to Terror. *Terrorism and Political Violence, 19,* 369–393. https://doi.org/10.1080/09546550701424075

Panda, D. (2006). Xinjiang and Central Asia: China's Problems and Policy Implications. *Indian Journal of Asian Affairs,* 19(2), 29-44. Retrieved from www.jstor.org/stable/41950474

Panke, D. (2019). Regional cooperation through the lenses of states: Why do states nurture regional integration? *The Review of International Organizations,* 15, 1-30. https://doi.org/10.1007/s11558-019-09348-y

Permanent Mission of the Peoples Republic of China to the United Nations. (2003, December 15). *China seeks cooperation worldwide to fight "East Turkistan" terrorists.* Retrieved from http://www.china-un.ch/eng/zt/zgfk/t89062.htm

Potter, P. (2013). Terrorism in China: Growing Threats with Global Implications. *Strategic Studies Quarterly, Winter,* 7(4), 70-92. Retrieved from www.jstor.org/stable/26270778

Reccia, F. (2018, January 22). The evolving terrorist threat to China's Central Asia projects. *Global Risk Insight.* Retrieved from: https://globalriskinsights.com/2018/01/china-central-asia-serb-projects-terrorism-risk/

Reeves, J. (2016). Ideas and Influence: Scholarship as a Harbinger of Counterterrorism Institutions, Policies, and Laws in the People's Republic of China. *Terrorism and Political Violence,* 28(5), 827-847. https://doi.org/10.1080/09546553.2014.955915

Ritchie, H., Hasell, J., Appel, C., & Roser, M. (2020, November). Terrorism. *Our world in data*. Retrieved from: https://ourworldindata.org/terrorism

Romaniuk , P. (2010). Institutions as swords and shields: multilateral counter-terrorism since 9/11. *Review of International Studies,* 36(3), 591-613. Retrieved from www.jstor.org/stable/40783287

Rosendorff, P., & Sandler, T. (2005). The Political Economy of Transnational Terrorism. *The Journal of Conflict Resolution,* 49(2), 171-182. Retrieved from www.jstor.org/stable/30045106

Schmid, A., & Jongman, A. (1988). *Political terrorism: a new guide to actors, authors, concepts, data bases, theories, and literature.* Amsterdam: Transaction Books.

Scobell, A., Ratner, E., & Beckley, M. (2014). *China's Strategy Toward South and Central Asia: An Empty Fortress.* Santa Monica, California: RAND Corporation.

Shanghai Cooperation Organisation . (2001, June). *The Shanghai Convention on Combating Terrorism, Separatism and Extremism. Shanghai Cooperation Organisation.* Retrieved from https://www.un.org/en/chronicle/article/role-shanghai-cooperation-organization-counteracting-threats-peace-and-security

Shanghai Cooperation Organisation . (2002, June 7). Agreement on Regional Anti-Terrorist Structure between the Member States of the Shanghai Cooperation Organization. *Shanghai Cooperation Organisation.* Retrieved from http://ecrats.org/en/

Shanghai Cooperation Organisation. (2020). About SCO. *Shanghai Cooperation Organisation* Retrieved from http://eng.sectsco.org/

Sutter, R. G. (2012). *Chinese foreign relations: Power and policy since the Cold War.*

Lanham: Rowman & Littlefield.

Tanner , M. S., & Bellacqua , J. (2016). *China's Response to Terrorism.* Washington Boulevard: CNA Analysis and Solutions.

Tschantret, J. (2018). Repression, opportunity, and innovation: The. *Terrorism and Political Violence, 30*(4), 569-588. https://doi.org/10.1080/09546553.2016.1182911

Tuttle, G. (2015). China's Race Problem: How Beijing Repress Minorities. Foreign Affairs,

    May/June, 39-46. Retrieved from www.jstor.org/stable/24483662

Wallace, T. (2014). China and the Regional Counter-Terrorism Structure: An Organizational Analysis. *Asian Security, 10*(3), 199-220. https://doi.org/10.1080/14799855.2014.976614

Xiang, L. (2013, September 14). SCO faces regional challenges: Xi. *Global Times*. Retrieved from http://www.globaltimes.cn/content/811187.shtml

Zenz, A. (2018, March 12). China's Domestic Security Spending: An Analysis of Available Data. *China Brief, 18*(4). Retrieved from https://jamestown.org/program/chinas-domestic-security-spending-analysis-available-data/

Zenz, A., & Leibold, J. (2019). Securitizing Xinjiang: Police Recruitment, Informal Policing and Ethnic Minority Co-optation. *The China Quarterly*, 242, 324-348. https://doi.org/10.1017/S0305741019000778

Chapter 3

AidData. (2020). Retrieved from https://www.aiddata.org/

American Enterprise Institute. (2020). *China Global Investment Tracker*. Retrieved from https://www.aei.org/china-global-investment-tracker/

Ameyaw-Brobbey, T. (2018). The Belt and Road Initiative: Debt Trap and its Implication on International Security. *Asian Journal of Multidisciplinary Studies, 1*(2), 9.

Beeson, M. (2018). Geoeconomics with Chinese characteristics: The BRI and China's evolving grand strategy. *Economic and Political Studies*, 6(3), 240–256. https://doi.org/10.1080/20954816.2018. 1498988

Blackwill, R. D., & Harris, J. M. (2016). *War by other means: Geoeconomics and statecraft*. Massachusetts: Harvard University Press.

Blank, S. (2012). Whither the New Great Game in Central Asia? *Journal of Eurasian Studies*, 3(2), 147–160. https://doi.org/10.1016/j.euras.2012.03.005

CADGAT. (2019). *Central Asia Data-Gathering and Analysis Team Research Project*. Retrieved from http://www.osce-academy.net/en/research/cadgat/.

Chen, J. Y.-W., & Jiménez-Tovar, S. (2017). China in Central Asia: Local Perceptions from Future Elites. *China Quarterly of International Strategic Studies*, 03(03), 429–445. https://doi.org/10.1142/S2377740017500178

Cheng, A. (2018, July 31). Will Djibouti Become Latest Country to Fall Into China's Debt Trap? *Foreign Policy*. Retrieved from https://foreignpolicy.com/2018/07/31/will-djibouti-become-latest-country-to-fall-into-chinas-debt-trap/

Chung, C. (2004). The Shanghai Co-operation Organization: China's Changing Influence in Central Asia. *The China Quarterly*, 180, 989–1009. https://doi.org/10.1017/S0305741004000712

Copeland, D. C. (2015). *Economic Interdependence and War*. Princeton: Princeton University Press.

Edwards, M. (2003). The New Great Game and the new great gamers: Disciples of Kipling and Mackinder. *Central Asian Survey*, 22(1), 83–102. https://doi.org/10.1080/0263493032000108644

Esakova, N. (2012). *European energy security: Analysing the EU-Russia energy security regime in terms of interdependence theory*. Germany: Springer VS.

Fengler, W., & Valley, P. (2019). Connecting Central Asia to the world. *Brookings Institute*. Retrieved from https://www.brookings.edu/blog/future- development/2019/09/09/connecting central-asi-a-to-the-world/

Ferchen, M. (2016). *China, economic development, and global security: Bridging the gaps.* Beijing: Carnegie-Tsinghua

Grant, J. (2019, December 18). China Looks to Central Asia as an Economic Alternative. *The Diplomat*. Retrieved from https://the-diplomat.com/2019/12/china-looks-to-central-asia-as-an-economic-alternative/

Goldstein, A. (2000). Great expectations: Interpreting China's arrival. In M.E. Brown, O. R. Coté, S. M., Lynn-Jones, & S. E. Miller (Eds.), *The rise of China* (3-40). Massachusetts: MIT Press.

Guangcheng, X. (2015). The Strategic Interests of China and Russia in Central Asia. In D. B. H.

Denoon (Ed.), *China, The United States, and the Future of Central Asia* (pp. 154–172). New York: NYU Press.

Hamm, G. (2013). Revisiting the Great Game in Asia: Rudyard Kipling and popular history. *International Journal: Canada's Journal of Global Policy Analysis*, *68*(2), 395–402. https://doi.org/10.1177/0020702013492534

Hauner, M. (1984). The Last Great Game. *Middle East Journal*, *38*(1), 72–84. www.jstor.org/stable/4326728

Horn, S., Reinhart, C., & Trebesch, C. (2019). *China's overseas lending* [Kiel Working paper, No 2132]. Retrieved from https://www.econstor.eu/bitstream/10419/200198/1/1668908891.pdf

Hsiung, J. C. (2009). The Age of Geoeconomics, China's Global Role, and Prospects of Cross-Strait Integration. *Journal of Chinese Political Science*, *14*(2), 113–133. https://doi.org/10.1007/s11366-009-9045-y

Hurley, J., Morris, S., & Portelance, G. (2019). Examining the debt implications of the Belt and Road Initiative from a policy perspective. *Journal of Infrastructure, Policy and   Development*, *3*(1), 139. https://doi.org/10.24294/jipd.v3i1.1123

Jaborov, S. (2018). Chinese Loans in Central Asia: Development Assistance or "Predatory Lending"? In M. Laruelle (Ed.), *China's Belt and Road Initiative and its impact in   Central Asia* (pp. 34–   40). Washington, D.C.: Central Asia Program, The George Washington University.

Jackson, R. H., & Sørensen, G. (2013). *Introduction to international relations: Theories and approaches* (Fifth edition). Oxford: Oxford University Press.

Jackson, S. F. (2016). Does China Have a Monroe Doctrine? Evidence for Regional Exclusion. *Strategic Studies Quarterly*, *10*(4), 64-89. Retrieved from   www.jstor.org/stable/26271530

Jarosiewicz, A., Strachota, K., Matusiak, M., & Wołowska, A. (2013). *China vs. Central Asia: The achievements of the past two decades*. Warsaw: Centre for Eastern Studies.

Kapyla, J., & Aaltola,   M. (2019a). Critical infrastructure in geostrategic competition: Comparing the US and Chinese Silk Road projects. In M. Wigell, S. Scholvin, & M. Aaltola (Eds.), *Geo-economics and power politics in the 21st century: The revival of economic statecraft* (pp. 43–59). London: Routledge, Taylor & Francis Group.

Keohane, R. O., & Nye, J. S. (2012). *Power and interdependence* (4th ed). Boston: Longman.

Konstantinas, A. (2013). China's Economic Penetration into Post-Soviet Central Asia and Eastern Europe. *Lithuanian Foreign Policy Review*, *30*, 113–131. Retrieved from https://www.researchgate.net/publication/290222879_China's_economic_penetration_into_post-soviet_central_Asia_and_Eastern_Europe

Kruglov, A. (2019, November 12). Sinophobia simmers across Central Asia. *AsiaTimes*. Retrieved from https://asiatimes.com/2019/11/ sinophobia-simmers-across-central-asia/

Kundnani, H. (2011). Germany as a Geo-economic Power. *The Washington Quarterly*, *34*(3), 31–45. https://doi.org/10.1080/0163660X.2011.587950

Kyrgyz Bank. (2020). Retrieved from https://www.nbkr.kg/index.jsp?-lang=ENG

Kyzy, U. (2019, October 8). Why Is Anti-Chinese Sentiment on the Rise in Central Asia? *The Diplomat*. Retrieved from https://thediplomat.com/2019/10/why-is-anti-chinese-   sentiment-on-the-rise-in-central-asia/.

Lain, S. (2018). The Potential and Pitfalls of Connectivity along the Silk Road Economic Belt. In Marlène Laruelle (Ed.), *China's Belt and Road Initiative and its impact in Central Asia* (pp. 1–10). Washington, D.C.: Central Asia Program, George Washington University.

Lanteigne, M. (2008). China's Maritime Security and the "Malacca Dilemma." Asian Security, 4(2), 143–161. https://doi.org/10.1080/14799850802006555

Laruelle, M., & Peyrouse, S. (2009). *China as a Neighbor: Central Asian Perspectives and Strategies*. Washington, D.C.: Central Asia-Caucasus Institute & Silk Road Studies   Program

Lee, G. (2014). The Merchants of Shanghai, the Mandarins of Beijing: Economic Interdependence in Chinese Foreign Policy. *The Korean Journal of International Studies*, *12*(Special   Issue), 79–88. https://doi.org/10.14731/kjis.2014.05.12.S.79

Levina, M. (2019, March 17). Can Central Asia countries pay their external debts? *The Times of Central Asia*. Retrieved from https://www.timesca.com/index.php/news/26-opinion-head/20949-can-central-asia-countries-pay-their-external-debts

Luttwak, E. (1990). *From Geopolitics to Geo-Economics: Logic of Conflict, Grammar of Commerce. 20*, 17–23. Retrieved from https://www.jstor.org/stable/42894676

Malashenski, A. (2013). *The Fight for Influence: Russia in Central Asia.* Washington, D.C.: Carnegie Endowment for International Peace.

Mariani, B. (2013). *China's role and interests in Central Asia.* London: Saferworld.

Ministry of Finance of the Republic of Tajikistan. (2019). Retrieved from https://www.developmentaid.org/#!/donors/view/145924/ministry-of-finance-of-the-republic-of-tajikistan-ministerstvo-finansov-respubliki-tadzhikistan.

Mirovalev, M. (2020, February 25). Why are Central Asian countries so quiet on Uighur persecution? *Aljazeera.* Retrieved from https://www.aljazeera.com/indepth/features/central-asian-countries-quiet-uighur-persecution-200224184747697.html

Mitchell, G. (2014). China in Central Asia: The beginning of the end of Russia? *Slovo, 26*(1), 18–31. https://doi.org/10.14324/111.0954-6839.0112

Morrison, W. M. (2013). *China's Economic Rise: History, Trends, Challenges, and Implications for the United States.* Washington, D.C.: Congressional Research Service. Retrieved from https://fas.org/sgp/crs/row/RL33534.pdf

National Bank of Kazakhstan. (2020). Retrieved from https://national-bank.kz/?switch=english

National Statistical Committee of the Kyrgyz Republic. (2020). Retrieved from http://www.stat.kg/en/

News Central Asia. (2019, February 4). *Uzbekistan takes steps to encourage FDI inflow and foreign trade.* Retrieved from http://www.newscentralasia.net/2019/02/04/uzbekistan-takes-steps-to-encourage-fdi-inflow-and-foreign-trade/

OEC. (2018). Retrieved from https://oec.world/en/

OECD. (2018). *Net ODA*. Retrieved from https://data.oecd.org/oda/net-oda.htm

Olcott, M. (2013, September 18). China's Unmatched Influence in Central Asia. *Carnegie Endowment for International Peace*. Retrieved from https://carnegieendowment.org/2013/09/18/china-s-unmatched-influence-in-central-asia-pub-53035

Peyrouse, S. (2007). *The economic aspects of the Chinese-Central Asia rapprochement*. Washington, D.C.: Silk Road Studies Program; Central Asia-Caucasus Institute.

Peyrouse, S. (2016). Discussing China: Sinophilia and sinophobia in Central Asia. *Journal of Eurasian Studies, 7*(1), 14–23. https://doi.org/10.1016/j.euras.2015.10.003

Rumer, E., Sokolsky, R., & Stronski, P. (2016). *U.S. policy toward Central Asia 3.0*. Washington,D.C.: Carnegie Endowment for International Peace.

Saidov, B. (2019, April 20). Reforms make Uzbekistan attractive to investors. *China Daily*. Retrieved from https://global.chinadaily.com.cn/a/201904/20/WS5cba7331a3104842260b74a6.html

Samruk-Kazyna. (2018). *Overview of investment attractiveness of Central Asian countries*. Retrieved from https://sk.kz/upload/iblock/05c/05cd94b6368a1aadd76795e999b7745d.pdf

Scholvin, S., & Wigell, M. (2018). Power politics by economic means: Geoeconomics as ananalytical approach and foreign policy practice. *Comparative Strategy, 37*(1), 73–84. https://doi.org/10.1080/01495933.2018.1419729

Scissors, D. (2018). China's global investment: Neither the US nor Belt and Road. *AEI Paper& Studies*. Retrieved from https://www.aei.org/research-products/report/chinas-global-investment-neither-the-us-nor-belt-and-road/

Scobell, A., Lin, B., Shatz, H., Johnson, M., Hanauer, L., Chase, M., Cevallos, A., Rasmussen, I., Chan, A., Strong, A., Warner, E., & Ma, L. (2018). *At the Dawn of Belt and Road: China in the Developing World*. California: RAND Corporation.

Scobell, A., Ratner, E., & Beckley, M. (2014). *China's strategy toward South and Central Asia: An empty fortress*. California: RAND Corporation.

Sharshenova, A., & Crawford, G. (2017). Undermining Western democracy promotion in Central Asia: China's countervailing influences, powers and impact. *Central Asian Survey, 36*(4), 453–472. https://doi.org/10.1080/02634937.2017.1372364

Sim, L.-C., & Aminjonov, F. (2020, February 1). Potholes and Bumps Along the Silk Road Economic Belt in Central Asia. *The Diplomat*. Retrieved from https://thediplomat.com/2020/02/potholes-and-bumps-along-the-silk-road-economic-belt-in-central-asia/

Stronski, P., & Ng, N. (2018). *Cooperation and competition: Russia and China in Central Asia, the Russian Far East, and the Arctic*. Washington, D.C.: Carnegie Endowment for International Peace.

Sutter, R. G. (2012). *Chinese foreign relations: Power and policy since the Cold War* (3rd ed). Lanham: Rowman & Littlefield Publishers.

Todaro, M. P., & Smith, S. C. (2015). *Economic development* (12th ed). Boston: Pearson.

UN Comtrade. (2020). Retrieved from https://comtrade.un.org/data/

UNCTAD. (2018). *Foreign direct investment: Inward and outward flows and stock, annual*. Retrieved from https://unctadstat.unctad.org/wds/TableViewer/tableView.aspx

UNCTAD STAT. (2020). Retrieved from https://unctadstat.unctad.org/wds/TableViewer/tableView.aspx

United Nations Development Programme. (2019). *Human development report 2019: Beyond income, beyond averages, beyond today: inequalities in human development in the 21stcentury*. New York: United Nations Development Programme.

Wigell, M., & Landivar, A. S. (2019). China's economic statecraft in Latin America: Geostrategic implications for the United States. In M. Wigell, S. Scholvin, & M. Aaltola (Eds.), *Geo-economics and power politics in the 21st century: The revival of economic statecraft* (pp. 164–181). London: Routledge, Taylor & Francis Group.

Scholvin, S., & Wigell, M. (2019b). Geo-economics power politics: An introduction. In M. Wigell, S. Scholvin, & M. Aaltola (Eds.), *Geo-economics and power politics in the 21st century: The revival of economic statecraft* (pp. 1-13). London: Routledge, Taylor & Francis Group.

World Bank. (2020a). *International Debt Statistics 2020*. World Bank. Retrieved from https://openknowledge.worldbank.org/bitstream/handle/10986/32382/9781464814617.pd f

World Bank. (2020b). [World Bank]. GDP (Current US$) - Kazakhstan, Kyrgyz Republic, Turkmenistan, Tajikistan, Uzbekistan. Retrieved from https://data.worldbank.org/indicator/NY.GDP.MKTP.CD?locations=KZ-KG-TM-TJ-UZ

World Bank. (2020c). Foreign Direct Investment, Net Inflows (% of GDP) - Kazakhstan, Kyrgyz Republic, Tajikistan, Turkmenistan, Uzbekistan. Retrieved from https://data.worldbank.org/indicator/BX.KLT.DINV.WD.GD.ZS?locations=KZ-KG-TJ-TM-UZ

Xinhua. (2020a, June 6). China, Russia agree to upgrade relations for new era. *Xinhua*. Retrieved from http://www.xinhuanet.com/english/2019-06/06/c_138119879.htm Xinhua. (2020b, June 11). Factbox: China's economic cooperation with Tajikistan, Kyrgyzstan reaps fruitful results. *Xinhua*. Retrieved from http://www.xinhuanet.com/english/2019- 06/11/c_138134440.htm

Chapter 4

Bell, J. (1999). Redefining National Identity in Uzbekistan: Symbolic Tensions in Tashkent's Official Public Landscape. *Cultural Geographies, 7*(2), 183-213.

Bohr, A. (1998). *Uzbekistan Politics and Foreign Policy.* London: The Royal Institute of International Affairs.

Critchlow, J. (1991). *Nationalism in Uzbekistan.* Boulder, Colorado: Westview Press.

Dollerup, C. (1998). Language and Culture in Transition in Uzbekistan. *Post-Soviet Central Asia.*

Drobizheva, L, et al. (1996). *Ethnic Conflict in the Post-Soviet World.* New York, New York: M.E. Sharpe, Inc.

Hechter, M. (2000). *Containing Nationalism.* Oxford, UK: Oxford University Press.

Karimov, I.A. (1992). *Uzbekistan the Road of Independence and Progress.* Tashkent: Uzbekiston.

Kellner-Heinkele, et al. (2001). *Politics of Language in the Ex-Soviet Muslim States.* Ann Arbor, Michigan: University of Michigan Press.

Lake, D, et al. (1996). Containing Fear: The Origins and Management of Ethnic Conflict. *International Security.*

Lewis, D. (2016). With Uzbekistan's Dictator Dead, Russia Seeks to Extend its Influence. *The Conversation.*

Posen, B. (1993). The Security Dilemma and Ethnic Conflict. *Survival.*

Putz, C. (2018). Kazakhstan makes arrests after deadly bus fire killed 52 Uzbek labor migrants. The Diplomat. Retrieved from https://thediplomat.com/2018/02/kazakhstan-makes-arrests-after-deadly-bus-fire-killed-52-uzbek-labormigrants/

Rashid, A. (1994). *The Resurgence of Central Asia: Islam of Nationalism?.* Oxford, UK: Oxford University Press.

Smith, A. D. (1986). *The Ethnic Origins of Nations*. Hoboken, New Jersey: Blackwell Publishers.

Snyder, J. (2000). *From Voting to Violence: Democratization and Nationalist Conflict*. New York, New York: WW Norton & Company.

Suny, R. (1993). *The Revenge of the Past*. Palo Alto, California: Stanford University Press.

Chapter 5

Allworth, E. (1994). **Central Asia** *130 Years of Russian Dominance, A Historical Overview*. Durham and London: Duke University Press.

Amirbek, A. & Aydin, T. (2015). 'Identity Politics of Turkey Towards Central Asia'. *Mediterranean Journal of Social Sciences, 2(6, 2) (November)*.

Aras, B. (2009). 'The Davutoğlu Era in Turkish Foreign Policy'. *Insight Turkey, 11(3), pp. 127-142*.

Aras, B. (2014). 'Davutoğlu Era in Turkish Foreign Policy Revisited'. *Journal of Balkan and Near Eastern Studies, pp.1-15*. DOI: 10.1080/19448953.2014.938451

Aras, B. (2019). 'The Crisis and Change in Turkish Foreign Policy After July 15'. *Alternatives: Global, Local, Political*. DOI: 10.1177/0304375419837415

Aydın, M. (2004). 'Foucault's Pendulum: Turkey in Central Asia and the Caucasus'. *Turkish Studies, 5(2)*.

Aydın, M. (2019). Foreign Policy, 1923-2018. In A. Özerdem and Matthew Whiting (Eds.), *The Routledge Handbook of Turkish Politics*. London and New York: Routledge.

Badem, C. (2010). *The Ottoman Crimean War (1853-1856)*. Leiden and Boston: Brill.

Badem, C. (2014). "Fourty Years of Black Days"? The Russian Administration of Kars, Ardahan, and Batum, 1878-1918. In L. J. Frary and M. Kozelsky (Eds.), *Russian-Ottoman Borderlands, The Eastern Question Reconsidered.* Wisconsin: The University of Wisconsin Press.

Bağcı, H. & Doganlar, A. A. (2009). 'Changing Geopolitics and Turkish Foreign Policy'. *ANNALES Universitatis Mariae Curie, Lublin – Polonia, 16(2).*

Bazarbayev, K. K. & Zulpiharova, E. (2013). 'Central Asian Knot of World Politics'. *Procedia – Social and Behavioral Sciences, 89.*

Beissinger, M. R. (1997). State Building in the Shadow of an Empire-State: The Soviet Legacy in Post-Soviet Politics. In K. Dawisha and B. Parrott (Eds.), *The End of Empire? The Transformation of the USSR in Comparative Perspective.* New York and London: M. E. Sharpe.

Bozdağlıoğlu, Y. (2003). *Turkish Foreign Policy and Turkish Identity, A Constructivist Approach.* New York and London: Routledge.

Breuning, M. (2007). *Foreign Policy Analysis: A Comparative Introduction.* New York: Palgrave Macmillan.

Bunce, V. (2005). 'The National Idea: Imperial Legacies and Post-Communist Pathways in Eastern Europe'. *East European Politics & Societies, 19(3).*

Davutoğlu, A. (1997). 'Orta Asya'daki Dönüşüm, Asya-içi Dengeler ve Türkiye'. *Yeni Türkiye, 3(15).*

Esenova, S. (2002). 'Soviet Nationality, Identity, and Ethnicity in Central Asia: Historic Narratives and Kazakh Ethnic Identity'. *Journal of Muslim Minority Affairs, 22(1).*

Fairey, J. (2014). Russia's Quest for the Holy Grail: Relics, Liturgics, and Great-Power Politics in the Ottoman Empire. In L. J. Frary and M. Kozelsky (Eds.), *Russian-Ottoman Borderlands, The Eastern Question Reconsidered.* Wisconsin: The University of Wisconsin Press.

Frenchman, M. (1993). 'Turkey reaches out to the Central Asian Republics', *Turkish Review, 7(31)*.

Fuller, G. E. (1993). The Growing Role of Turkey in the World. In G. E. Fuller, I. O. Lesser, P. B. Henze, and J. F. Brown (Eds.), *Turkey's New Geopolitics: From Balkans to Western China*. Colorado: Westview Press.

Gerd, L. (2014). Russia, Mount Athos, and the Eastern Question, 1878-1914. In L. J. Frary and M. Kozelsky (Eds.), **Russian-Ottoman Borderlands,** *The Eastern Question Reconsidered*. Wisconsin: The University of Wisconsin Press.

Gharabaghi, K. (1994). 'Development Strategies for Central Asia in the 1990s: In Search of Alternatives'. *Third World Quarterly, 15(1)*.

Gleason, G. (1993). Uzbekistan: From Statehood to Nationhood. In Ian Bremmer and Ray Taras (Eds.), *Nation and Politics in the Soviet Successor States*. Cambridge: Cambridge University Press.

Golden, P.B. (2011). *Central Asia in World History*. New York: Oxford University Press.

Goshulak, G. (2003). 'Soviet and Post-Soviet: Challenges to the Study of Nation and State Building', *Ethnicities, 3(4)*.

Green, W. C. (1993). 'The Historic Russian Drive for a Warm Water Port, Anatomy of a Geopolitical Myth'. *Naval War College Review, 46(2), pp. 80-100*.

Hasanli, J. (2011). *Stalin and the Turkish Crisis of the Cold War 1945-1953*. Lanham: Lexington Books.

Karpat, K. H. (1992/94). 'The Foreign Policy of the Central Asian States, Turkey and Iran', *International Journal of Turkish Studies, 6(1-2)*.

Kösebalaban, H. (2011). **Turkish Foreign Policy** *Islam, Nationalism, and Globalization*. New York: Palgrave Macmillan.

Kuru, A. T. (1999). Türkiye'nin Orta Asya'ya Yönelişi: Dokuz Asır Sonra Politika Değişimi. In M. K. Öke (Ed.), *Geçiş Sürecinde Orta Asya Türk Cumhuriyetleri*. İstanbul: Alfa.

Landau, J. M. (1995). *Pan-Turkism: From Irredentism to Cooperation.* London: Hurst&Company.

Lapidus, G. W. (2002). Ethnicity and State-Building: Accomodating Ethnic Differences in Post-Soviet Eurasia. In Mark R. Beissinger and Crawford Young (Eds.), *Beyond State Crisis? Postcolonial Africa and Post-Soviet Eurasia in Comparative Perspective.* US: Woodrow Wilson Center Press.

LeDonne, J. P. (1997). *The Russian Empire and the World, 1700-1917, The Geopolitics of Expansion and Containment.* New York: Oxford University Press.

Manisalı, E. (1992). 'Turkey and the new Turkic Republics'. *Turkish Review, 6(29).*

Manz, B. F. (1989). *The Rise and Rule of Tamerlane.* New York: Cambridge University Press.

Mütercimler, E. (1993). *Türkiye-Türk Cumhuriyetleri İlişkiler Modeli.* İstanbul: Anahtar Kitaplar.

Nezihoglu, H. and Sayin, F. M. (2013). 'Two Options among Numerous Directions: Eurasianism on Moscow's Terms or Regional Integration between Sovereign Neighbors in Central Asia'. *The Journal of International Social Research, 6(26).*

Olcott, M. B. (2001). 'Revisiting the Twelve Myths of Central Asia'. *Carnegie Endowment for International Peace, Russian and Eurasian Program, Working Paper, (23).*

Öniş, Z. (2010). *Multiple Faces of the "New" Turkish Foreign Policy: Underlying Dynamics and a Critique.* GLODEM Working Paper Series (04/2010), Center for Globalization and Democratic Governance, Koç University, pp.1-23.

Saray, M. (1982). 'The Russian Conquest of Central Asia'. *Central Asian Survey, 1(2-3).*

Saray, M. (1994). *Osmanlı Devleti ile Türkistan Hanlıkları Arasındaki Siyasi İlişkiler (1775-1875).* Ankara: TTK.

Slezkine, Y. (1994). 'The USSR as a Communal Apartment, or How a Socialist State Promoted Ethnic Particularism'. *Slavic Review, (53)*.

Soucek, S. (2000). *A History of Inner Asia*. New York: Cambridge University Press.

Starr, S. F. (2013). *Lost Enlightenment Central Asia's Golden Age from the Arab Conquest to Tamerlane*. Princeton and Oxford: Princeton University Press.

Turnbull, S. (2003). *Essential Histories, The Ottoman Empire, 1326-1699*. New York and London: Routledge.

Tüfekçi, Ö. (2012). 'Another Last Eurasianist: Davutoğlu's Eurasianist Rhetoric'. *Caucasus International, 2(3)*.

Yilmaz, Ş. (1999). 'An Ottoman Warrior Abroad: Enver Paşa as an Expatriate'. *Middle Eastern Studies, 35(4)*.

Chapter 6

Alexeeva, E. (2012). Osobennosti I perspektivy obrazovatelnoi migratsii v epokhu globalnykh transformatsii. (Specific features and prospectives of educational migration in the era of global transformations). *Vestnik Moskovskogo universiteta*. Series 18. Sociology and Political Science. 2012. No. 4, 113-136.

Anderson, K.H. & Heyneman, S.P. (2005). Education and Social Policy in Central Asia: The Next Stage of the Transition. *Social Policy & Administration*. Vol. 39, No. 4, August 2005, 361-380.

Brunner, J.J., Tillett, A. (2007). *Higher Education in Central Asia. Challenges of Modernization. Case Studies from Kazakhstan, Tajikistan, The Kyrgyz Republic and Uzbekistan*. Washington, DC: The World Bank. Retrieved from: http://documents1.worldbank.org/curated/en/266211468235483571/pdf/689260ESW0P0850rnization00200700eng.pdf

Bulatova, T., Glukhov, A. (2019). Faktiry privlecheniya obrazovatelnykh migrantov (na primere sibirskih vuzov) (Attracting factors for student migrants (the case of Siberian universities). *Vestnik RUDN*. Series: Sociology. 2019. Vol. 19. No. 1, 40-52.

Chernykh, A., Kiseleva, E. (2015). 'Rossiya naraschivaet import studentov dlya prodvizheniya svoikh interesov v mire' (Russia increases imports of students in order to promote its interests in the world). *Kommersant*. 24 April 2015. Retrieved from: http://www.kommersant.ru/doc/2715149.

Confucius Institute. (2020). About Confucius Institute / Classroom. Retrieved from: http://english.hanban.org/node_10971.htm

Del Sordi, A. (2017). Sponsoring student mobility for development and authoritarian stability: Kazakhstan's Bolashak programme. *Globalizations*, DOI:10.1080/14747731.2017.1403780

Dementyeva S. (2008). Uchebnaya migratsiya v Rossiyu v fokuse tolerantnosti. (Student migration to Russia in the focus of tolerance). *Vestnik Tomskogo universiteta*. 2008. No. 317, 39-46.

Fierman, W. (2012). Russian in the Post-Soviet Central Asia: a Comparison with the States of the Baltic and South Caucasus. *Europe-Asia Studies*. 2012, 64:6, 1077-1100.

Gareva, M. (2019). Kazakhstan iz-za utechki mozgov finansiruet ekonomiku Rossii - Senator Bakhtiyaruly (Because of the brain drain, Kazakhstan is financing Russia's economy: Senator Bakhtiyaruly). *Inform-Buro*. 15 Feb. 2018. Retrieved from: https://informburo.kz/novosti/kazahstan-iz-za-utechki-mozgov-finansiruet-ekonomiku-rossii-senator-bahtiyaruly.html

Gavrilov, K., Gradirovskiy, S., Pismennaya, E., Ryazantsev, S., Yatsenko, E. (2012). *Uchebnaya migratsiya iz stran SNG i Baltii: potentsial i perspektivy dlya Rossii* (Student migration from CIS and Baltic states: potential and prospective for Russia). Moscow: Eurasia Heritage Foundation.

Gutek, G. L. (1993). *American education in a global society: internationalizing teacher education.* New York u.a.: Longman.

Khorsandi Taskoh, A. (2014). *A Critical Policy Analysis of Internationalization in Postsecondary Education: An Ontario Case Study.* Ontario: Western University. Retrieved from: https://ir.lib.uwo. ca/cgi/viewcontent.cgi?article=3340&context=etd

Knight, J. (2003). *Updating the definition of internationalization.* International Higher Education. No. 3 (33), pp. 2–3. Retrieved from: https://ejournals.bc.edu/index.php/ihe/article/view/7391/6588

Kosachev, K. (2012). Rossotrudnichestvo kak instrument 'myagkoy sily. (Rossotrudnichestvo as a tool of soft power), *Federalnyi Spravochnik.* Vol. 26 (2012), 185–194.

Migration Portal. (2017). Retrieved from: https://migrationdataportal. org/themes/international-students

Ministry of Science and Higher Education of the Russian Federation. (2018). *Export of Russian educational services: Statistical Collection.* Issue 8 Moscow: Center for Social Forecast and Marketing.

Mitin, D. (2010). Obrazovatelnaya (uchebnaya) migratsiya: ponyatie, problemy I puti resheniya. (Educational (student) migration: the term, problems and solutions). *Vestnik RUDN.* Series: Political Sciences. 2010. No. 3, 123-134.

Najibullah, F. (2020). Education Exodus: Uzbek Students Rushing Home To Study After Tashkent Eases Transfers. *Radio Free Europe / Radio Liberty Uzbekistan,* February 14, 2020. Retrieved from: https://www.rferl.org/a/uzbek-students-rushing-home-to-study-after-tashkent-eases-transfers/30434095.html

Nessipbayeva, O. (2015). The Bolashak Program In Building A Democratic And Prosperous Society. *Procedia - Social and Behavioral Sciences.* 191 (2015), 2275 – 2279.

Nurbek, S., Tulegenova, J., Abrayev, A., Janabylov, A., Madiev, E. & Kab-
lasova, L. (2014). *Mezhdunarodnaya stipendiya Prezidenta respubliki Kazakhstan "Bolashak" kak factor razvitiya chelovechesk-
ogo kapitala* (International scholarship of the President of the
Republic of Kazakhstan "Bolashak" as the factor of human capital development). Astana: Shanyrak-Media.

Nye, J. (2005). 'Soft Power and Higher Education.' *Forum Futures 2005*,
pp. 11-14.

OECD. (2012). *Education at a glance 2012: OECD indicators.* Paris.

Peyrouse, S. (2008). *The Russian Minority in Central Asia: Migration, Politics, and Language*, Occasional Paper no. 297. Washington, DC:
Kennan Institute.

Poletaev, D. (2012). Uchebnaya migratsiya v Rossiyu: sustschestvuyus-
chie praktiki i vozmozhnye perspektivy (Student migration to
Russia: existing practices and possible prospectives). *Nauchnye
trudy: Institut narodnohozyaistvennogo prognozirovaniya RAN.*
2012. No. 10, 390-406.

Rakisheva, B., Poletaev, D. (2011). Uchebnaya migratsiya iz Kazakhstana
v Rossiyu kak odin iz aspektov strategicheskogo sotrudnichestva
v ramkah razvitiya Tamozhennogo soyuza (Student migration
from Kazakhstan to Russia as one of the aspects of strategic interaction within the framework of the Customs union). *Evraziyska-
ya ekonomicheskaya integratsiya.* No. 3 (12). August 2011, 84-101.

REGNUM News (2018). *Olimpiadu rossiyskogo vuza obyavili nezakon-
noy v Kazakhstane.* (Olympiad of the Russian university has
been declared illegal in Kazakhstan). 13 April 2018. Retrieved
from: https://regnum.ru/news/society/2403896.html

Ryazantsev, S. & Korneev, O. (2014). Russia and Kazakhstan in Eurasian
Migration System: Development Trends, Socio-Economic Consequences of Migration and Approaches to Regulation. *Regional
Migration Report: Russia and Central Asia* (pp.5-54). Di Barto-
lomeo, A., Makaryan, S. & Weinar, A. (Eds). European University Institute. San Domenico di Fiesole, Italy.

Sagintayeva, A. & Jumankulov, Z. (2015). Kazakhstan's Bolashak Program. *International Higher Education*. Number 79: Winter 2015, 21-23.

Shneyder, V. (2019). The main aspects of educational cooperation between Russia and Uzbekistan at the present time. *Journal Post-Soviet Studies*. 2019. Vol. 2. No. 7, 1472-1476.

Ukrainian International Education Council. (2018). Why study in Ukraine. Retrieved from: https://uiec.org/en/education-in-ukraine/why-study-in-ukraine

UNESCO Institute of Statistics. (2015). *UIS Glossary*. Retrieved from: http://glossary.uis.unesco.org/glossary/en/home

UNESCO Institute of Statistics. (2019a). *Education: Outbound internationally mobile students by host region*. Retrieved from: http://data.uis.unesco.org/Index.aspx?queryid=172

UNESCO Institute of Statistics. (2019b). Global Flow of Tertiary-Level Students. Retrieved from: http://uis.unesco.org/en/uis-student-flow?=undefined&wbdisable=true

Vsemirnaya assotsiatsiya vypusknikov vysshikh uchebnykh zavedeniy (2020) (Global Alumni Alliance of Soviet/Russian Academic Institutions). Official website. Retrieved from: http://www.alumnirussia.org/

Zakon Respubliki Belarus ot 26.01.1990 No. 3094-XI "O yazykakh v Respublike Belarus" (1990). (Law of the Republic of Belarus from 26.01.1990 No. 3094-XI "On languages in the Republic of Belarus"). Retrieved from: http://pravo.levonevsky.org/bazaby/zakon/zakb1527.htm

Zhuravsky, A., Vyhovanets, O. (2013). 'Compatriots: Back to the Homeland', *Russian International Affairs Council*. 31 May 2013. Retrieved from: https://russiancouncil.ru/en/analytics-and-comments/analytics/compatriots-back-to-the-homeland/

Chapter 7

Abdullaev Evgeniy (2005), "Uzbekistan between Traditionalism and Westernization", in B. Rumer (ed.), Central Asia at the End of Transition, N.Y, London: M. E. Sharpe.

Amrebayev Aydar (2020), "Kazakhstan – Kyrgyzstan: The Border of Friendship and Cooperation or Misunderstanding and Rivalry?" CABAR.asia, 30 March

Retrieved from: https://cabar.asia/en/kazakhstan-kyrgyzstan-the-border-of-friendship-and-cooperation-or-misunderstanding-and-rivalry/ (2020.05.12)

Fazendeiro, Bernardo Teles (2017), "Uzbekistan's defensive self-reliance: Karimov's foreign policy legacy", International Affairs, 93: 2, 409–427

Haggard S. (2018), Developmental States, Cambridge: Cambridge University Press

Indeo F. (October 30 2019), "Uzbekistan ed Unione Economica Euroasiatica: un mutamento epocale nella politica estera di Tashkent?". Eurasian Business Dispatch Newsletter, n. 55; Retrieved from: http://eurasianbusinnessdispatch.com/ita/archivio/Uzbekistan-ed-Unione-Economica-Euroasiatica-un-mutamento-epocale-nella-politica-estera-di-Tashkent--di-Fabio-Indeo-713-ITA.asp (2019.11.02)

Karavayev A.V. (2019), "Uzbekistan – EAES: vliyaniye evraziyskogo integratsionnogo protsessa na ekonomiku respubliki". Ekspertnyy doklad, Moscow.

Makszimov V, (2019), "Central Asia leaders meet again in sign of increased regional cooperation", EURACTIV, Dec 3, https://euractiv.com/section/central-asia/news/central-asia-leaders-meet-again-in-sign-of-increased-regional-cooperation/ (2020.12.01)

Molchanov M. (2018), «New regionalism and Eurasia», in Shiping Hua (ed.), Routledge Handbook of Politics in Asia, London and New York: Routledge, pp. 506-521.

Molchanov M. (2015), «Eurasian Regionalism: Ideas and Practices», in R. E. Kanet & M. Sussex (Eds.), Power, Politics and Confrontation in Eurasia: Foreign Policy in a Contested Region, New York: Palgrave Macmillan, 135-160.

Mukhtarov D. (2014 May 24), "Single Hydrocarbons Market of Eurasian Economic Union to Be Created by 2025," Trend, Retrieved from: https://en.trend.az/business/energy/2277110.html (2020.02.20)

Nyematov A. (2020), "Detal'no izuchit', prezhde chem prinyat' «pravila igry»", Narodnoe Slovo, February 19; Retrieved from: http://xs.uz/ru/post/detalno-izuchit-prezhde-chem-prinyat-pravila-igry (2020.02.24)

Peacenexus (2019), "Development of Transport Corridors in Central Asia and effect of the "Belt and Road" Initiative", Retrieved from: https://peacenexus.org/wp-content/uploads/2020/01/Repot_DSC_PN_2019_eng.pdf (2020.01.22)

Perović, J. (2019), "Russia's Eurasian Strategy" in Thompson, Jack, Thränert, Oliver, Strategic Trends 2019. Key Developments in Global Affairs, Zürich, 45–63.

Perović Jeronim (2018), "Russia's Turn to Eurasia", Policy Perspectives, 6:5, Center for Security Studies, Retrieved from: https://css.ethz.ch/content/dam/ethz/special-interest/gess/cis/center-for-securities-studies/pdfs/PP6-5_2018.pdf (2019.11.10)

Romashov V. (2016), "Uzbekistan's Balancing Act: A Game of Chance for Independent External Policies", in Helena Rytövuori-Apunen (ed.), The Regional Security Puzzle around Afghanistan. Bordering Practices in Central Asia and Beyond, Leverkusen: Verlag Barbara Budrich, 161-190.

Shagina M. (2020), "The Collateral Damage of Russia's Counter-Sanctions for the EAEU", Russian Analytical Digest, n. 247, 17 February.

Söderbaum F., Shaw T. (eds., 2003), Theories of New Regionalism: A Palgrave Reader, Basingstoke: Palgrave Macmillan UK.

Solozobov Yuriy, Shibutov Marat (2019, May 20), "Demografiya stavit krest na Ukraine, vozvyshaya Azerbaydzhan i Uzbekistan", Regnum, Retrieved from: https://regnum.ru/news/polit/2631132. html (2019.12.20)

Stronski P., Sokolsky R. (2020, Jan. 1), Multipolarity in Practice: Understanding Russia's Engagement With Regional Institutions, Carnegie Endowment for International Peace, pp. 30. Retrieved from: https://carnegieendowment.org/2020/01/08/multipolarity-in-practice-understanding-russia-s-engagement-with-regional-institutions-pub-80717 (2020-02-25).

Tolipov F. (2019), "Uzbekistan-2.0 and Central Asia-2.0 New Challenges and New Opportunities", Monitoring Central Asia and the Caspian Area, Eurasiatica, 94-106.

Tolipov F. (2012). "Uzbekistan's New Foreign Policy Concept". CACI Analyst. Central Asia and Caucasus Institute. URL http://cacianalyst.org/publications/analytical-articles/item/12557-analytical-articles- (2019-12-10).)

Trickett N. (April 26, 2018), "Reforming Customs, Uzbekistan Nods toward the Eurasian Economic Union", The Diplomat. Retrieved from: https://thediplomat.com/2018/04/reforming-customs-uzbekistan-nods-toward-the-eurasian-economic-union/ (2020.02.20)

Vinokurov, Evgeny (2018). Introduction to the Eurasian Economic Union. Basingstoke: Palgrave MacMillan.

Weitz, R. (2018). "Uzbekistan's New Foreign Policy", Silk Road Paper, Central Asia and Caucasus Institute. Retrieved from: https://silkroadstudies.org/resources/pdf/SilkRoadPapers/1801Weitz.pdf (2019-12-10)

Chapter 8

(* indicates a primary source)

* Federation of Indian Chamber of Commerce and Industry (FICCI). (2017). "India-EAEU FTA Survey Report". New Delhi, India. http://ficci.in/spdocument/20978/India-EAEU-FTA-Survey-Report-revised.pdf

MEA. (December, 2018). 'India-Kazakhstan Relations', Ministry of External Affairs, Government of India. https://mea.gov.in/Portal/ForeignRelation/december_2018.pdf

* MEA. (2019, 13 January). Joint Statement on the outcome of the First meeting of the Foreign Ministers of Dialogue "India- Central" with participation of Afghanistan, Media Centre, Ministry of External Affairs, Government of India. https://www.mea.gov.in/bilateral-documents.htm?dtl/30908/Joint Statement on the outcome of the First meeting of the Foreign Ministers of Dialogue India Central Asia with participation of Afghanistan

Abbasova, Vusala. (2015). "Turkmenistan ends construction of its section of TAT railway", *Azer News*. Accessed on 24 May 2020. https://www.azernews.az/region/89871.html.

Afghan Voice Agency (2019, 6 August). "Turkmenistan lobbies transport corridor from Afghanistan to Europe via Azerbaijan". https://www.avapress.com/en/news/189633/turkmenistan-lobbies-transport-corridor-from-afghanistan-to-europe-via-azerbaijan.

Ahmad, Talmiz. (2018), "Why India needs to take a fresh look at China's Belt and Road Initiative". *The Wire*. Accessed on 25 May 2020. https://thewire.in/diplomacy/india-needs-to-take-a-fresh-look-at-the-belt-and-road-initiative-proposal.

ANI (2019, February 11). "Kazakhstan expresses confidence in trade with India through Chabahar". https://www.aninews.in/news/world/asia/kazakhstan-expresses-confidence-in-trade-with-india-through-chabahar20190210234342/.

Azernews. (2016, 19 November). "Iran to inaugurate Qazvin-Rasht-Astara railway in 2017". https://www.azernews.az/region/105333.html.

Borah, Rupajyoti. (2019). "India responds to Belt and Road Initiative with infrastructure push". *Nikkei Asian Review*. Accessed on 25 May 2020. https://asia.nikkei.com/Opinion/India-responds-to-Belt-and-Road-Initiative-with-infrastructure-push?fbclid=IwAR0gfI6XSh2yB-vArP6ijSsqPz36bc_Km-6vbBRNNwkybk2yxgwk_yP9MLcU.

Brzezinski, Zbigniew. (1997). *The Grand Chessboard: American Primacy and Its Geostrategic Imperatives*. Basic Books.

Gulati, Monish. (2015). "India's Central Asia connect may lie through Ashgabat". *Indian Defence Review*. Accessed on 25 May 2020. http://www.indiandefencereview.com/indias-central-asia-connect-may-lie-through-ashgabat/.

Haidar, Suhasini. (2020), "Iran drops India from Chabahar rail project, cites funding delay". *The Hindu*. Accessed on 30 July 2020. https://www.thehindu.com/news/national/iran-drops-india-from-chabahar-rail-project-cites-funding-delay/article32072428.ece.

Hasanov, Huseyn. (2017). "Afghanistan-Turkmenistan-Azerbaijan-Georgia-Turkey project discussed in Ashgabat". Accessed on 25 May 2020. https://en.trend.az/business/economy/2333563.html.

Hashmi, Sana. (2019), "India's response to China's BRI linked to its territorial concerns". *The Indian Express*. Accessed on 25 May 2020. https://indianexpress.com/article/opinion/columns/belt-and-road-form-india-china-5689217/

Kalsotra, Rajan. (2015a). "A challenge for Delhi diplomacy". *The Pioneer*. Accessed on 26 May 2020. http://www.dailypioneer.com/columnists/oped/a-challenge-for-delhi-diplomacy.html.

Kalsotra, Rajan. (2015b). "India should build on its historic ties with Iran". *The Tribune*. Accessed on 26 May 2020. http://www.tribuneindia.com/news/comment/india-should-build-on-its-historical-ties-with-iran/131498.html.

Kapoor, Nivedita. (2019). "SCO 2019: Opportunities and challenges for India". *Observer Research Foundation*. Accessed on 26 May 2020. https://www.orfonline.org/expert-speak/sco-2019-opportunities-and-challenges-for-india-51614/?fbclid=IwAR33HyO-xC VmfJl jHDpFdRag6HxdV384r7IMsOVOjwo2w359TAYal-4H2w.

Karle, Prathamesh. (2019). "Time for India to enhance engagement with Central Asia". *Observer Research Foundation*. Accessed on 26 May 2020. https://www.orfonline.org/expert-speak/time-india-enhance-engagement-central-asia-48519/?fbclid=IwAR1oXiLC2Erco40CBrU5atnATvqQYShIJrkn-l9k05Vo4Ru50YLaxYcON9HU.

Kaul, Ajay. (2009). "India hands over strategic Zaranj-Delaram highway to Afghan". *Hindustan Times*. Accessed on 26 May 2020. https://www.hindustantimes.com/world/india-hands-over-strategic-zaranj-delaram-highway-to-afghan/story-WSbFNMguM-WjvY39V7fR46H.html.

Khan Saif, Shadi. (2018). "Trade corridor from Afghanistan to Turkey inaugurated". *Anadolu Agency*. Accessed on 27 May 2020. https://www.aa.com.tr/en/economy/trade-corridor-from-afghanistan-to-turkey-inaugurated/1337767.

Mackinder, H.J. (1904). "The Geographical Pivot of History". *The Geographical Journal*, 23 (4), 421–444.

Mammadova, Leman. (2018). "Qazvin-Rasth railway opens today". *Azernews*. Accessed on 27 May 2020. https://www.azernews.az/region/141401.html?fbclid=IwAR0p0iJUPCx50oswDZ-rqEaZ_8CdUuxkRzq36fEXd8MH5z6slMU5lZWIXZBs.

Panda, Ankit. (2019). "A First: Afghan Shipment Heads to India via Iran's Chabahar Port". *The Diplomat*. Accessed on 27 May 2020. https://thediplomat.com/2019/02/a-first-afghan-shipment-heads-to-india-via-irans-chabahar-port/.

Pandit, Rajat. (2020). "India may invite Australia for Malabar naval exercise with US & Japan". *The Times of India*. Accessed on 27 May 2020. https://timesofindia.indiatimes.com/india/india-planning-to-invite-australia-for-malabar-naval-exercise/articleshow/73715057.cms?fbclid=IwAR0yFaqKdZ4ud0Pz83g8Fhm-9d_2CmQ_W7qQONQeyn0kuAPVam_mJFWe1LN4.

RailwayPro. (2018, 26 November). "Trial begin on Qazvin-Rasht line". https://www.railwaypro.com/wp/trials-begin-on-qazvin-rasht-line/?fbclid=IwAR0sIbYgXPQI0UKSmWBJZn-nbMnwolrzg2rl0-rNhVaGyMyTMgi-2cTRuWhU

Roy Chaudhury, Dipanjan. (2018). "Eurasian Economic Union trade ties with India independent of China". *The Economic Times*. Accessed on 28 May 2020. https://economictimes.indiatimes.com/news/economy/foreign-trade/eurasian-economic-union-trade-ties-with-india-independent-of-china/articleshow/65450137.cms?from=mdr&fbclid=IwAR1JtwwT67JXLegB-Bo7cUWpR-WqlMdBxdo7WGAyAAGhpLNe_hijH0zKwocY.

Roy Chaudhury, Dipanjan. (2020c). "India, Central Asia region have exclusively positive dynamics: Uzbek Foreign Minister". *The Economic Times*. Accessed on 28 May 2020. https://economictimes.indiatimes.com/news/politics-and-nation/india-central-asian-region-have-exclusively-positive-dynamics-uzbek-foreign-minister/articleshow/73301936.cms?fbclid=IwAR25rWz0XdJs8lJjyZtOhkEj67LaYul9tPOppSLS-jbe2Rpi8UmHrs2kzCtw&from=mdr.

Roy Chaudhury, Dipanjan. (2020b). "India, Uzbekistan explore PTA to push bilateral trade and business with Central Asia". *The Economic Times*. Accessed on 28 May 2020. https://m.economictimes.com/news/economy/foreign-trade/india-uzbekistan-explore-pta-to-push-bilateral-trade-and-business-with-central-asia/articleshow/73253086.cms?fbclid=IwAR25S92wZZyzU_UDXhSuBJ8Btv4268I-p9hIIQl3tPB6mPChjSBEurvYXvgw.

Roy Chaudhury, Dipanjan. (2020a). "Russia pushes India's entry into Eurasian Economic Union strengthening third country coop". *The Economic Times*. Accessed on 28 May 2020. https://economictimes.indiatimes.com/news/economy/foreign-trade/russia-pushes-indias-entry-into-eurasian-economic-union-strengthening-third-country-coop/articleshow/73108911.cms?from=mdr.

Sachdeva Gulshan & Lisbonne de Vergeron Karine. (2018). "European and Indian Perceptions of the Belt and Road Initiative". EU-India Think Tanks Twinning Initiative.

Sen, Aveek. (2019). "Iran looks to Chabahar and a new transit corridor to survive US sanctions". *Atlantic Council*. Accessed on 28 May 2020. https://www.atlanticcouncil.org/blogs/iransource/iran-looks-to-chabahar-and-a-new-transit-corridor-to-survive-us-sanctions/.

Simes, Dimitri. (2020), "Russia woos India to sign trade pact with Eurasian Economic Union". *Nikkei Asian Review*. Accessed on 28 May 2020. https://asia.nikkei.com/Politics/International-relations/Russia-woos-India-to-sign-trade-pact-with-Eurasian-Economic-Union?fbclid=IwAR0VWerYhSemLQTlcp3edkkYbIs1KrmvLx-LLgBPfUHJ0_HEY4UvM5T1I_PA.

Singh Roy, Meena. (2015). "International North South Transport Corridor: Re-energising India's gateway to Eurasia". IDSA Issue Brief. Accessed on 29 May 2020. https://idsa.in/issuebrief/InternationalNorthSouthTransportCorridor_msroy_180815.

Singh Roy, Meena. (2017). "Eminem asked: What does India stand to gain if the membership of SCO is granted?" IDSA. Accessed on 29 May 2020. https://idsa.in/askanexpert/membershipofSCO?fbclid=IwAR11FsungaMMTwZ6aFnmhLshrlq2vIA3y13MO3W-iVUNeO_T3tQsNC9gZdjA.

Sood, Jyotika. (2017), "India clears the decks for multi-modal transnational connectivity play". *Livemint*. Accessed on 29 May 2020. http://www.livemint.com/Politics/rveanjGrWWuFfjfnbM-w3qN/India-clears-the-decks-for-multimodal-transnational-connect.html.

Sood Jyotika & Bhaskar, Utpal. (2017). "Dry run for Russia-Iran-India transport project likely tomorrow". *Livemint*. Accessed on 29 May 2020. https://www.livemint.com/Politics/dio3cLF9lcJp8s-rblf1ccO/Dry-run-for-RussiaIranIndia-transport-project-likely-tomor.html.

Stobdan, P. (2018). "Significance of India joining the Ashgabat Agreement". IDSA. Accessed on 28 May 2020. https://idsa.in/idsa-comments/significance-of-india-joining-the-ashgabat-agreement_p-stobdan-120218.

The Economic Times. (2020, 28 April). "Moody's slashes India growth forecast to 0.2 percent for 2020". https://economictimes.indiatimes.com/news/economy/indicators/moodys-slashes-india-growth-forecast-to-0-2-per-cent-for-2020/articleshow/75432876.cms?from=mdr.

The Hindu. (2019, August 14). "India-Turkmenistan holds talks on crucial transit corridor via Iran, Oman". *Business Line, The Hindu*. http://www.thehindubusinessline.com/economy/policy/india-turkmenistan-hold-talks-on-crucial-transit-corridor-via-iran-oman/article9818197.ece.

Conclusion

Khan, K. H., & Kuszewska, A. (2020). The Significance of India's (Re) connectivity Strategy in Central Asia: An Introduction. In K. H. Khan (Ed.), *The Strategy of (Re) connectivity: Revisiting India's Multifaceted Relations with Central Asia.* New Delhi, India: KW Publishers.

Roberts, Paul Craig. (2015). The Neoconservative Threat to World Order: America's Perilous War for Hegemony. Atlanta, USA: Clarity Press, INC

Sorensen, Georg. (2016). Rethinking the New World Order. London, UK: Palgrave Macmillan

Stewart, Dona J. (2013). The Middle East Today: Political, Geographical and Cultural Perspectives. New York, USA: Routledge

Xing Li, Mammo Muchie. (2010). The Myths and Realities of the Rising Powers: Is China a Threat to the Existing World Order? In Li Xing (Ed), The Rise of China and the Capitalist World Order. England, UK: Ashgate Publishing Limited

Index